Pro-poor Tourism: Who Benefits?

CURRENT THEMES IN TOURISM
Series Editors: Professor Chris Cooper, *University of Queensland, Australia*
Dr C. Michael Hall, *University of Canterbury, New Zealand*

Other Books in the Series
Global Ecotourism Policies and Case Studies: Perspectives and Constraints
Michael Lück and Torsten Kirstges (eds)
The Politics of World Heritage: Negotiating Tourism and Conservation
David Harrison and Michael Hitchcock (eds)

Other Books of Interest
Tourism Marketing: A Collaborative Approach
Alan Fyall and Brian Garrod
Music and Tourism: On the Road Again
Chris Gibson and John Connell
Tourism Development: Issues for a Vulnerable Industry
Julio Aramberri and Richard Butler (eds)
Nature-Based Tourism in Peripheral Areas: Development or Disaster?
C. Michael Hall and Stephen Boyd (eds)
Tourism, Recreation and Climate Change
C. Michael Hall and James Higham (eds)
Shopping Tourism, Retailing and Leisure
Dallen J. Timothy
Wildlife Tourism
David Newsome, Ross Dowling and Susan Moore
Film-Induced Tourism
Sue Beeton
Rural Tourism and Sustainable Business
Derek Hall, Irene Kirkpatrick and Morag Mitchell (eds)
The Tourism Area Life Cycle, Vol. 1: Applications and Modifications
Richard W. Butler (ed.)
The Tourism Area Life Cycle, Vol. 2: Conceptual and Theoretical Issues
Richard W. Butler (ed.)
Tourist Behaviour: Themes and Conceptual Schemes
Philip L. Pearce
Tourism Ethics
David A. Fennell
North America: A Tourism Handbook
David A. Fennell(ed.)
Lake Tourism: An Integrated Approach to Lacustrine Tourism Systems
C.Michael Hall and Tuija Härkönen (eds)
Codes of Ethics in Tourism: Practice, Theory, Synthesis
David A. Fennell and David C. Malloy
Managing Coastal Tourism Resorts: A Global Perspective
Sheela Agarwal and Gareth Shaw (eds)

For more details of these or any other of our publications, please contact:
Channel View Publications, Frankfurt Lodge, Clevedon Hall,
Victoria Road, Clevedon, BS21 7HH, England
http://www.channelviewpublications.com

CURRENT THEMES IN TOURISM
Series Editors: Chris Cooper (*University of Queensland, Australia*),
C. Michael Hall (University of Canterbury, New Zealand)

Pro-poor Tourism: Who Benefits?

Perspectives on Tourism and Poverty Reduction

Edited by
C. Michael Hall

CHANNEL VIEW PUBLICATIONS
Clevedon • Buffalo • Toronto

Library of Congress Cataloging in Publication Data
Pro-poor Tourism : Who Benefits?: Perspectives on Tourism and Poverty reduction
Edited by C. Michael Hall
Current Themes in Tourism
Includes bibliographical references.
1. Tourism–Economic aspects. 2. Poverty. I. Hall, Colin Michael. II. Title. III. Series.
G155.A1P7557 2007
338.4'791–dc22   2007029620

British Library Cataloguing in Publication Data
A catalogue entry for this book is available from the British Library.

ISBN-13: 978-1-84541-075-9 (hbk)

Channel View Publications
An imprint of Multilingual Matters Ltd

UK: Frankfurt Lodge, Clevedon Hall, Victoria Road, Clevedon BS21 7HH.
USA: 2250 Military Road, Tonawanda, NY 14150, USA.
Canada: 5201 Dufferin Street, North York, Ontario, Canada M3H 5T8.

The contents of this book also appear in Journal *Current Issues in Tourism, Vol.10, No. 2&3*

The policy of Multilingual Matters/Channel View Publications is to use papers that are
natural, renewable and recyclable products, made from wood grown in sustainable forests.
In the manufacturing process of our books, and to further support our policy, preference is
given to printers that have FSC and PEFC Chain of Custody certification. The FSC and/or
PEFC logos will appear on those books where full certification has been granted to the
printer concerned.

Typeset by Techset Composition.
Printed and bound in Great Britain by the Cromwell Press.

Contents

1 *Editorial* **Pro-Poor Tourism: Do 'Tourism Exchanges Benefit
   Primarily the Countries of the South'?**
   by C. Michael Hall 1

2 **Tourism and Poverty Alleviation: An Integrative
   Research Framework**
   by Weibing Zhao and J. R. Brent Ritchie 9

   Introduction 9
   Conceptualising APT: An Integrative Research Framework 12
      Poverty alleviation and determinants 13
      Three APT themes 14
      APT stakeholders 19
      APT and other poverty alleviation approaches 21
      Environments of APT 22
   Identifying Research Needs and Opportunities:
   The Use of the Framework 23
      Three general approaches to guide research through
         the framework 23
      Highlights of research needs and opportunities 25
   Conclusion 27
      Correspondence 29
      Notes 29
      References 29

3 **Tourism as a Tool for Poverty Alleviation: A Critical
   Analysis of 'Pro-Poor Tourism' and Implications for
   Sustainability**
   by Stephanie Chok, Jim Macbeth and Carol Warren 34

   Introduction 34
   Pro-Poor Tourism: Where Tourism Benefits the Poor
         (Along with the Rich) 37
      PPT principles and strategies 37
      The argument for tourism as a poverty alleviation tool 38
      PPT and other 'tourisms' 38
      Limitations of tourism as a poverty alleviation strategy 40
      The sustainability positions of PPT stakeholders 41

PPT and the Challenge of Global Sustainability 43
  Environmental considerations from a weak to very
    weak sustainability perspective 43
  Socioeconomic considerations from a weak to very
    weak sustainability perspective 44
Conclusion 49
  Correspondence 51
  References 51

**4 Growth Versus Equity: The Continuum of Pro-Poor Tourism
    and Neoliberal Governance**
    by Daniela Schilcher 56

Introduction 56
Tourism, Poverty and Economic Growth 58
The Issue of Inequality 59
Economic Restructuring and 'the Poor' 61
Political Practice: The Nebuleuse of Neoliberalism 63
Making Tourism More Pro-Poor 69
Conclusion 73
  Acknowledgements 75
  Correspondence 75
  References 75
  Web addresses 83

**5 Lao Tourism and Poverty Alleviation: Community-Based
    Tourism and the Private Sector**
    by David Harrison and Steven Schipani 84

Tourism as 'Development' 84
Lao PDR: The Background 89
The Development of Tourism in Lao PDR 90
The Organisation of Tourism in Lao PDR 92
  The Nam Ha Ecotourism Project 92
  The Asian Development Bank 94
  SNV (The Netherlands development organisation) 95
  The Lao National Tourism Administration 96
  The private sector 97
Lao Tourism and Poverty Alleviation 99
  The Nam Ha Ecotourism Project 99
  The Nam Ha Project and the Asian Development Bank 102
  The private sector 107
Conclusion 112
  Acknowledgements 116
  Correspondence 116
  Notes 116
  References 117

6 **Exploring the Tourism-Poverty Nexus**
by Regina Scheyvens 121

Introduction 121
The Poverty Agenda 123
The Evolution of Pro-Poor Tourism 125
Theoretical Perspectives on Tourism and Development 126
    Liberal perspectives 126
    Critical perspectives 128
    Neoliberal perspectives 129
    Alternative perspectives 130
    Post-structuralist perspectives 131
Different Approaches to Pro-Poor Tourism 132
    The PPT partnership 133
    World Tourism Organisation and ST-EP
        (sustainable tourism–eliminating poverty) 134
    World Bank 135
Reflections on Different Approaches to Pro-Poor Tourism 136
Conclusion 140
    Correspondence 141
    Notes 141
    References 141

7 **Nature-Based Tourism and Poverty Alleviation: Impacts of
Private Sector and Parastatal Enterprises In and Around
Kruger National Park, South Africa**
by Anna Spenceley and Harold Goodwin 145

Introduction 145
    South African context 146
    Poverty and tourism 147
Assessment of Tourism Interventions 150
    Study methods 150
Socioeconomic Impacts 155
    Local employment 155
    Procurement 157
    Corporate social responsibility initiatives 158
    Local economic dependency and access 159
Conclusions 160
    Correspondence 164
    Acknowledgements 164
    References 164

Editorial
Pro-Poor Tourism: Do 'Tourism Exchanges Benefit Primarily the Countries of the South'?

Poverty reduction has become an important item on the tourism agenda. The United Nations World Tourism Organization (UNWTO) (2007) has identified poverty reduction, along with climate change, as a global challenge to the tourism industry. According to UNWTO Secretary-General Francesco Frangialli:

> ... they require innovative and changed behaviour to effectively respond over time and Tourism can and must play its part in the solutions to both ... the UNWTO has been actively working on these issues for some years and is committed to seek balanced and equitable policies to encourage both responsible energy related consumption as well as anti-poverty operational patterns. This can and must lead to truly sustainable growth within the framework of the Millennium Development Goals. (UNWTO, 2007)

In the same press release the UNWTO states that 'Tourism exchanges benefit primarily the countries of the South' (UNWTO, 2007) and provide a list of characteristics that would be familiar to all first year university students of tourism:

- The number of international tourist arrivals has risen from 25 million in 1950 to 842 million in 2006; this rise is equivalent to an average annual growth of about 7%.
- The revenues generated by these arrivals – not including airline ticket sales and revenues from domestic tourism – have risen by 11% a year (adjusted for inflation) over the same span of time; this outstrips that growth rate of the world economy as a whole.
- International tourism receipts reached US$680 billion in 2005 (€547 billion), making it one of the largest categories of international trade.
- Depending on the year, this trade volume equals or exceeds that of oil exports, food products, or even cars and transport equipment.
- Tourism, taken in the narrow sense, represents one quarter of all exports of services – 40% if air transport is included.
- Tourism's share of direct foreign investment flows, though still limited, has increased spectacularly between 1990 and 2005. (UNWTO, 2007)

Such figures are impressive with respect to international tourism. Yet if examining tourism exchange from a global perspective the actual share of international tourist arrivals which the south enjoys is relatively small. For example, Africa which accounts for 13.3% of the world's population and 3.8% of world gross domestic product (GDP) had a global market share of 4.6% (Table 1). Similarly, one of the fastest growing areas in terms of international tourism, the Asia-Pacific, and which accounts for just over half of the world's population, only accounts for 19.3% of the world's arrivals. In contrast, Europe, with just over 10% of the world's population has over 50% of market share. Another way of comparing the relative balance of arrivals is through an international arrivals mobility ratio. If comparing approximate population to international arrivals (2002 figures are used for population and 2003 for arrivals in this instance), the global 2002 ratio was $1:9.1$. However, the imbalances in the world tourism system are well illustrated if one compares differences between the north and the south. The Asia-Pacific, which includes developed countries such as Japan, Australia and New Zealand, had a ratio of $1:30.8$, while Africa had a ratio of $1:26.6$. In contrast, Europe had a ratio of $1:1.6$ and North America $1:5.5$. Given this situation the potential of tourism to contribute to the economic development of the developing countries, at least at a macro-level, would appear to be questionable unless there are massive shifts in flows of international arrivals.

The use of tourism as tool for economic development in developing countries has been a focus of research in tourism studies since the 1970s (e.g. De Kadt, 1979; Lea, 1988; Smith & Eadington, 1992). In the 1990s this research interest was widened with the integration of economic development in the broader rubric of sustainability, and the establishment of new forms of tourism such as ecotourism in which the economic benefits received by destination communities were a significant concern (e.g. Cater, 1993; Hall & Lew, 1998; Murphy, 2000; Smith & Eadington, 1992). The current decade has seen further revisions of the development concept in tourism with increased attention being given to the equity dimension of sustainable development and which has lead to renewed interest in the community as a critical element in achieving development goals (e.g. Reid, 2003; Scheyvens, 2002; Weaver, 2004).

One particularly important aspect of the interest in equity and human well-being as a tourism development goal has been the growth of academic and development agency interest in the relationship between tourism development and poverty-reduction strategies – what is often referred to as pro-poor tourism (PPT). Significantly, as with the tourism and sustainable development relationship, the PPT field has developed in great part as a result of interchange between academics and researchers and public and non-government organisations (NGOs) with interests in the less-developed countries. For example, one of the strongest advocates for PPT, as well as researchers on the subject, is the Pro-Poor Tourism Partnership (http://www.propoortourism.org.uk/) a collaborative research initiative between the International Centre for Responsible Tourism (ICRT), the International Institute for Environment and Development (IIED), and the Overseas Development Institute (ODI). However, also as with sustainable development, the PPT field has become increasingly open to contestation and critical debate, as the contents of the

Table 1 International tourism, GDP and population by region

Region	GDP (PPP$US billions estimated) 2002	GDP as % of world GDP	GDP per capita (PPP$US estimated per person) 2002	Population 2002 (million)	Population as % of world population	International tourist arrivals 2000 (million)	International tourist arrivals 2003 (million)	International tourist arrivals 2005 (million)	Market share (%) 2005	Average annual growth 2000/05 (%)	Inbound mobility ratio – arrivals (2003): population (2002)
Europe	12,297	25.2	18,803	654	10.5	395.8	407.1	441.5	54.8	2.2	1 : 1.6
Asia Pacific	16,631	34.1	4,470	3479	55.7	110.5	113.3	155.4	19.3	7.1	1 : 30.8
Americas	15,091	30.9	17,609	857	13.7	128.1	113.1	133.5	16.6	0.8	1 : 7.6
N. America	12,144	24.9	28,597	425	6.8	91.4	77.3	89.9	11.2	−0.3	1 : 5.5
Africa	1,897	3.8	2,280	832	13.3	28.2	31.0	36.7	4.6	5.4	1 : 26.8
Middle East	2,866	5.8	6,795	422	6.8	24.2	29.5	39.1	4.8	10.1	1 : 14.3
World	48,781	100	7,815	6,242	100	687	694	806	100	3.3	1 : 9.1

Notes: PPP refers to purchasing power parity; purchasing power is a measure of what can be bought in the territory in which that money is earned; percentage figures have been rounded.
Source: derived from UNDP, 2004; UNWTO, 2006.

present volume illustrate. The range of opinions regarding PPT and its potential to act as a positive force for human well-being is well summed up by Hall and Brown (2006: 13), 'does PPT simply offer another route by which economic imperialism, through tourism, may extend its tentacles, or is it an appropriately liberating and remunerative option?'

In one sense, the focus on providing tourism employment to the presently unemployed is perhaps not far removed from the goals of any regional econ-omic development programme. PPT advocates tend to suggest that there are qualitative differences with respect to its approach with respect to the poor (e.g. Ashley *et al.*, 2000). However, critics suggest that it is another form of neo-liberalism that fails to address the structural reasons for the north–south divide, as well as internal divides within developing countries (e.g. Chok *et al.*, 2007; Scheyvens, 2007; Schilcher, 2007). These debates are not just aca-demic as NGOs have also been highly critical of the notion of fighting poverty through tourism. For example, Ecumenical Coalition on Tourism Executive Director Ranjan Solomon stated:

> For as long as the rich and powerful are going to draw up the parameters and architecture of tourism policy, nothing will change – not much, in any case. How can it? For after all, the investor is there to make profits. Social responsibilities do not factor – evidence of this is too thin to be counted or weighed in. The occasional burst of charity is not what we are talking about and asking for. Tourism is, virtually, for all intents and purposes, one with a purely economic function in-so-far as the industry is concerned ...

> Tourism is largely an avenue and instrument for the rich and affluent whose wealth has been accumulated in the context of unjust structures and systems of society. Incremental changes in policy which slogans like 'liberalization with a human face' will stop far short of what is needed – an overhauling of tourism practice to guarantee it is just, parti-cipatory, and geared to authentic human advancement. (Solomon, 2005)

Solomon's comments were in part a response to the Declaration on Tourism and the Millennium Development Goals launched by the UNWTO and other agencies and NGOs in September 2005. According to WTO Secretary-General Francesco Frangialli in releasing the declaration:

> Tourism needs greater recognition by governments and development institutions for its capacity to generate economic, environmental and social benefits ... It is also a sector that promotes inter-cultural under-standing and peace among nations ... For poor countries and small island states, tourism is the leading export- often the only sustainable growth sector of their economies and a catalyst for many related sectors. It can play a key role in the overall achievement of the Millennium Development Goals by 2015. (eTurboNews, 2005a)

The release of the declaration also highlighted that developing countries received US$177 billion in tourism receipts in 2004 with tourism being the primary source of foreign exchange earnings in 46 of the 49 poorest nations that the UN describes as the Least Developed Countries (eTurboNews, 2005b). For those in support of tourism as a means of poverty reduction, these figures are indicative of the value of tourism as a means of improving welfare and living standards. Yet, the argument may well be put forward that these figures perhaps illustrate the problems associated with tourism, development and globalisation and the impacts of trade liberalisation. Indeed, while the declaration calls for tourism to be integrated into all development and poverty reduction strategies, with an emphasis on positive linkages with local economic activities (see http://www.unwto.org/step/). However, poverty reduction is integrated with UNWTO's desire for increased liberalisation of trade in tourism services ('with a human face') as local linkages must, in turn, be connected to international linkages, as part of the commodity chain of international tourism. As the 2003 addendum report of the UNWTO Secretary General to the General Assembly with respect to liberalisation of trade in tourism services (available for download from the UNWTO website under the heading of 'improving competitiveness' [http://www.unwto.org/quality/trade/en/trd_01.php?op=3&subop=15]) states:

> It is recalled that the Osaka Millennium Declaration adopted at the outcome of the fourteenth General Assembly concluded that *'the liberalization of the conditions governing trade in services is compatible with sustainable tourism development and the protection of social and cultural values and identities'*, the elements now included in the Organization's concept of *'tourism liberalization with a human face'*.

In the report presented by the Secretary-General to the last General Assembly it was stressed that: 'an expression of freedom by nature and an international phenomenon by definition, tourism has everything to gain from the conquest of extensive new territory in the realm of freedom'. The Secretary-General added that:

> everyone stands to benefit from a development in tourism exports. First of all, the Third World countries which are on the whole net beneficiaries of international tourism trade in that their cumulative tourism balances of payments reflect a surplus in relation to the industrialized countries, a surplus that can help to finance their development and reduce their foreign debt. And the industrialized countries stand to benefit as well for two reasons: first, because through tourism they fulfill the wishes of their consumer citizens who would like to be able to travel abroad more freely and easily: and second, because their large enterprises, in particular the multinationals, have everything to gain from cheaper travel and easier access to foreign markets, not to mention the associated possibility of exporting their tourism engineering or that of their sub-contractors to those markets. (Secretary General, UNWTO, 2003: 2)

The idea that openness is good for growth and human development has become deeply ingrained in development institutions (e.g. see Dollar & Kray, 2000). Indeed, there is perhaps insufficient recognition in the discussion on pro-poor tourism that the focus on poverty reduction actually received its impetus since the early 1990s as a result of the interests of the World Bank.

The World Bank's *World Development Report 1990* relaunched poverty reduction as a primary objective of the Bank. As Culpeper (2002: 2) observed, 'other agencies, notably the principal multilateral development banks and bilateral aid agencies, soon followed suit'. The World Banks' policy descriptions focused on the development potential of greater openness to trade and foreign investment as part of a broader globalisation policy agenda.

> Consequently, 'openness' has come to mean trade liberalization plus pro-motion of longer-term foreign investment, particularly FDI. Along with sound domestic economic policies, developing countries were now being told that openness (in this sense) is central to poverty-reducing growth. (Culpeper, 2002: 3)

Such ideas have clearly been embraced by the UNWTO and other public, private and NGO stakeholders as part of the tourism and poverty-reduction and pro-poor tourism agenda.

Nevertheless, as the United Nations Development Programme (UNDP) has recognised:

> In practice, the relationship between trade and growth is determined by a complex array of domestic and external factors. Cross-country evidence provides little foundation for the use of loan conditions or world trade rules to promote rapid liberalization. (UNDP, 2005: 120)

The UNDP as with many other commentators do argue that liberalisation of trade in services, such as tourism, offers potential benefits to developing countries. 'The problem is that industrial countries have focussed on areas that threaten to undermine human development prospects, while failing to liberalize areas that could generate gains for poor countries' (UNDP, 2005: 137).

The counter-institutional argument with respect to pro-poor tourism is that while projects at the local level may be beneficial to some communities and individuals the bigger picture remains the problem. Unless structural changes are made, particularly with respect to agricultural trade, the hopes for poverty-reduction in many parts of the developing world remain poor indeed. While 'poorer countries' do have the capacity to 'harness their assets of natural beauty and cultural wealth for development gains' (Secretary General of the UN Conference on Trade and Development, Dr. Supachai Panitchpakdi in eTurboNews, 2005b) it is often difficult to eat a view. The notion espoused by the UNWTO that 'tourism exchanges benefit primarily the countries of the South' is a ridiculous one and hides the reality that not only is the consumption of tourism the domain of the wealthy, but in many ways so is its production. Pro-poor tourism initiatives will be of value to some communities, as is usually the case with the transfer of economic and intellectual capital, yet issues of the location of those places in the international and domestic tourism commodity chains still remain. Pro-poor tourism initiat-ives are also of some value to consultants, researchers and companies who benefit financially from such trade aid support initiatives, and who, together with tourists and government agencies, may also be able to assuage their need to 'do something about the gap between rich and poor without changing their own lifestyles. These comments are not to deny the importance of poverty reduction. It is clearly one of the most important issues of our time. Yet whether tourism is a means of reducing poverty gaps beyond isolated instances or is perhaps symptomatic of a causal relationship, at least with respect to the broader scope of north-south trade, needs to be debated much further than is presently the case in tourism policy circles.

C. Michael Hall
Editor

References

Ashley, C., Boyd, C. and Goodwin, H. (2000) *Pro-Poor Tourism: Putting Poverty at the Heart of the Tourism Agenda*. Natural Resource Perspectives, Number 51. London: Overseas Development Institute.

Cater, E.A. (1993) Ecotourism in the third world: Problems for sustainable development. *Tourism Management* 14 (2), 85–90.

Chok, S., Macbeth, J. and Warren, C. (2007) Tourism as a tool for poverty alleviation: A critical analysis of 'pro-poor tourism' and implications for sustainability. *Current Issues in Tourism* 10 (2&3), 144–165.

De Kadt, E. (ed.) (1979) *Tourism – Passport to Development?* Oxford: Oxford University Press.

Dollar, D. and Kray, A. (2000) *Growth Is Good for the Poor*. Washington, DC: World Bank, Development Research Group. On WWW at http://www.worldbank.org/research/growth/pdfiles/growthgoodforpoor.pdf.

eTurboNews (2005a) World leaders: Use tourism in war on poverty, WTO praised. *eTurboNews*, September 16. On WWW at http://www.travelwirenews.com/eTN/16SEP2005.htm.

eTurboNews (2005b) Leaders call for harnessing of tourism to combat poverty. *eTurboNews*, September 15. On WWW at http://www.travelwirenews.com/eTN/15SEP2005.htm.

Hall, C.M. and Lew, A.A. (eds) (1998) *Sustainable Tourism Development: Geographical Perspectives*. Harlow: Addison Wesley Longman.

Hall, D. and Brown, F. (eds) (2006) *Tourism and Welfare: Ethics, Responsibility and Sustained Well-being*. Wallingford: CABI.

Lea, J. (1988) *Tourism and Development in the Third World*. London: Routledge.

Murphy, P.E. (1994) Tourism and sustainable development. In W. Theobold (ed.) *Global Tourism: The Next Decade* (pp. 274–290). Oxford: Butterworth Heinemann.

Reid, D.G. (2003) *Tourism, Globalization and Development: Responsible Tourism Planning*. London: Pluto Press.

Scheyvens, R. (2002) *Tourism for Development: Empowering Communities*. Harlow: Prentice Hall.

Scheyvens, R. (2007) Exploring the tourism-poverty nexus. *Current Issues in Tourism*.

Schilcher, D. (2007) Growth versus equity: The continuum of pro-poor tourism and neo-liberal governance. *Current Issues in Tourism*.

Secretary General UNWTO (2003) *Report of the Secretary-General, Addendum 1, Liberalization of Trade in Tourism Services*. A/15/7 Add.1, Madrid, September 2003. 15th session, Beijing, China, 19–24 October 2003, Provisional agenda item 7.

Smith, V.L. and Eadington, W.R. (eds) (1992) *Tourism Alternatives: Potentials and Problems in the Development of Tourism*. Philadelphia: University of Pennsylvania Press.

Solomon, R. (2005) Tourism: A challenger for the 21st century. *eTurboNews*, September 25. On WWW http://travelwirenews.com/eTN/27SEPT2005.htm.

United Nations Development Programme (UNDP) (2005) *Human Development Report 2004: Cultural Liberty in Today's Diverse World*. New York: UNDP.

United Nations Development Programme (UNDP) (2005) *Human Development Report 2005: International Cooperation at a Crossroads: Aid, Trade and Security in an Unequal World*. New York: UNDP.

UNWTO (2006) *Tourism Highlights 2006*. Madrid: UNWTO.
UNWTO (2007) Tourism will contribute to solutions for global climate change and poverty challenges. Press release, UNWTO Press and Communications Department, March 8, Berlin/Madrid.
Weaver, D. (2004) Tourism and the elusive paradigm of sustainable development. In A. Lew, C.M. Hall and A. Williams (eds) *Companion to Tourism* (pp. 510–520). Oxford: Blackwell.

Tourism and Poverty Alleviation: An Integrative Research Framework

Weibing Zhao
Tourism Management, Haskayne School of Business, University of
Calgary, Calgary, Alberta, Canada

J. R. Brent Ritchie
Tourism Management Area and World Tourism Education and Research
Centre, Haskayne School of Business, University of Calgary, Calgary,
Alberta, Canada

The past decade has seen an upsurge of interest from the governments and development organisations in a tourism-based approach to poverty alleviation. More specifically, poverty alleviation has been established as a major priority within the United
Nations World Tourism Organisation (UNWTO) itself, as is evidenced by the launch-
ing of the concept of ST-EP (Sustainable Tourism as an effective tool for Eliminating
Poverty). In contrast, the implications of tourism for poverty alleviation have been
largely neglected by the tourism academic community. Relevant research to date is
fragmented, limited in scope, and lacks a consistent methodological development.
To address these deficiencies, this paper presents an integrative research framework,
which synthesises multiple perspectives and can be used as an overarching guideline
to stimulate and guide other future enquiries on tourism and poverty alleviation.
Towards this end, a number of research needs and opportunities have also been identified and suggested along with the presentation of the framework.

doi: 10.2167/cit296.0

Keywords: tourism development, poverty alleviation, research framework, stakeholders, Third World

Introduction

Although the economic significance of tourism for developing countries is
long established (UNWTO & UNCTAD, 2001), noticeably in generating
foreign exchange earnings, attracting international investment, increasing tax
revenues and creating new jobs, it is not until recently that tourism has begun
to be exalted as a powerful weapon to attack poverty. Dated back to the late
1990s, the Pro-Poor Tourism Partnership in the United Kingdom, a
collaborative research initiative of the International Center for Responsible
Tourism (ICRT), the International Institute for the Environment and
Development (IIED) and the Overseas Development Institute (ODI), has been
committed to investigating the ways to tap the potential of tourism in poverty
alleviation and is responsible for most of the early research and documentation
(Ashley *et al.*, 2001). Inspired by the vision and innovative work of the Pro-Poor
Tourism Partnership, UNWTO (2002, 2004a) launched the Sustainable Tourism

for Eliminating Poverty programme (hereafter ST-EP),[1] aiming to promote socially, economically and ecologically sustainable tourism as a gateway to development and reduction of poverty among the world's least developed countries. Recent years have also witnessed a wide range of large-scale, tourism-based development projects around the world, for example in Vietnam (UNWTO, 2004b), Nepal (MoCTCA, 2001) and China (CNTA, 2003).

The confluence of tourism and poverty, previously two separate domains (Bowden, 2005), reflects an essential change in the philosophy of tourism development and poverty alleviation, which is illustrated by Figure 1. Traditionally, regional economic growth is predominantly set as the premier target of local tourism development, while poverty alleviation is either considered a sub-goal or a natural outcome of regional economic growth (Ashley *et al.*, 2000; Deloitte & Touche *et al.*, 1999). A commonly held belief is that as long as the whole region gets wealthier, the benefits brought by economic growth will eventually trickle down to the local poor through multiple channels, such as employment, public welfare and family network (Zeng *et al.*, 2005). Thus, policymakers usually pay considerable attention to the expansion of the tourism sector, but much less to the real issue – to what extent tourism development in practice contributes to poverty alleviation (Christie, 2002). As a result, the impact of tourism on poverty alleviation has been indirect and thus non-phenomenal. In contrast, contemporary approaches, for example pro-poor tourism and ST-EP, aim to establish a direct link between tourism and poverty alleviation and emphasise the voices and needs of the poor in tourism development (Ashley *et al.*, 2001; UNWTO, 2002). The poor become the focus of concern; whether they can reap net benefits from tourism now is the primary criterion for justifying any tourism-based development initiative. Such a new philosophy is believed to greatly enhance the chance of the poor to benefit from tourism.

Despite the potential of tourism as a development tool and the worldwide, mushrooming interest in tourism-based poverty alleviation initiatives, the relationship between tourism and poverty alleviation largely remains *terra incognita* among tourism academics. Until very recently, poverty alleviation and relevant issues have only attracted a small cohort of researchers within tourism, and the existing literature is basically case study driven and oriented to practical aspects.[2] In addition, related research work was produced in a

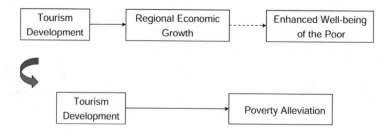

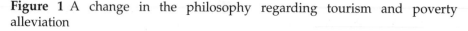

Figure 1 A change in the philosophy regarding tourism and poverty alleviation

diversity of sources, considerably in the form of grey literature, thus failing to explicitly contribute to methodological development in this field of research.

The complexity of poverty-related issues may partly account for the sparse attention of tourism researchers paid to poverty alleviation research. Nowadays, poverty not only means inadequate income and human development, but also embraces vulnerability and a lack of voice, power and representation (World Bank, 1990, 2000). Due to the multidimensional nature of poverty, understanding any poverty-related issue is always a challenge as a wide range of interwoven factors, such as economic, sociopolitical and cultural forces, need to be taken into account. In addition, unfamiliarity with the research settings (poverty-stricken areas) and remoteness to the research subjects (poor people) may also deter many researchers, especially those in economically advanced countries, from delving into poverty research. Anyhow, the severe mismatch between research and practice highlights an urgent need for a more systematic, comprehensive and coherent approach to guide the enquiries of this emerging field of research. Despite the practical difficulties in studying poverty as mentioned above, this field is obviously worth greater research efforts given that poverty has become one of the biggest enemies of humankind into the 21st century. The Millennium Development Goals (MDGs) has made a historic pledge to halve the proportion of the world's people whose income is less than one dollar a day by the year 2015 (United Nations, 2000). We believe that tourism, as one of the largest economic drivers in the contemporary world, should and also can play a more active role in achieving such an ambitious goal.

In this study, 'anti-poverty tourism' (APT) will be used as a unifying concept to refer to any tourism development in which poverty alleviation is set as the central or one of the central objectives. To address the deficiencies in the literature as discussed above, this paper aims to provide an integrative research framework on APT, which is intended to serve as a catalyst that can stimulate more future, in-depth investigations in this emerging field of research. A similar approach has been utilised on urban tourism (Pearce, 2001), sport tourism (Hinch & Higham, 2001), wildlife tourism (Reynolds & Braithwaite, 2001), special interest tourism (Trauer, 2006), mountaineering (Pomfret, 2006) and human resource development (Liu & Wall, 2006). The unique value of integrative frameworks lies in their strength in offering 'both a general overview of the field and a means of putting specific studies and problems in context, so as to understand better the existing interrelationships, to develop a sense of direction and common purpose, and to provide more integrated solutions to problems that may arise' (Pearce, 2001: 928). Thus, integrative frameworks are especially useful for the formation and maturing of emerging research topics or fields like APT.

Discussions below are organised as follows. In the next section, the integrative framework that represents a holistic, conceptual understanding of the APT domain will be introduced and explained. The later section is intended to illustrate the usefulness of the integrative framework for analysis, and will identify and suggest a number of research needs and opportunities associated with the framework. The last section will conclude, with some discussions on the managerial implications of the framework.

Conceptualising APT: An Integrative Research Framework

Figure 2 is an illustration of the integrative APT research framework proposed in this paper. Its content and structure arose out of a deliberate, comprehensive consideration of a wide range of related literature (see the references of this section), combined with some of the present authors' personal thoughts and theoretical constructs. An overview of the framework will be presented first, followed by detailed explanation and justification for each of the constituents and their relationships.

The central part of the integrative framework – the ladder, is basically concerned with the process and mechanisms as to how tourism development can contribute to the reduction of poverty. It consists of four levels – 'poverty alleviation', 'determinants', 'APT themes' and 'stakeholders', each of which is further specified as a cluster of several interrelated components. 'Poverty alleviation', being the convergent point of the whole framework, is the essential objective of any development initiative including APT. 'Determinants' in this framework refers to those prerequisites that must be met in order to achieve the objective of poverty alleviation in a sustainable manner. Specifically, three determinants – 'opportunity', 'empowerment' and 'security' have been identified and included on the basis of a review of contemporary development studies and practices. They conjointly represent a highly generalised model to poverty alleviation, and any development effort or approach, to be justified and successful, should address and contribute to at least one of them. The third level of the ladder is a list of three crucial themes that require serious consideration in APT. From a tourism development perspective, it is proposed that to effectively reduce poverty, an impoverished destination needs to build up its competitiveness, ensure adequate local participation and follow the principles of sustainable development; deficiency in any aspect may severely weaken the positive impacts of tourism on the life of the poor. Given the significance of stakeholders in tourism planning, development and management, the framework also includes six salient stakeholder groups as deemed most relevant to APT.

The upper parts on both sides of the ladder address the relationships of APT with other poverty alleviation approaches. Research on this will provide

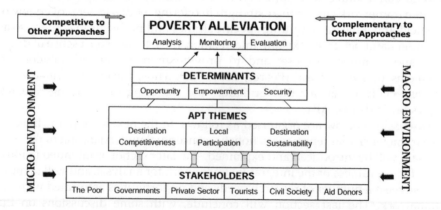

Figure 2 An integrative framework for anti-poverty tourism research

information on the comparative benefits and costs of APT, which can be used as the basis for fitting APT into broader poverty alleviation initiatives. The over-hanging parts, namely 'macro environment' and 'micro environment', high-light the facts that tourism is an open system and APT is thus subject to various influences and pressures that arise within and outside the system.

Poverty alleviation and determinants

In accordance with the multidimensional nature of 'poverty', 'poverty alle-viation' has also been widely recognised as a multidimensional objective (World Bank, 1990, 2000). That said, understanding both 'poverty' and 'poverty alleviation' is obviously beyond simply tracking economic measures, and inherently requires special treatment by more comprehensive research. This research need has been adequately considered by the integrative framework, which highlights the importance of the research regarding the analysis, monitoring and evaluation of poverty and poverty alleviation. Typically, for this part, the following basic questions will be investigated: (1) What is poverty and who are the poor? (2) What are the root reasons of poverty? (3) How to measure poverty and track the progress towards poverty alleviation? The relevance of these questions to APT research is evident as researchers need to be well-informed on them so that research subjects can be selected, appropriate indicators developed, and the effective-ness of APT monitored and evaluated. Although answers to these basic questions can be directly 'borrowed' from generic poverty studies, there is still a situational need for tourism researchers to adapt the answers to the context of tourism. This is especially true when it comes to the monitoring and evaluation of the particular contributions of tourism to the reduction of poverty. The big challenge is that it is not always easy to differentiate the impacts of tourism from those of other development activities. The recently developed Tourism Satellite Account (TSA) by UNWTO (2001) provides a promising solution in this regard, but only in the economic sense. In addition, TSA only measures the contribution of tourism to the macro economy rather than specifically to a certain social group like the poor. Tracing and mapping tourists' cash flows to the local poor could be another relevant approach in exploring the correlation between tourism and poverty alleviation. However, this approach requires extensive work in data collection and validation, and may be less feasible in large-scale destinations with a diverse economy.

The level of 'determinants' includes three components – 'opportunity', 'empowerment' and 'security', which collectively reflect the guiding prin-ciples of contemporary development practices under the leadership of the World Bank (2000).[3] 'Opportunity' means the poor must have access to econ-omic opportunity of which they can take advantage to change their destiny. Much research and evidence have demonstrated the ineffectiveness and unsustainability of the traditional, charity-based approach in poverty allevia-tion (World Bank, 1998). This is mainly because the poor could become overly dependent on donations and lose their motivations to improve their life by themselves. Therefore, nowadays more emphasis has been put on the income generation capacity building of the poor (UNIDO, 2001), in which economic opportunity plays a significant, incubating role. The second component – 'empowerment', is also well entrenched in poverty studies (see PREM, 2002). In the political sense, 'empowerment' aims to enhance the capacity of the poor to influence the state and social institutions, and thus strengthen their participation in political processes and local decision making. In the economic sense, it highlights removing the barriers that work against the poor and building their assets to enable them to engage effectively in markets. The poor being socially, economically and politically marginalised, both forms of empowerment represent the essential processes for them to pursue and benefit from any economic opportunity (World Bank, 2000). The third component 'security', is concerned with reducing the vulnerability of the poor to various risks such as ill health, economic shocks and natural disasters. Since poor households have fewer assets and less diversified sources of income to manage any crisis, they could be easily thrown into despair when these adverse impacts happen to them (Dhanani & Islam, 2002). Therefore, simply expanding opportunity and empowerment are insufficient; to consolidate the fruits of poverty alleviation, a social security system specifically for the poor also requires establishing. These three components, each from a distinct angle, have manifested three requisite but supplementary ways to assist the poor. Evidently, to achieve the most desired effect in poverty alleviation, all of the three components should be concurrently strengthened.

The above discussion indicates that the three components under the category of 'determinants', as the key conditions for poverty alleviation in the general sense, actually serve as the bridge linking development initiatives and the objective of poverty alleviation. Judging the appropriateness and efficacy of a certain poverty alleviation approach can be as straightforward as to examine whether it contributes to the opportunity, empowerment or/and security of the poor. As an immediate example, the usefulness of tourism development for poverty alleviation can be evaluated by employing these three criteria. Doing so is expected to reveal valuable information that helps specify the functioning mechanisms of APT in poverty alleviation, and thus provide theoretical support for APT.

Three APT themes

Destination competitiveness

The last decade has seen a rapid expansion of literature in tourism addressing destination competitiveness, which reflects the escalating competition in contemporary global and regional tourism markets (e.g. Kozak & Rimmington, 1999; Pearce, 1997; Ritchie & Crouch, 2000, 2003). From discussions on destination image and attractiveness to comprehensive considerations of a wide range of destination attributes (Enright & Newton, 2004), this line of enquiry has developed into a significant field of research in tourism and now destination competitiveness has been widely recognised as a decisive factor influencing the performance of destinations. Yet a close examination of the literature reveals that few studies to date have paid serious attention to the destination competitiveness of the developing world, especially impoverished destinations. Although admittedly it is less likely for a newly developing, still fragile tourism economy to build up its competitiveness in a manner that could overpower leading competitors, appropriate competitiveness is still required in order to survive and thrive, at least to differentiate itself from the most immediate competitors (Ritchie, 2004). UNWTO (2002: 94) reinforces this view, stating that 'commercial viability is paramount ... the poor do not have sufficient resources ... to risk engaging in initiatives which do not have strong links to demonstrably viable markets for their goods and services'.

In terms of Ritchie and Crouch (2000), destination competitiveness combines both comparative advantages and competitive advantages. The former involves the endowed resource base that, both naturally and built, makes a destination attractive to visitors, while the latter refers to the ability to mobilise and deploy this resource base. In comparison to wealthy and established destinations, which have abundant resources to build up their strength in all or most aspects, impoverished destinations may only have comparative advantages on a very limited number of destination attributes like core attractions and cost/value. For this sake, it might be a more productive strategy if impoverished destinations were centred on seeking competitive advantages by wise deployment of the limited resources in hand and effective utilisation of second-mover advantages (Ritchie, 2004). Emphasis on competitive advantages will naturally put a high demand on such high-end functions as destination management on a daily, operational basis, and destination policy, planning and development in the long term (Ritchie & Crouch, 2003). Notably, due to the difference in the quality of human resource base, there could be a larger gap in these functions between wealthy, established destinations and impoverished destinations. Reducing such a gap obviously requires strategic, consistent commitment from the government in human resource development and the presence of an education and training-conscious private sector (Esichaikul & Baum, 1998; Liu & Wall, 2006). However, before the establishment of a strong human resource base, which evidently takes time and demands huge financial input, it is often necessary for impoverished destinations to procure external technical assistance in order to meet the most immediate needs in search of appropriate competitiveness, especially in the initial planning phase. The value of technical assistance in this regard has been well demonstrated by the development of Bali and Caribbean in early time (Miller, 1983) and Greater Mekong Sub-Region (GMS) recently (ADB, 2004).

Other related research has indicated additional insights for the competitiveness building of impoverished destinations with resource constraints. For example, seeking competitiveness in a smaller geographical scope and among reachable markets, rather than simply targeting at the global, continental or national level, has been recognised as a more practical and promising competitive strategy for destinations in the developing world (Ghimire, 2001; Saayman *et al.*, 2001). Implementation of such a strategy inherently requires a change of focus from dependency on inbound tourism to parallel development of domestic tourism. A direct advantage of domestic tourism is that it comparatively has much less resource demand on the destination and thus helps accumulate competitive elements in a gradual, manageable manner (Seckelmann, 2002; Sindiga, 1996). This may be best illustrated by the rise of China as a nation destination in the global tourism market, which benefits a lot from the sustained boom of China's domestic tourism that not only

EXAMPLE

contributes to the development of infrastructure, facilities and human resource base, but more importantly, has stimulated a strong, positive political will towards tourism (Wu *et al.*, 2000; Xu, 1999; Zhang, 1997). Another well-founded competitive strategy for impoverished destinations is to promote certain forms of tourism that are largely built upon or have wide linkages with resources locally available and distinct, such as cultural tourism (UNWTO, 2004b), agrotourism (Torres & Momsen, 2004) and rural tourism (Briedenhann & Wickens, 2004). Embedded in local features, these forms of tourism are usually the big attraction to foreign tourists, and in addition, can be organised without intensive investment and development. A logical extension of this strategy is to focus on attracting and marketing to non-institutional (Cohen, 1972) or allocentric-oriented (Plog, 1973) tourists, the tourists who have intense interests in experiencing the authentic local lifestyle but do not care much about the physical built environment. In recent years, the importance of developing partnerships among neighbouring destinations, for example, in resource sharing and collaborative destination marketing, has also been seriously noticed by academics and practitioners. The above-mentioned GMS tourism development project (ADB, 2004), for instance, is exactly intended to promote tourism and reduce poverty of this broad region by strengthening interregional cooperation in the fields like product design, service consistency, marketing and cross-border transit. Development of destination/attraction clusters (Jackson, 2006) and deliberate design of tour routes (Briedenhann & Wickens, 2004), two additional approaches recently suggested for impoverished destination, actually follow a similar principle, both aiming to enhance the destination competitiveness through partnerships.

Local participation

Despite the significance of destination competitiveness, it cannot be taken for granted that poverty will be automatically alleviated as a destination becomes more competitive in the tourism market. The high percentage of economic leakage and unequal benefit distribution caused by excessive and inappropriate use of nonresidents and the 'neocolonial' travel trade structure have been long noticed in the destinations of the developing world (e.g. Britton, 1982; Brohman, 1996; Brown, 1998). The inclusion of the second theme – local participation, demonstrates the need to emphasise the adequate involvement of local poor residents in the APT development process. The rationale for local participation is straightforward: if the poor, the targeted beneficiary, remain outside of the circle of the tourism economy, tourism means nothing or little to them. Specifically, local participation is believed to be able to create larger and balanced economic opportunities for the local poor, increase local tolerance and positive attitudes to tourism development, and facilitate the implementation of the principles of sustainable tourism (Tosun, 2005).

In terms of the different roles the poor play in APT development, their participation basically takes two forms, as shown in Figure 3. One form of participation is to be engaged in public councils and related decision making as community members, and the other is to pursue tourism-related economic activities as the input of local human resources, either wage/paid work or self-employment. In the theoretical sense, both forms of local participation

- Community Member   ⟺   • Public Participation

- Human Resource   ⟺   • Employment
  - Wage worker   - Wage/Paid employment
  - Self-employed   - Self-employment
    - Own-account worker   - Non-business self-employment
    - Entrepreneur   - Small/micro business

Figure 3 Roles of the poor and corresponding modes of participation in tourism

represent the indispensable processes for successful APT development (Ashley *et al.*, 2001; UNWTO, 2002, 2004a). Public participation not only serves to protect and promote the holistic well-being of the community to which the poor belong, but also contributes to democracy, equity and equality by making the voice of the poor heard and in full consideration (Keogh, 1990; Simmons, 1994); in contrast, participation by employment is mainly driven by individual endeavours to reap economic benefits tourism brings and thus has more direct impacts on the life of poor households. Although both forms of local participation are equivalently important, a scan of the tourism literature reveals that they have been unevenly treated. Previous research has been heavily focused on employment, with scanty attention to public participation. On one hand, the overt emphasis on employment reflects the fact that the creation of employment opportunities has been dominantly set as a top priority of tourism development in the developing world. On the other hand, this comparative neglect of public participation may also be partly due to the short history of the participatory tourism development approach in the developing world and thus little evidence available for analysis (Tosun, 2005). Noticeably, as for research on employment, there also exists an unbalanced treatment of wage/paid employment and self-employment. Relevant research to date has been narrowly tilted to the study of formal wage/paid employment, mostly hospitality services (Liu & Wall, 2006), whereas self-employment, especially in the informal sector, is largely neglected. For example, research on family business, entrepreneurship and small business – a significant, quickly expanding body of literature in tourism, has not yet paid serious attention to the initiatives of socially disadvantaged groups such as the disabled, women, children, indigenous people and ethnic minorities, which account for most of the poor of this world. Such a weakness, evidently, should be rectified in the future research.

Recently, the practicability and effectiveness of local participation in the context of the developing world have been somewhat questioned (Dahles & Keune, 2002; Tosun, 2000; Zimmerman, 2000). In essence, APT development is not simply a form of charity (Ritchie, 2004). The economic performance of the poor in tourism development still to a large extent depends upon their own rent appropriation capability, which is especially true in decentralised economies. However, the disadvantaged socioeconomic status of the poor, characterised by lack of human and financial capital, greatly constrains their abilities to identify and pursue well-rewarding employment opportunities in the tourism sector (Liu & Wall, 2006). It is not uncommon that in many destinations of developing countries, nearly all or most well-remunerated management positions are occupied by foreign professionals; in addition, local small enterprises and vendors could be easily squashed out of the market by multinationals and other better-standing competitors (Brohman, 1996; Brown, 1998). Besides employment, public participation of the poor in tourism is also not encouraging. According to Tosun (2000), due to a variety of operational, structural and cultural barriers embedded in impoverished areas, real mass public participation actually seldom happens to the poor. In local tourism development, spontaneous participation that provides full managerial responsibility and authority to the host community is believed to be a form the most beneficial to locals in comparison to induced participation and coercive participation (Tosun, 1999). Nevertheless, the reality is that induced and coercive participation are much more common modes to be found in developing countries (Tosun, 2006).

The above discussion has indicated a gap between the theoretical soundness and practical invalidity of local participation in the context of the developing world. To bridge this gap essentially requires an adapted model of local participation, which should be based upon the development of a deep understanding of the participatory behaviors of the poor at the grassroots level. Correspondently, a bottom-up approach in research and policymaking should be necessarily adopted in order to replace or supplement the traditional top-down approach (Altieri & Masera, 1993; Murray & Greer, 1992). Some more concrete methods to foster local participation in impoverished destinations have also been recommended, such as decentralisation of public administration system, fundamental changes in socio-political, legal and economic structure, involvement of non-government organisations (NGOs) and donor agencies, collaboration and cooperation of international tour operators and multinationals, and dissolution of cultural barriers (Tosun, 2000, 2006). However, a challenge to the implementation of these methods is that they involve a wide range of stakeholder groups whose interests in local participation may even conflict with each other. In addition, some of the methods require transformation of the political system and culture (e.g. decentralisation of public administration system and dissolution of cultural barriers, as specified above), which obviously goes beyond the scope of tourism and is less likely to be realised in the short term.

Destination sustainability

The third theme – destination sustainability, highlights the need to view APT development from a long-term perspective. In recognition of the fundamental importance of sustainability to the ongoing competitiveness of a destination, Ritchie and Crouch (2003: 33) pointed out that 'a destination which, for short-term profit, permits the rape and pillage of the natural capital on which tourism depends is destined for long-term failure'.

For impoverished destinations, sustainability especially should be a focus of concern in that ample evidence has indicated an overlap between unsustainable actions and poverty (Dasgupta *et al.*, 2005). Poorer households are more resource dependent than are the rich. Environmental degradation lowers agricultural and other incomes of the poor, and conversely the poor become even more relied on natural resources, furthering the process of environmental degradation and increasing poverty (Duraiappah, 1998). Such a poverty-environment trap has been seen in many areas struggling with poverty (Dasgupta *et al.*, 2005). The tendency of unsustainable development in APT is further intensified by the fact that tourism is a sector heavily built upon natural capital (Collins, 1999). Although tourism can directly contribute to sustainability by providing rationality and funding for conservation and by replacing certain resource extraction economies like mining, hunting and logging, a wide variety of economic, social and environmental problems resulting from poor planning and management of tourism should not be neglected or underestimated (May, 1991; Romeril, 1989). This is especially true for impoverished destinations in that their tourist products are mostly nature-based and sensitive, and they often lack resources to monitor any tourists, let alone mass tourism. In addition, the sociopolitical and legal environment of impoverished destinations is often characterised by incompleteness, ineffectiveness and poor governance, thus counterproductive to sustainability (Mowforth & Munt, 1998). Based upon the experience of Turkey and other developing countries with tourism development, Tosun (1998, 2001) concluded that unsustainable tourism development in the developing world is largely attributed to inappropriate economic policy, backward development approaches, ineffective public administration, over commercialisation and unfavourable international tourism system. Hence, although the general principles and approaches of sustainable tourism development also apply to impoverished destinations, these particular issues and problems attached to impoverished destinations obviously require special consideration. As commonly pointed out by many researchers (see Wahab & Pigram, 1997), probably what is the most crucially needed in Third World tourism development is a fundamental change in policy and decision making from a short-term, money driven mind-set to a long-term, future-oriented vision.

So far, the first three levels of the ladder, inclusive of the components, have been individually detailed. These three levels – 'poverty alleviation', 'determinants' and 'APT themes', together with the links among them, holistically communicate a central proposition that in APT development, the increase in destination competitiveness, local participation and destination sustainability can enhance the opportunity, empowerment and security of the poor, and further contribute to the reduction of poverty. Although the validity of this proposition is pending upon empirical tests, which is beyond the scope of this present work, the soundness of this proposition lies with providing a more concrete roadmap to explore the theoretical foundations for the tourism-based approach to poverty alleviation. In this sense, it mainly serves to inspire future enquiries at this stage.

APT stakeholders

Over the past decade, the significance of stakeholder involvement and collaboration in tourism planning and development has been well entrenched in tourism literature. Appropriate stakeholder management is believed to be cost saving in the long run, contribute to the integration of knowledge, lead to well-informed decisions, and ensure equity and equality by reducing power imbalance among different stakeholders (Jamal & Getz, 1995; Reed, 1997; Ryan, 2002; Sautter & Leisen, 1999). The inclusion of a stakeholder dimension in the framework reflects this growing importance of the concept 'stakeholder' and highlights the necessity to give full consideration to the primary stakeholders and their interactions in APT, which can to a great extent shape the nature, impacts and even destiny of this kind of development initiative. Admittedly, the composition of primary stakeholders may vary significantly across different specific contexts, with changes in salience, interests and relations. However, intended to serve as a conceptual starting point, the list of stakeholders in the framework has been identified in the broadest sense.

Among the six primary stakeholder groups, as listed at the bottom of the framework, the poor, private sector and governments are relatively straightforward (Ashley *et al.*, 2001; Roe & Urquhart, 2001; UNWTO, 2002, 2004a). The poor are the targeted beneficiary of APT, and thus their interests absolutely should be accorded full consideration in the planning and development process. It is worth reminding that although presented as a single stakeholder group in the framework, the poor are not necessarily homogeneous in terms of assets, skills, social networks, confidence, etc. Special attention should be paid to the well-being of the poorest of the poor as they are least capable of directly participating in tourism enterprises. The private sector is the fundamental power that energises the development of tourism and plays a wide range of essential roles such as investment, product development, marketing and operation (Ashley & Roe, 2003). So, without the strong support of the private sector, the tourism sector can hardly grow to the extent that phenomenally benefits the impoverished destination and local poor. The involvement of governments in APT development is also inevitable and necessary. For one thing, poverty alleviation has been among the top agenda of most, if not all, governments in developing countries (World Bank, 1990, 2000). Second, given the fragmented nature of tourism and the escalating competition in the global tourism market, the development of a robust tourism economy is nearly impossible in the absence of the leadership and appropriate intervention of the public sector (Jenkins & Henry, 1982; Pearce, 1998). In addition, if sustainable tourism development is to be achieved, the public sector will also need to play a strong role in terms of education, coordination, regulation and even implementation (Mowforth & Munt, 1998; Wahab & Pigram, 1997).

Tourists, as the customers and money source of destinations, should be a salient stakeholder group in the normative sense, but unfortunately they are seldom given full consideration in the practical planning and development process. The premier difficulty in embracing tourists in stakeholder management lies in their indefinite identity in that the tourists of a certain destination are a quite fragmented, dynamic and amorphous body with diverse interests. For this sake, questions as to who should represent tourists in general and what kind of interests to represent are extremely difficult to be decided. However, the practical difficulty for the direct involvement of tourists in stakeholder management does not discount the value to consider tourists a key stakeholder. Demand analysis on tourists, for example, can have a decisive impact on the product design and market development of the destination. In addition, if guided appropriately, tourists can play a more active role in poverty alleviation by being pro-poor during their travels in impoverished host places. Prior research is heavily limited to the discussion of the economic benefits tourists bring to the poor, with a few notable exceptions, for example Wearing's (2001) seminal book on volunteer tourism and Selzer's (2004) pioneer work on travelers' philanthropy. Actually, tourists can help the local poor in a variety of non-economic ways, such as temporary voluntary work, small charitable donation, cultural exchange and knowledge transfer in the encounters, and so on (UNWTO, 2004a). These non-economic benefits may have a more profound influence on the life of the poor. Of course, since APT is in essence commercial tourism, the traveling experience of tourists cannot be compromised for these non-economic pro-poor favours. However, in a related comment, the process of helping others itself might be able to bring great pleasure to philanthropic tourists, and if they are organised, this type of tourists could form a distinct force to attack the poverty of impoverished destinations.

The identification of civil society as a primary stakeholder reflects the rising significance of civil society in contemporary development practices (World Bank, 2000). Civil society, as a collective concept, refers to a multi-level group of voluntary and non-profit organisations that, independent from the state, market and family spheres, are dedicated to promoting public good, especially for marginalised or disadvantaged social groups (Hadenius & Uggla, 1996). Due to its independence and distinct roles, it has been promoted as an effective tool to address the failure in the governance of the state and market. Civil society is also an important medium through which aid is channelled in that it has a common interest in development and is able to reach to the poorest of the poor (Edwards & Hulme, 1996). In APT development, civil society can play a positive role in a variety of ways, for example to seek development funds, campaign for business ethics, amplify the voice of the poor at the policy level, provide free training and guidance, support small/micro business initiatives and promote a democratic participatory process (Ashley *et al.*, 2001; UNWTO, 2004a). These functions, though supplementary in nature, are often indispensable in the developing world, especially when both the state and market have proved to be dysfunctional and against the poor.

Aid donors, in the framework, specifically refer to those entities that generously provide loans, grants or other kind of assistance to support APT development projects. Although aid donors usually do not directly participate in development, they have the legitimacy to ensure that the money or other resources they have donated are used for the purposes they desire. The aids, especially those channeled through international development agencies, have been one of the most important sources of development funds for impoverished nations (World Bank, 1990). Thus, the salience of aid donors as a primary stakeholder group in APT is expected to grow fast as their interest in this kind of development initiatives increases.

APT and other poverty alleviation approaches

The upper parts on both sides of the central ladder are concerned with the relationship between the tourism-based approach and other customary approaches to poverty alleviation, such as charity and philanthropy, debt relief, education and training, information and communication technologies (ICTs), agrotechnology transfer, microfinance, voluntary resettlement, etc. Although all of these approaches purportedly work towards the same end – poverty reduction, they are not necessarily complementary to each other due to differences in the principle, priority and resource demand. For example, resettlement of the poor to places with better living conditions, a popular approach to address poverty in mountain regions, is obviously contradictive to the principle of APT since the latter emphasises finding economic opportunity exactly from the previous residence and surroundings rather than escaping from these. APT is also not consistent with charity and philanthropy in that it focuses on the capacity building of the poor and income generation rather than directly giving to them. In contrast, some other approaches like education and training, ICTs and microfinance (UNWTO, 2005) are basically close partners to APT. On one hand, these approaches, from different angles (human capital, information access and financial capital), can enhance the capability of the poor to participate in and benefit from tourism development. Thus, in the presence of these approaches, it is relatively easier to achieve the targeted objectives of APT. On the other hand, the success of APT will also provide supports for the implementation of these complementary approaches. However, it is cautioned that there are also potential conflicts between APT and these 'buddy' approaches. A brutal reality in most impoverished places is that resources available to poverty alleviation are usually quite limited and do not allow plural implementation of all or most of these approaches. For this sake, the practical decision as to which approach or approaches should be adopted is largely dependent upon the comparative effectiveness and efficiency of each approach in poverty alleviation. In this sense, those complementary approaches are actually competitive to APT. It should be admitted that each poverty alleviation approach has its own merits and tourism is not a panacea for any impoverished place. In planning APT, there is a crucial need to comparatively evaluate the pros and cons of the tourism-based approach to poverty alleviation, a need that has been largely neglected by previous research. A meaningful but also challenging thesis in this regard is to investigate the ways in which tourism can effectively team up with other poverty reduction strategies. So far, some valuable work has been done on the agriculture-tourism link and its implications for poverty reduction (e.g. Torres & Momsen, 2004).

Environments of APT

Tourism, as an open system, is subject to a variety of influences and pressures that, arising within or outside the tourism domain, constitute the development environments of tourism. In the framework, the macro environment of APT represents the forces that, often global in scope, broadly affect all human activities. Although these forces may be not directly related to tourism, they can result in events that are profound in their implications for world tourism and thus APT development. For example, events like the 9/11 terrorist attack, the breakout of the severe acute respiratory syndrome (SARS), the Indian Ocean tsunami and more recently, the rocketing of oil price, have caused fundamental changes in some destinations' attractiveness to tourists, shifts in the pattern of travel flows, adjustments of tourism businesses and transformations of tourism philosophy. Noticeably, for a certain destination, a change in the macro environment may mean challenges, opportunities, or both. It is important that APT planners maintain a monitoring system to identify and analyse the global forces they believe are relevant to the needs of tourism development so that they can strategically adapt to the macro environment, which is in a constant state of change and evolution.

The micro environment of APT is made up of entities, influences and forces that lie within the immediate arena of tourism activities and competition. Because of its proximity and greater sense of immediacy, the micro environment to a great extent determines the destination's ability to serve its visitors, local poor and other stakeholders. Basically, the micro environment of a given destination can be divided into two parts – internal and external. The internal part involves the entities that participate in the operation and delivery of the destination's tourism product or experience, such as suppliers, attractions, travel trade, related and supporting industries and destination management organisations. Consideration of these internal entities and their interactions can help identify potential conflicts among the entities and align the variety of interests with the central development objective of APT – poverty allevia-tion. In comparison, the external part of the micro environment mainly refers to the competitive environment posed by rival destinations. A scrutiny of the external environment of the destination will greatly facilitate APT planners to conduct competitive/collaborative analysis and take strategic actions in order to enhance the destination competitiveness.

Identifying Research Needs and Opportunities: The Use of the Framework

So far, the proposed integrative framework on APT has been portrayed, with the components individually examined. Although some major issues and themes relating to tourism and poverty alleviation have surfaced in the process, the implications of the framework for research largely remain unclear, especially given that the linkages in the framework are not adequately con-sidered. This section seeks to fill this gap. In the following, three general approaches to use the framework to inform research will be first suggested and based on that, a number of research needs and opportunities will be highlighted.

Three general approaches to guide research through the framework

The most straightforward approach to examine and use the framework is to focus on each of the components. The presentation of the framework in the pre-vious section has indicated that each component actually represents a relatively independent research domain with its own distinct problems and issues. If research were organised around the same component, significant research problems and issues concerning that component would be systematically and thoroughly identified and researched; as a result, a deep understanding of the nature and roles of the component in APT will be developed. In accordance with the main purpose of this study, this paper has only provided an overview of each component. Following the above-suggested approach, a natural extension of the present work will be to open up and flesh out each of the boxes (components) in the framework, as illustrated by Figure 3 that has decomposed 'local participation' into several more specific, researchable factors.

   Although each component has their own discourse, it also should be noted that there are frequent information, resource and other kind of exchanges or interactions occurring among the components. In full recognition of this, the second suggested approach is to horizontally examine the linkages among the components of the same dimension. Since this approach focuses on the relations of two or more components rather than a single component, it can reveal many additional research problems and issues that the first approach cannot. The first venue in which such an approach may lead to productive results is the stakeholder dimension. In APT, primary stakeholders are usually closely interconnected via a variety of geographic, sociocultural, economic and political nexus. It is through these nexus that the behaviours and performance of a certain stakeholder is influenced or even shaped by other stakeholders. Thus, examination of these nexus is expected to result in more insights with respect to stakeholder management. The same approach certainly can be equally employed to understand the theme and determinant dimensions. As for the theme dimension, research can be focused on the interrelations among destination competitiveness, local participation and destination sustainability. The affinity between destination competitiveness and sustainability is well established in the literature (Ritchie & Crouch, 2003), and so is between local participation and destination sustainability (Mitchell & Eagles, 2001; Tsaur *et al.*, 2006). By comparison, the relation between local participation and destination competitiveness largely remains unexplored. A positive correlation between these two themes cannot be taken for granted in that local participation in impoverished destinations is usually characterised by small capitalisation, inexperience and lack of expertise; thus, deep involvement of foreign companies and professionals is often required in order to keep competitive, especially in the early stages of tourism development (Ashley & Jones, 2001; Endo, 2006). So, further research is clearly needed to advance the current poor understanding of their relationship.

   A more advanced approach to use the framework to guide research is to examine the linkages of two or more dimensions, which is expected to better reflect or reveal the dynamics and operating laws of APT development. Maybe the most prominent thesis using such an approach is to test the propositions put forward in the last section concerning the relations among APT themes, determinants of poverty alleviation and the final end – poverty alleviation, as described by the arrows in the central ladder of the framework. From a theoretical perspective, pursuing these propositions may provide sound foundations for the tourism-based development approach to poverty alleviation. From a practical perspective, these propositions can serve as the guidelines to evaluate and monitor the effects of APT development. The approach can be similarly applied to understand the roles of the primary stakeholders in the building or enhancement of destination competitiveness, local participation and destination sustainability. Any combination of the components in the theme and stakeholder dimensions could be a distinct research topic. For example, research can be conducted on how civil society can contribute to local participation, or how the private sector can be better organised to build destination competitiveness. Along this line of enquiry, more significant research issues will emerge.

Highlights of research needs and opportunities

Based upon a comprehensive consideration of the literature and related discussions so far, the following research needs and opportunities have been identified and recommended as thought worth immediate or considerable attention in future enquires relating to tourism and poverty alleviation:

- *Themes–determinants–poverty alleviation nexus*: The significance of investigating the relations among these three levels has been iterated throughout the text. The nexus represents the central proposition of the framework regarding the principles of APT, and definitely should be among the top agenda of research.
- *Appropriate competitiveness*: Although seeking appropriate competitiveness may be the wisest competitive strategy for impoverished destinations, the content of appropriate competitiveness has not yet been specified. There is a considerable amount of literature on tourism policy and tourism management, but relatively little is suitable to the needs of those in impoverished destinations. Thus, there is a need to develop a conceptual model of appropriately competitive destination based on the realities of the developing world. A possibility in this regard is to adapt an existing, well-accepted framework, which, developed by Ritchie and Crouch (2003), identifies the factors that determine the competitiveness and sustainability of tourism destinations in developed countries. The adaptation of such a framework requires a deep understanding of the fundamental differences between developed and impoverished destinations, which can be achieved by exploring the views of relevant stakeholders, especially views from the stakeholders in impoverished destinations.
- *Entrepreneurship of the poor*: Entrepreneurship of the poor, as a big component of self-employment, has been severely under-reported in primary literature, especially in tourism (Echtner, 1995). Previous research is largely limited to the discussion of two types of entrepreneurs – growth and profit-driven and lifestyle (Getz & Carlsen, 2000; Getz & Petersen, 2005). Although poor entrepreneurs also fantasy growth/profits and desired lifestyle, their immediate goal of running a small/micro business may be just to shake off poverty and earn a comfortable life. Another particular characteristic of poor entrepreneurs is that they are often pushed, rather than pulled, to get involved in business activities, especially when there are few livelihood options available to them. The wide involvement of the poor in the informal sector further complicates their entrepreneurial phenomenon because the informal sector economy is very difficult to monitor, measure and research. Possible research topics relating to the entrepreneurship of the poor in tourism could be to investigate the nature and roles of entrepreneurial participation, antecedents and factors, ways of resource procurement, survival and growth strategy, etc. All these research topics highlight a need to focus on the

grassroots-level initiatives, and will lead to valuable information for the bottom-up policymaking process.

- *Involvement of the private sector*: Given that the rise of the APT movement around the world is a recent phenomenon, the acceptance by the private sector of the development philosophy requires time. At this stage, research on the private sector is critically needed to address two levels of the question. First, the private sector is basically concerned with customers and profits, and its engagement in APT to a large extent is driven by commercial opportunity, not simply ethical appeal (Ashley & Haysom, 2004). So, the question as to how impoverished destinations can create an attractive investment environment to motivate the private sector to participate in APT development should be paid close attention of research. However, on the other hand, it also should be noted that in the past the poor of many destinations have failed to benefit significantly, if not have suffered, from the deep involvement of the private sector (Brohman, 1996; Brown, 1998). As in the case of Quintana Roo, Mexico, Torres and Momsen (2005) found that while tourism development generated profit for transnational corporations and entrepreneurial elites, it did not achieve backward linkages that may have improved conditions for local impoverished population. Thus, there is a cry for some fundamental changes in traditional business practices. Although the endorsement and promotion of certain worldwide ethics campaigns such as the Global Code of Ethics for Tourism, Fair Trade and Corporate Social Responsibility is helpful, it is also necessary to investigate the ways in which APT planners can work together with the private sector to better serve the needs of the poor based on a win–win principle. The Pro-Poor Tourism Pilots in Southern Africa, a project dedicated to facilitating and enhancing the contribution of companies to the poor, has resulted in some very valuable tips and tools in this regard (Ashley, 2006), which can serve as an initial guide and literature base for further enquiries.
- *Travellers' philanthropy*: Travellers' philanthropy, as a newly promoted campaign, is founded on the assumption that there exist a considerable proportion of altruistic tourists who would love to visit impoverished destinations and volunteer to help the poor. To evaluate the possible impacts of such a campaign on poverty alleviation, the assumption should be first empirically tested. The testing can be based upon a general survey of tourists visiting impoverished destinations regarding their overall belief, attitude and intention about travellers' philanthropy. For a given impoverished destination, a detailed segmentation analysis can be conducted to identify those pro-poor, or potentially pro-poor, market segments. Although the phenomenon of travellers' philanthropy has been in evidence, there is a wide recognition that sporadic, spontaneous efforts must be organised and coordinated if it is to play a more influential role. In the implementation of travellers' philanthropy, a very important part of work is to bridge the helps that could be offered by tourists and those in the needs of the visited destination, which essentially requires the establishment of global or regional information and research networks. There is also a crucial research need to understand and address

the concerns of tourists interested in travellers' philanthropy, especially the barriers that limit their opportunity to pursue philanthropic behaviours, e.g. safety and security.

- *Integration of APT with other poverty alleviation approaches*: It is worth remen- tioning that for a given impoverished area, tourism is just one of the many development options. Since poverty usually results from a complex array of root causes, the elimination of poverty inherently requires an optimum combination of multiple approaches. Although the previous conceptual consideration of the relationships between tourism and other poverty alle- viation approaches has provided some insights in this regard, empirical research is especially valuable in the search of an optimum combination because the appropriateness of a certain development approach is highly dependent upon the specific circumstances under consideration. Given that APT is not yet widely practiced, more pilot project-based research, with a special focus on the integration of tourism with other poverty allevia- tion approaches, may be necessarily conducted before some general rec- ommendations can be made for impoverished destinations. From a practical perspective, these pilot projects should seek to explore the effective ways in which APT development practitioners can take full advantage of the currently operated poverty alleviation networks.

Conclusion

As pointed out earlier, researchers being engaged in the field of tourism and poverty alleviation are still a small community, and related research to date is quite fragmented. The ST-EP programme, as a global action framework to harness tourism to reduce poverty, candidly recognises the significance of research for the success of APT and calls for the establishment of a worldwide research base so that research initiatives in this field can be coordinated, concerted and shared (UNWTO, 2002). The website, www.propoortourism.org.uk, launched and managed by the Pro-Poor Tourism Partnership, provides an initial model in this regard. The proposed integrative research framework is also intended to serve a similar purpose. It has been shown that it not only contributes to the clar- ification of the boundary and scope of APT research, but also functions as a public platform for researchers with diverse background and interests to identify and discuss common themes and issues embedded in the framework.

The framework represents one of the exploratory attempts to specify the principles and mechanisms of the tourism-based approach to poverty allevia- tion. From a tourism development perspective, 'destination competitiveness', 'local participation' and 'destination sustainability' have been independently presented as the three must-be-addressed themes in APT development and research. Under the guidance of stakeholder theory, the primary stakeholders that play influential roles in APT have also been identified. Another note- worthy feature of the framework is that it sets APT in a broader context for examination and thus brings more insights into the research of this field. First of all, an adequate understanding of the linkages between tourism and the general principles of poverty alleviation is emphasised. Although these linkages are subject to empirical testing, they provide concrete clues to seek theoretical foundations for APT. Second, previous research mostly limits the scope of enquiries within the boundary of the tourism system. In contrast, this framework fully recognises tourism is an open system, and suggests research should consider the impacts of both macro and micro environments on APT. Furthermore, the potential limitation of tourism in alleviating poverty is also appropriately acknowledged in the framework by considering the competitive and complementary relations of tourism with other customary poverty alleviation approaches. It is cautioned that tourism is not suitable to all impoverished areas and that even if in the impoverished areas where tourism works, tourism also should be wisely combined with, rather than simply replace, other effective poverty alleviation approaches. Overall, the framework not only contributes to the formulation and maturation of APT as a distinct field of enquiry by making the link between tourism and poverty alleviation clearer, but also can be used as an organising device to unite a wide variety of research initiatives. Studying the phenomenon of APT is no longer perceived as solely the responsibility of researchers in tourism. Rather, inputs from various disciplines are welcome as long as they address certain components of the framework.

Although originally intended to inspire research, the framework also has practical implications for the planning, development and management of APT. One of its direct contributions in this regard is that the framework provides planners and managers a holistic picture of the APT development system through which they will gain a clear sense of the factors and relations that need close consideration. Second, as indicated earlier, the components and their inter-relationships embodied in the framework can serve as the major indicators so that the performance of APT development initiatives can be regularly evaluated. Furthermore, the framework also reminds planners and managers of the importance of stakeholder involvement and collaboration.

It should be noted that as a way of facilitating future research on APT, the framework just describes a skeleton of this emerging research field, and the components and embedded relationships in the framework are conceptualised in a highly abstract format. A logical step in extending the current work is to examine and use it in the ways suggested in this paper, which will enable the generic modeling to be tested and refined and thus provide further insights into the peculiarities of the APT phenomenon. Since APT research is cross-disciplinary in nature, relating to both tourism and poverty, a broader review of the development literature on poverty rather than narrowly focusing on the tourism literature is also very meaningful and necessary in order to seek more theoretical justification for the constituent components and structure of the framework. In addition, considering that APT research is essentially oriented to solving the real-world problem – poverty, it is strongly suggested that theoretical development should be well aligned with simultaneous close attention to the progresses made in practical APT development projects. That said, the framework should be developed on an ongoing 'learning' basis as researchers conduct research around it on a continuous, iterative basis, as well as continuing to monitor contributions to the literature, and to observe the activities and performance of organisations such as ST-EP.

Correspondence

Any correspondence should be directed to Weibing Zhao, Tourism Management, Haskayne School of Business, University of Calgary, Calgary, Alberta, Canada T2N 1N4 (weibing.zhao@haskayne.ucalgary.ca).

Notes

1. The ST-EP programme consists of four components. The first component is a research base that seeks to identify linkages, principles and model applications regarding sustainable tourism and poverty alleviation. The second component is an operating framework to promote and develop incentives for good practice among companies, consumers and communities. The third component is in the form of forums through which a diversity of stakeholders (private, public and non-govenmental) can be brought together, and information, ideas and plans shared and exchanged. The fourth component is the ST-EP Foundation dedicated to attracting financing from business, philanthropic and government sources. More information about ST-EP is available at the official website 'www.unwtostep.org'.
2. The Pro-Poor Tourism Partnership has contributed to the majority of extant literature on tourism and poverty alleviation, which was collectively published on the website 'www.propoortourism.org.uk' for free access and download by researchers world-wide. The Partnership has a special interest in experimenting and implementing the pro-poor tourism strategies crafted by Deloitte and Touche, *et al.* (1999), and so far nearly all of the research reports and papers posted on the website are deeply built upon empirical evidence. Another important outlet of research on this topic is UNWTO (2002, 2004a, 2005), which also heavily focuses on issues relating to planning, operation and implementation. By comparison, theoretical discussion and conceptualisation of the relationship between tourism and poverty alleviation are paid much less attention.
3. While the proposed framework adopts the World Bank's (2000) model for development and poverty alleviation that has received prominence in recent years, it should be acknowledged that the model is not without controversy among researchers and development practitioners. Serving as a powerful actor in international development, the World Bank is often criticised for taking a particular slant on neoliberalism, which advocates privatisation, market reform and external policy intervention in the developing world (Goldman, 2005). Not surprisingly, its current development and poverty alleviation approach generally represents such a neoliberal stance. For example, as to the concept 'empowerment', the World Bank (2000) mainly considered it in both a political and an economic sense, but there was no discussion of other ideas on empowerment such as John Friedmann's (1992) book that accords equivalent attention to psychological and social empowerment. Similarly, in interpreting the component 'opportunity', the World Bank (2000) only highlighted the importance of economic opportunity to the poor. By absorbing the World Bank's model into the research framework, we may risk blocking a more holistic view on development and poverty alleviation, and as such, there is a justified need to look beyond the World Bank's neoliberal stance. We will not venture further in this regard, but we do want to convey the point that the framework, essentially designed as a tool to stimulate thoughts and discussion, is open to debate and should be developed on a continuous, iterative basis.

References

Altieri, M.A. and Masera, O. (1993) Sustainable rural development in Latin America: Building from the bottom-up. *Ecological Economics* 7 (2), 93–121.

Ashley, C. (2006) Facilitating pro-poor tourism with the private sector: Lessons learned from PPT pilots in Southern Africa. PPT Report No 2, ODI, IIED, and CRT, February 2006.

Ashley, C. and Jones, B. (2001) Joint ventures between communities and tourism investors: Experience in southern Africa. *International Journal of Tourism Research* 3 (2), 407–423.

Ashley, C. and Haysom, G. (2004) From philanthropy to a different way of doing business: Strategies and challenges in integrating pro-poor approaches into tourism business. Paper presented at ATLAS Africa Conference, October 2004, Pretoria, South Africa.

Ashley, C. and Roe, D. (2003) Working with the private sector on pro-poor tourism: Opinions and experience from two development practitioners. Pro-Poor Tourism Working Paper. London: Overseas Development Institute.

Ashley, C., Boyd, C. and Goodwin, H. (2000) Pro-poor tourism: Putting poverty at the heart of the tourism agenda. *Natural Resource Perspectives* 51, 1–6.

Ashley, C., Roe, D. and Goodwin, H. (2001) Pro-poor tourism strategies: Making tourism work for the poor – a review of experience. PPT Report No 1, ODI, IIED, and CRT, April 2001.

Asia Development Bank (ADB) (2004) *Technical Assistance for the Greater Mekong Sub-Region Tourism Sector Strategy.* Manila: ADB.

Bowden, J. (2005) Pro-poor tourism and the Chinese experience. *Asia Pacific Journal of Tourism Research* 10 (4), 379–398.

Briedenhann, J. and Wickens, E. (2004) Tourism routes as a tool for the economic development of rural areas: Vibrant hope or impossible dream? *Tourism Management* 25 (1), 71–79.

Britton, S.G. (1982) The political economy of tourism in the Third World. *Annals of Tourism Research* 9 (3), 331–358.

Brohman, J. (1996) New directions in tourism for Third World development. *Annals of Tourism Research* 23 (1), 48–70.

Brown, D.O. (1998) In search of an appropriate form of tourism for Africa: Lessons from the past and suggestions for the future. *Tourism Management* 19 (3), 237–245.

China National Tourism Administration (CNTA) (2003) *The Plan for the Investment in Western Regional Tourism.* Beijing: CNTA.

Christie, I.T. (2002) Tourism, growth and poverty: Framework conditions for tourism in developing counties. *Tourism Review* 57 (1/4), 35–41.

Cohen, E. (1972) Towards a sociology of international tourism. *Sociological Research* 39 (2), 164–182.

Collins, A. (1999) Tourism development and natural capital. *Annals of Tourism Research* 26 (1), 98–109.

Dahles, H. and Keune, L. (eds) (2002) *Tourism Development and Local Participation in Latin America.* New York: Cognizant Communication Corporation.

Dasgupta, S., Deichmann, U., Meisner, C. and Wheeler, D. (2005) Where is the poverty-environment nexus? Evidence from Cambodia, Lao PDR, and Vietnam. *World Development* 33 (4), 617–638.

Deloitte and Touche, IIED and ODI (1999) *Sustainable Tourism and Poverty Elimination: A Report for the Department for International Development.* UK: DFID.

Dhanani, S. and Islam, I. (2002) Poverty, vulnerability and social protection in a period of crisis: The case of Indonesia. *World Development* 30 (7), 1211–1231.

Duraiappah, A.K. (1998) Poverty and environmental degradation: A review and analysis of the nexus. *World Development* 26 (12), 2169–2179.

Echtner, C.M. (1995) Entrepreneurial training in developing countries. *Annals of Tourism Research* 22 (1), 119–134.

Edwards, M. and Hulme, D. (1996) Too close for comfort? The impact of official aid on nongovernmental organizations. *World Development* 24 (6), 961–973.

Endo, K. (2006) Foreign direct investment in tourism: Flows and volumes. *Tourism Management* 27 (4), 600–614.

Enright, M.J. and Newton, J. (2004) Tourism destination competitiveness: A quantitative approach. *Tourism Management* 25 (6), 777–788.

Esichaikul, R. and Baum, T. (1998) The case for government involvement in human resource development: A study of the Thai hotel industry. *Tourism Management* 19 (4), 359–370.

Friedmann, J. (1992). *Empowerment: The Politics of Alternative Development.* Oxford: Blackwell.

Getz, D. and Carlsen, J. (2000) Characteristics and goals of family and owner-operated businesses in the rural tourism and hospitality sectors. *Tourism Management* 21 (6), 547–560.

Getz, D. and Petersen, T. (2005) Growth and profit-oriented entrepreneurship among family business owners in the tourism and hospitality industry. *International Journal of Hospitality Management* 24 (2), 219–242.

Ghimire, K.B. (2001) The growth of national and regional tourism in developing countries: An overview. In K.B. Ghimire (ed.) *The Native Tourist: Mass Tourism Within Developing Countries* (pp. 1–29). London: Earthscan.

Goldman, M. (2005) *Imperial Nature: The World Bank and Struggles for Social Justice in the Age of Globalization.* New Haven: Yale University Press.

Hadenius, A. and Uggla, F. (1996) Making civil society work, promoting democratic development: What can states and donors do? *World Development* 24 (10), 1621–1639.

Hinch, T.D. and Higham, J.E.S. (2001) Sport tourism: A framework for research. *International Journal of Tourism Research* 3 (1), 45–58.

Jackson, J. (2006) Developing regional tourism in China: The potential for activating business clusters in a socialist market economy. *Tourism Management* 27 (4), 695–706.

Jamal, T.B. and Getz, D. (1995) Collaboration theory and community tourism planning. *Annals of Tourism Research* 22 (1), 186–204.

Jenkins, C.L. and Henry, B.M. (1982) Government involvement in tourism in developing countries. *Annals of Tourism Research* 9 (4), 499–521.

Keogh, B. (1990) Public participation in community tourism planning. *Annals of Tourism Research* 17 (3), 449–465.

Kozak, M. and Rimmington, M. (1999) Measuring tourist destination competitiveness: Conceptual considerations and empirical findings. *International Journal of Hospitality Management* 18 (3), 273–283.

Liu, A. and Wall, G. (2006) Planning tourism employment: A developing country perspective. *Tourism Management* 27 (1), 159–170.

May, V. (1991) Tourism, environment and development: Values, sustainability and stewardship. *Tourism Management* 12 (2), 112–118.

Miller, D. (1983) United Nations: Projects from Benin to Bali. *Tourism Management* 4 (4), 303–308.

Ministry of Culture, Tourism and Civil Aviation (MoCTCA) (2001) *Tourism for Rural Poverty Alleviation Programme.* Nepal: MoCTCA.

Mitchell, R.E. and Eagles, P.F.J. (2001) An integrative approach to tourism: Lessons from the Andes of Peru. *Journal of Sustainable Tourism* 9 (1), 4–28.

Mowforth, M. and Munt, I. (1998) *Tourism and Sustainability: New Tourism in the Third World.* London: Routledge.

Murray, M.R. and Greer, J.V. (1992) Rural development in Northern Ireland: Policy formulation in a peripheral region of the European community. *Journal of Rural Studies* 8 (2), 173–184.

Pearce, D.G. (1997) Competitive destination analysis in Southeast Asia. *Journal of Travel Research* 35 (4), 16–25.

Pearce, D.G. (1998) Tourism development in Paris: Public intervention. *Annals of Tourism Research* 25 (2), 457–476.

Pearce, D.G. (2001) An integrative framework for urban tourism research. *Annals of Tourism Research* 28 (4), 926–946.

Plog, S.C. (1973) Why destination areas rise and fall in popularity? *Cornell Hotel and Restaurant Administration Quarterly* 14 (3): 13–16.

Pomfret, G. (2006) Mountaineering adventure tourists: A conceptual framework for research. *Tourism Management* 27 (1), 113–123.

Poverty Reduction and Economic Management (PREM) (2002) *Empowerment and Poverty Reduction: A Sourcebook.* New York: World Bank.

Reed, M.G. (1997) Power relations and community-based tourism planning. *Annals of Tourism Research* 24 (3), 566–591.

Reynolds, P.C. and Braithwaite, D. (2001) Towards a conceptual framework for wildlife tourism. *Tourism Management* 22 (1), 31–42.

Ritchie, J.R.B. and Crouch, G.I. (2000) The competitive destination: A sustainability perspective. *Tourism Management* 21 (1), 1–7.

Ritchie, J.R.B. and Crouch, G.I. (2003) *The Competitive Destination: A Sustainable Tourism Perspective.* Oxon, UK: CABI Publishing.

Ritchie, J.R.B. (2004) *Lecture at the 2004 UNWTO Ulysses Award Inaugural Ceremony,* 7 June 2004. Madrid, Spain.

Roe, D. and Urquhart, P. (2001) Pro-poor tourism: Harnessing the world's largest industry for the world's poor. *World Summit on Sustainable Development Opinion,* May 2001. UK: IIED.

Romeril, M. (1989) Tourism and the environment: Accord or discord? *Tourism Management* 10 (3), 204–208.

Ryan, C. (2002) Equity, management, power sharing and sustainability – issues of the 'new tourism'. *Tourism Management* 23 (1), 17–26.

Saayman, M., Saayman, A. and Rhodes, J.A. (2001) Domestic tourist spending and economic development: The case of the North West Province. *Development Southern Africa* 18 (4), 443–455.

Sautter, E.T. and Leisen, B. (1999) Managing stakeholders: A tourism planning model. *Annals of Tourism Research* 26 (2), 312–328.

Seckelmann, A. (2002) Domestic tourism: A chance for regional development in Turkey? *Tourism Management* 23 (1), 85–92.

Seltzer, M. (2004) Travelers' philanthropy: Helping communities build economic assets and sustain environmental and cultural resources in an era of rapid globalization. In Travelers' Philanthropy Conference Proceedings, April 12–15th, Centre on Ecotourism and Sustainable Development, Stanford University, Washington, DC, USA.

Simmons, D.G. (1994) Community participation in tourism planning. *Tourism Management* 15 (2), 98–108.

Sindiga, I. (1996) Domestic tourism in Kenya. *Annals of Tourism Research* 23 (1), 19–31.

Torres, R. and Momsen, J.H. (2004) Challenges and potential for linking tourism and agriculture to achieve pro-poor tourism objectives. *Progress in Development Studies* 4 (4), 294–318.

Torres, R. and Momsen, J.H. (2005) Planned tourism development in Quintana Roo, Mexico: Engine for regional development or prescription for inequitable growth? *Current Issues in Tourism* 8 (4), 259–285.

Tosun, C. (1998) Roots of unsustainable tourism development at the local level: The case of Urgup in Turkey. *Tourism Management* 19 (6), 595–610.

Tosun, C. (1999) Towards a typology of community participation in the tourism development process. *Anatolia: An International Journal of Tourism and Hospitality Research* 10 (2), 113–134.

Tosun, C. (2000) Limits to community participation in the tourism development process in developing countries. *Tourism Management* 21 (6), 613–633.

Tosun, C. (2001) Challenges of sustainable tourism development in the developing world: The case of Turkey. *Tourism Management* 22 (4), 289–303.

Tosun, C. (2005) Stages in the emergence of a participatory tourism development approach in the developing world. *Geoforum* 36 (3), 333–352.

Tosun, C. (2006) Expected nature of community participation in tourism development. *Tourism Management* 27 (3), 493–504.

Trauer, B. (2006) Conceptualizing special interest tourism: Frameworks for analysis. *Tourism Management* 27 (2), 183–200.

Tsaur, S-H., Lin, Y-C. and Lin, J-H. (2006) Evaluating ecotourism sustainability from the integrated perspective of resource, community and tourism. *Tourism Management* 27 (4), 640–653.

United Nations (2000) *Millennium Summit Goals*. New York: United Nations.
United Nations Industrial Development Organization (UNIDO) (2001) *Building Productive Capacity for Poverty Alleviation in Least Developed Countries (LDC's): the Role of Industry*. Vienna: UNIDO.
United Nations World Tourism Organization (UNWTO) (2001) *Tourism Satellite Account: Recommended Methodological Framework*. Madrid: UNWTO.
United Nations World Tourism Organization (UNWTO) (2002) *Tourism and Poverty Alleviation*. Madrid: UNWTO.
United Nations World Tourism Organization (UNWTO) (2004a) *Tourism and Poverty Alleviation: Recommendations for Action*. Madrid: UNWTO.
United Nations World Tourism Organization (UNWTO) (2004b) *Final Report on Ministerial Conference on Cultural Tourism and Poverty Alleviation*, 11–12 June 2004, Hue, Vietnam. Madrid: UNWTO.
United Nations World Tourism Organization (UNWTO) (2005) *Tourism, Microfinance and Poverty Alleviation*. Madrid: UNWTO.
United Nations World Tourism Organization (UNWTO) and United Nations Conference on Trade and Development (UNCTAD) (2001) *Tourism in the Least Developed Countries*. Madrid: UNWTO.
Wahab, S. and Pigram, J.J. (eds) (1997) *Tourism, Development and Growth: The Challenge of Sustainability*. London: Routledge.
Wearing, S. (2001) *Volunteer Tourism: Experiences that Make a Difference*. New York: CAB International.
World Bank (1990) *World Development Report 1990: Poverty*. New York: Oxford University Press.
World Bank (1998) *Assessing Aid: What Works, What Doesn't, and Why*. World Bank Policy Research Report. New York: Oxford University Press.
World Bank (2000) *Attacking Poverty: World Development Report 2000/01*. New York: Oxford University Press.
Wu, B., Zhu, H. and Xu, X. (2000) Trends in China's domestic tourism development at the turn of the century. *International Journal of Contemporary Hospitality Management* 12 (5), 296–299.
Xu, G. (1999) Socio-economic impacts of domestic tourism in China: Case studies in Guilin, Suzhou and Beidaihe. *Tourism Geographies* 1 (2), 204–218.
Zeng, B., Carter, R.W., Lacy, T. and Bauer, J. (2005) Effects of tourism development on the local poor people: Case study in Taibai Region China. *Journal of Services Research* 5 (S), 131–148.
Zhang, W. (1997) China's domestic tourism: Impetus, development and trends. *Tourism Management* 18 (8), 565–571.
Zimmerman, F.J. (2000) Barriers to participation of the poor in South Africa's land redistribution. *World Development* 28 (8), 1439–1460.

Tourism as a Tool for Poverty Alleviation: A Critical Analysis of 'Pro-Poor Tourism' and Implications for Sustainability

Stephanie Chok and Jim Macbeth
School of Tourism, Social Sciences and Humanities, Murdoch University, Western Australia

Carol Warren
Asian Studies, Social Sciences and Humanities, Murdoch University, Western Australia

Forecasts of high tourism growth in developing nations, where widespread poverty exists, has led to considerable interest in tourism as a tool for poverty alleviation. Powerful bureaucratic and business alliances have been forged to expand this programme. International development agencies are also turning to tourism as a way of alleviating poverty. This is sometimes termed 'pro-poor tourism' (PPT). Distinguished from other forms of 'alternative tourisms' such as ecotourism and community-based tourism, the stakeholders involved in this enterprise are no less divided. Ideological divisions manifest themselves in the political struggle over how tourism in developing countries should unfold. This paper identifies the different sustainability positions of prominent pro-poor tourism stakeholders and considers the implications for meeting pro-poor and sustainability objectives. Generally, tourism is too often regarded a panacea without an attendant recognition that, like any other industrial activity, tourism is highly political. As a global industry, tourism operates within a neo-liberal market economy which presents severe challenges to meeting pro-poor and sustainable development objectives. This paper therefore recommends a fundamental re-evaluation of tourism's pro-poor potential in the absence of significant commitment to directly address structural inequities which exacerbate poverty and constrain pro-poor attempts.

doi: 10.2167/cit303

Keywords: pro-poor tourism, poverty alleviation, sustainability, political economy of tourism development

Introduction

The convergence of high tourism growth in poverty-stricken countries has generated a large amount of interest in tourism as a poverty alleviation strategy (Sofield *et al.*, 2004; UNESCAP, 2003; WTO-OMT, 2004a). This is sometimes termed 'pro-poor tourism' (PPT). Touted as an 'alternative' approach to mainstream tourism development models, PPT strategies are directed towards generating net benefits for the poor (DFID, 1999). The stakeholders involved in this enterprise are varied in background and value positions, as well as divided over approaches and strategies.

A prominent stakeholder is the World Tourism Organization (WTO-OMT), an inter-governmental organisation and specialised agency of the United Nations (UN). The WTO-OMT launched its Sustainable Tourism-Eliminating Poverty (ST-EP) programme at the World Summit for Sustainable Development in Johannesburg in 2002. The corporate sector has also shown considerable interest, most notably the World Travel and Tourism Council (WTTC), a powerful private sector group made up of 'the presidents, chairs and CEOs of 100 of the world's most foremost companies' (WTTC, 2005: para. 1). International financial institutions like the Asian Development Bank and the World Bank are also supporting tourism projects as part of their broader 'pro-poor growth' objectives (ADB, 2002; Sofield *et al.*, 2004).

The UK Department for International Development (DFID), which coined the term 'pro-poor tourism' (PPT), has played a significant role in exploring tourism's potential for poverty reduction (DFID, 1999; Sofield *et al.*, 2004) and is closely linked with the Overseas Development Institute (ODI). The ODI is part of the Pro-Poor Tourism Partnership (PPT Partnership), a key source of literature on PPT. Oft-cited authors Ashley *et al.* (1999, 2000, 2001) and Ashley and Haysom (2005) are part of the PPT Partnership, a collaborative research initiative between the International Centre for Responsible Tourism (ICRT), the International Institute for Environment and Development (IIED), and the ODI. Bibliographies of recent work related to tourism and poverty elimination – including reports from global organisations like the World Tourism Organization and the United Nations – would typically include literature from the PPT Partnership.

It is noted that the term pro-poor tourism is contested. It is considered pejorative by some and potentially alienates tourism stakeholders, including investors and tourists (Sofield *et al.*, 2004). Authors like Sofield *et al.* (2004) prefer to use the World Tourism Organization's term, Sustainable Tourism-Eliminating Poverty (ST-EP). Other industry sources may refer to tourism as a tool for 'poverty alleviation', 'poverty reduction' or 'poverty elimination'. These concerns are acknowledged but PPT has been adopted in this discussion to reflect its continued usage in key policy documents. It is also difficult to avoid in an article which draws heavily on material from the Pro-Poor Tourism Partnership. The use of the term 'pro-poor tourism' in this paper includes the myriad of stakeholders – corporate bodies, international bureaucracies, aid agencies, research institutes, global financial institutions, etc. – who are promoting tourism as a tool for poverty alleviation, regardless of what they term it.

While pro-poor tourism is seen as a relatively 'new' discourse (Ashley *et al.*, 1999), the 'poverty agenda' has existed for decades (Storey *et al.*, 2005). PPT reflects shifts in dominant development thinking as a result of disillusion-ment with the failures of modernisation theory to bring about economic and social justice (Chambers, 1998; Kabeer, 1994; McMichael, 2000). There is a notable convergence of PPT with other disciplines and social movements; indeed, the membership of the PPT Partnership means the discourse has likely grown out of a multi-disciplinary process linked to years of experience in the field of international development. PPT's underlying principles – such

Hall criticises

as a holistic livelihoods approach (Ashley *et al.*, 2000) – echo those of sustainable development.

Similarly, the pro-poor tourism discourse, like the sustainable development (SD) debate, is wrought with diverse views and competing values (Beder, 1996; Birkeland *et al.*, 1997; Dale, 2001). Like sustainable development, it is a morally-charged concept valued for its unifying qualities, yet remains vulnerable to political hijacking (Irwin, 2001; Jacobs, 1999; Macbeth, 2005). It is therefore important to critically analyse the ideologies which underpin pro-poor tourism and distinguish between the diversity of views (and values) within the debate. In researching ecotourism initiatives in Belize, Duffy (2002) exposes ideological divisions within the environmental movement and illustrates how these varied and occasionally overlapping ethical positions shape policy, constrain individual agency and undermine efforts at sustainability. Pro-poor tourism, if it is to contribute meaningfully to progressive change needs to be deconstructed in a similar fashion.

Tourism is too often regarded as a panacea – an economic, social and environmental 'cure-all'. Globally, there is a lack of convincing empirical evidence to justify the claim that increased tourism development will lead to significant benefits for the poor. Such a presumed causal link must also be judged against considerable evidence that tourism is causing much environmental, socio-economic and cultural damage (Christ *et al.*, 2003; ECTWT, 2005; Leepreecha, 1997; Madely, 1999; Mastny, 2002). Furthermore, tourism development, as an economic activity, operates within the same socio-political confines as other forms of development that have failed struggling economies (Kabeer, 1994; McMichael, 2000). If persistent structural inequities are not addressed, relying on tourism (pro-poor or not) as a last resort 'rescue plan' is unlikely to reap significant and long-term benefits for the already marginalised, particularly if their communities are already fractured and inhabit environmentally vulnerable areas.

While this article does not seek to promote tourism as a poverty alleviation tool, it should not be seen as 'anti-tourism' in its critical analysis of strategies that do. This paper offers a critique of the global political economy within which tourism development, as a global industry, operates. The aim is to temper the misplaced optimism many place on tourism as the solution to socioeconomic woes and environmental degradation.

To set the context, the first section begins with a broad overview of pro-poor tourism – including its key principles and strategies – and outlines the main arguments of its advocates. The distinction between pro-poor tourism and 'alternative tourisms' is highlighted and a brief discussion of PPT's limitations follows. This leads into an analysis of the differential ethics of pro-poor tourism's main stakeholders through identifying their sustainability positions. The environmental and socioeconomic implications for meeting pro-poor and sustainability challenges are then discussed with these perspectives in mind. In conclusion, this paper provides a critical summary of the main issues which complicate PPT discourse, with a particular emphasis on the political dimensions of tourism development.

Pro-Poor Tourism: Where Tourism Benefits the Poor (Along with the Rich)

PPT principles and strategies

Pro-poor tourism is broadly defined as tourism that generates net benefits for the poor (PPT Partnership, 2004a). 'Net benefits' means benefits outweigh costs (Ashley *et al.*, 1999). This encompasses economic as well as environmental, social, and cultural dimensions (Ashley *et al.*, 1999; UNESCAP, 2003; WTO-OMT, 2002). PPT arises from a belief that tourism *can* and *should* contribute to pro-poor economic growth. Pro-poor growth is 'growth that enables the poor to actively participate in and significantly benefit from economic activity' (PPT Partnership, 2004b: 2).

As an approach, pro-poor tourism is guided by underlying principles. These key principles are outlined in Table 1.

These principles recognise that poverty is multi-dimensional; they extend beyond income generation to include a range of livelihood impacts from tourism. The lack of rigid blue-print approaches emphasises the need to be context-specific – such flexibility is governed by an unequivocal core focus on the poor in the South. Pro-poor tourism's emphasis is on 'unlocking opportunities for the poor within tourism, rather than expanding the overall size of the sector' – in other words, 'tilting' rather than expanding the cake (DFID, 1999: 1).

Roe and Urquhart (2004) summarise the core focus areas of PPT into three distinct but overlapping strategies that include economic benefits, non-economic

Table 1 PPT principles

PPT principles
Participation. Poor people must participate in tourism decisions if their livelihood priorities are to be reflected in the way tourism is developed.
A holistic livelihoods approach. Recognition of the range of livelihood concerns of the poor (economic, social, and environmental; short-term and long-term). A narrow focus on cash or jobs is inadequate.
Balanced approach. Diversity of actions needed, from micro to macro level. Linkages are crucial with wider tourism systems. Complementary products and sectors (for example, transport and marketing) need to support pro-poor initiatives.
Wide application. Pro-poor principles apply to *any* tourism segment, though strategies may vary between them (for example between mass tourism and wildlife tourism).
Distribution. Promoting PPT requires some analysis of the distribution of both benefits and costs – and how to influence it.
Flexibility. Blue-print approaches are unlikely to maximise benefits to the poor. The pace or scale of development may need to be adapted; appropriate strategies and positive impacts will take time to develop; situations are widely divergent.
Commercial realism. PPT strategies have to work within the constraints of commercial viability.
Cross-disciplinary learning. As much is untested, learning from experience is essential. PPT also needs to draw on lessons from poverty analysis, environmental management, good governance and small enterprise development.

Source: Ashley *et al.* (2000); DFID (1999); Roe and Urquhart (2004).

impacts and reforming the policy process. Enhancing the participation of the poor through capacity building and skills transfer, as well as reforming decision-making processes so that their needs are prioritised are recognised as key. These broad strategies need to be pursued across sectors and levels (both micro and macro) and involve a variety of stakeholders (from governments to international donors and investors, tour operators, tourists and the poor) (DFID, 1999).

The principles and strategies listed in this discussion are not exhaustive but are generally reflective of the PPT Partnership's approach to pro-poor tourism. As a 'relatively untried and untested' (Roe & Urquhart, 2004: 321) area, there is limited (though growing) case study material and much of the discussion on PPT is based on theory and preliminary research at this stage.

The argument for tourism as a poverty alleviation tool

Proponents of pro-poor tourism highlight the advantages tourism offers to developing nations. In countries with few competitive exports, tourism is believed to offer a viable development option where few others exist. Poor countries are seen to have comparative advantage as they possess 'assets' prized by the tourism industry, namely wildlife, landscape and cultural experiences sought after by a growing number of tourists (DFID, 1999; PPT Partnership, 2004b; WTO-OMT, 2004a). The poor can build on the natural and cultural capital upon which tourism is dependent, even if they lack the financial resources (Ashley *et al.*, 2001).

Tourism is already a significant economic sector among the world's poorest countries (PPT Partnership, 2004c; Sofield *et al.*, 2004; WTO-OMT, 2004a). Currently, 12 countries account for 80% of the world's poor; in 11 of these countries, tourism is either growing or already significant to the economy (Ashley *et al.*, 2001). This means the livelihoods of millions of poor people are already affected – both negatively and positively – by tourism, a trend likely to continue (DFID, 1999; Roe & Urquhart, 2004; Sofield *et al.*, 2004; WTO-OMT, 2002).

It is also highlighted that tourism offers better labour-intensive and small-scale opportunities compared with other non-agricultural sectors and employs a high proportion of women (WTO-OMT, 2002). As a diverse industry, tourism increases the scope for wide participation, including that of the informal sector, where women are most involved (Sofield *et al.*, 2004). With tourism, consumers come to the product, 'providing considerable opportunities for linkages' (Roe & Urquhart, 2004: 310).

PPT and other 'tourisms'

PPT advocates stress that it is not a specific product or sector of tourism but an approach to tourism development and management (PPT Partnership, 2004a; Sofield *et al.*, 2004). The view is that 'it is possible for almost any tourism attraction or product to meet pro-poor tourism objectives' (UNESCAP, 2003: 4). A pro-poor approach 'identifies the thrust to direct all efforts to poverty reduction' (UNESCAP, 2003: 4). While the constructive pro-poor elements of many sustainable tourism initiatives are welcomed, Ashley *et al.* (2001: 50) stress their different starting points. The sustainable tourism agenda, like the traditional tourism industry, focuses on mainstream destinations. Environmental and other concerns are then added on, with social issues edged towards the periphery. It then moves out to less important destinations, leaving the poor in the South at the edge of the picture. As a result, industry guidelines, which tend to be developed in the North for popular tourism destinations, may be ill-suited to the 'pressing poverty constraints of countries of the South' (Ashley *et al.*, 2001: 3). In contrast, pro-poor tourism focuses directly on tourism destinations in the South, and on developing tourism good practice particularly relevant to conditions of poverty. In the PPT framework, poor people and poverty are placed in the centre. From there, tourism is viewed as 'one component of the household, local and national economies and environment that affects them' (Ashley *et al.*, 2001: 50).

According to Ashley *et al.* (2000: 1), ecotourism and community-based tourism focus on preserving the environmental and cultural base on which tourism depends, but do not adequately consider the 'full range of impacts on the livelihoods of the poor'. In ecotourism, conservation approaches stress local benefits either as incentives for environmental protection, or as a means of promoting alternatives to unsustainable activity (Ashley *et al.*, 2001). Benefits to local people assume secondary importance and are expressed in a protectionist or defensive way, for example in terms like 'preserving local culture' or 'minimising costs' (DFID, 1999: 2). Pro-poor tourism differs in its emphasis on expanding opportunities, and identifies net benefits to the poor as an explicit goal in itself; environmental concerns should contribute to this goal (Ashley *et al.*, 1999). In other words, what ecotourism uses as means, pro-poor tourism views as 'the end'.

Similarly, community-based tourism aims to increase local involvement in tourism and this is also a key component of PPT strategies. However, PPT is more than just a community focus, 'it requires mechanisms to unlock opportunities for the poor at all levels and scales of operation' (Ashley *et al.*, 2001: 3). This might mean 'maximising the use of local labour, goods and services in the formal sector ... expanding informal sector linkages ... and creating a supportive policy framework and planning context that addresses needs of poor producers and residents within tourism' (Ashley *et al.*, 1999: 14). Though distinguished from other forms of tourism, PPT strategies need to be combined with 'general tourism development strategies which aim to develop the sector as a whole' (Ashley *et al.*, 1999: 6). This is because PPT strategies are 'dependent on the health of the overall industry' (Ashley *et al.*, 2000: 9).

Pro-poor tourism means 'doing business differently, whether the business is a large beach resort or a luxury wilderness lodge' (Ashley & Haysom, 2005: 2). It involves more than just small, medium and micro enterprises. Ashley and Haysom (2005) stress a need for businesses to adapt their practices in pro-poor ways, including a move towards more 'people-focused development'. This poses severe challenges to a globalising market economy which favours rapid development. Indeed, Ashley and Haysom (2005: 1) concede that 'tourism business remains a business' and marginal change is all one can hope for. At the same time, the authors believe that 'marginal change in a massive sector' (Ashley & Haysom, 2005: 1) can result in significant benefits for the poor, particularly at a local or district level.

Limitations of tourism as a poverty alleviation strategy

There appear to be severe limits to what PPT can achieve as a poverty reduction strategy, particularly at a global level. Tourism systems, like natural ecosystems, are 'dynamic, operational realities, being changeable, largely unpredictable, and only minimally explainable by linear cause and effect science' (Farrell & Twining-Ward, 2005: 113). Successful PPT that aims to be sustainable is therefore dependent on a complex multitude of factors ranging from favourable geographical location (Roe & Urquhart, 2004) to secure land tenure (PPT Partnership, 2004d), supportive policy frameworks (DFID, 1999; Roe & Urquhart, 2004) and point of intervention in tourism cycles (Ashley *et al.*, 1999). Pro-poor growth thus demands considerable time inputs, attitudinal changes and flexibility (Ashley & Haysom, 2005).

As DFID (1999) emphasises, commercial reality places constraints on the extent that tourism can be made pro-poor. The PPT approach stresses commercial viability. Seeking positive outcomes for the poor requires 'close attention to demand, product quality, marketing, investment in business skills and inclusion of the private sector' (Roe & Urquhart, 2004: 321). This will place considerable demands on local capacities and, in its absence, could lead to a high dependence on foreign input and intervention. While some level of local-foreign collaboration is clearly necessary, what is of concern are the uneven socioeconomic relations that govern such 'collaborations' within the context of tourism development in developing countries (Cooper, 2003; Mbaiwa, 2004; Mowforth & Munt, 2003; Reid, 2003). As Williams (2002: 2) points out, 'tourism and travel related services are still strongly dominated by Northern countries'. Core tools of tourism such as air travel, hotel, Internet and e-commerce are concentrated in the North and advances in these fields tend to allow a greater consolidation of their stronghold as opposed to any diffusion in favour of developing countries. Generally, in terms of controlling access and retention of tourist expenditures, developing countries have weak bargaining power vis-à-vis international tour operators and experience discrimination (Williams, 2002).

At the same time, distributive justice, while a desired outcome, is not an explicit objective of PPT. While pro-poor tourism is keen to maximise returns for poor people, the relative distribution of benefits is not an immediate concern. This means that 'as long as poor people reap net benefits, tourism can be classified as "pro-poor" (even if richer people benefit more than poorer people)' (Ashley *et al.*, 2001: 2). In fact, DFID (1999) warns against the expectation that all poor people will benefit equally; it is acknowledged that 'some will lose' (DFID, 1999: 4). The 'fairly poor' are more likely to reap net benefits than the 'poorest', who lack the 'capital and skills to exploit the economic opportunities, but are likely to suffer the negative impacts on local resources' (DFID, 1999: 1). This stance goes against the central argument of authors like Reid (2003: 2), who argues that the tourism industry urgently needs to 'address more directly the goal of distributive justice'. This is especially the case in developing nations, where 'tourism is characterized by uneven development, ensuring erratic returns and unequal incomes' (Reid, 2003: 4).

Despite acknowledging that tourism is a profit-driven business dominated *(Conclusion* by private sector interests, PPT advocates maintain that tourism offers better prospects for pro-poor growth than most other sectors (DFID, 1999; Roe & Urquhart, 2004; UNESCAP, 2003; WTO-OMT, 2004a). It is emphasised that negative fallouts from tourism are common to most forms of industrial activity in our current global economy (DFID, 1999; Roe & Urquhart, 2004; Sofield *et al.*, 2004). The bottom-line recognition appears to be that tourism is an expanding industry interlinked with powerful global interests and already involves many poor people, either directly or indirectly.

Pro-poor tourism thus springs from a mixture of optimism and opportunism. This is not an inherently negative combination. It does become problematic, however, if powerful stakeholders manipulate opportunities to serve their self-interests and are able to do so under the veil of 'humanitarian' concern. As Reid (2003: 3) points out, regardless of how altruistic pro-poor claims may sound, it is 'doubtful whether those who are intended to benefit – at least according to the rhetoric – have gained nearly as much as those promoting *money)* tourism though corporate globalization'.

It is important at this stage to emphasize that pro-poor tourism advocates are not a homogenous group. Despite distinct convergences in rhetoric at a framework level, there are conflicts in value positions within PPT proponents. This needs to be highlighted as the primacy of some values over others – anthropocentric/ecocentric, patriarchal/egalitarian, utilitarian/prioritarian – critically shape key decision-making processes and thereby outcomes.

The sustainability positions of PPT stakeholders

Distinguishing between the differential ethics of tourism's varied stakeholders – even as they appear to present a global 'consensus' on the need to eliminate poverty and protect the environment – is a necessary challenge. There are various analytical frameworks that can be used for this purpose. Duffy (2002), for example, differentiates ideological divisions within ecotourism discourse into blue-green, red-green and deep-green perspectives and demonstrates that far from the 'cost-free strategy' suggested by its advocates, ecotourism is a 'highly-politicised strategy that does not offer a neutral path to sustainable development for the South' (Duffy, 2002: 156). Firmly locked into notions of 'green capitalism', ecotourism remains a 'business that has to compete alongside other businesses, and it focuses on profit rather than conservation' (Duffy, 2002: x). Ecotourism, therefore, does not require a 'radical or fundamental shift, but operates within existing social, economic and political structures' (Duffy, 2002: 156).

PPT discourse, similarly, is not politically neutral. Despite a veneer of consensus on the benefits of tourism as a tool for poverty alleviation, PPT stakeholders are varied and divided. Ideological divisions are manifested not so much in 'mainstream' recommendations but in professional attitudes, practices and priorities. In fact, pro-poor tourism shares the same crisis as sustainable development – widespread acceptance at a general or framework level but fierce political contest over its actual implementation (Jacobs, 1999; Macbeth, 2005).

As Hunter (1997) notes, competing interpretations of sustainability belie differences in ethics and management strategies. These varied interpretations represent different positions along the 'sustainable development spectrum', from the very weak (a traditionally resource exploitative perspective) to the very strong (an extreme preservationist perspective) (Hunter, 1997: 852–853). Defining characteristics of these positions are outlined in Table 2.

These sustainability positions explain the disparities and conflicts within the sustainability debate. Problems with planning and implementation often occur when stakeholders and interest groups battle over the primacy of their preferred and fiercely defended sustainability positions. Even within a single organisation, institution or community group, stakeholders may sit anywhere along the sustainability spectrum. Moreover, 'because values, politics, and our understanding of the Earth and its systems will evolve, notions of what is sustainable will never be static' (Prugh & Assadourian, 2003: 11). This further muddies the SD discourse and, more importantly, its implementation. These varied sustainability positions, however, are a useful analytical tool for

Table 2 Characteristics of very weak to very strong sustainability positions

Very weak	*Weak*	*Strong*	*Very strong*
Anthropocentric and utilitarian	Anthropocentric and utilitarian	(Eco) systems perspective	Bioethical and eco-centric
Resource exploitative	Resource conservationist	Resource preservationist	Extreme resource preservationist
Natural resources utilised at economically optimal rates through 'free market economy'; operates to satisfy individual consumer choice	Concern for distribution of development costs and benefits through intra- and inter-generational equity	Adherence to intra- and inter-generational equity; interests of the collective given more weight than those of individual consumer	Recognises nature's rights and intrinsic value in nature, encompassing non-human living organisms
Growth-oriented	Growth managed and modified	Zero economic and population growth	Anti-economic growth and reduced human population
Infinite substitution possible between natural and human-made capital; continued well-being assured through economic growth and technical innovation	Rejection of infinite substitution between natural and human-made capital; recognition of some aspects of natural world as critical capital (e.g. ozone layer)	Recognises primary value of maintaining functional integrity of ecosystems over and above secondary value through human resource utilisation	Strongly influenced by Gaianism; nature's rights respected, including abiotic elements

Source: Hunter (1997).

they expose the competing values and contradictory strategies of diverse stakeholders within the sustainable development debate.

Within this framework, the Pro-poor Tourism Partnership appears to
embody a weak sustainability position. The focus on poor people in the
South reflects a strong anthropocentric view. Although ecological damage is
to be minimised, environmental benefits are secondary to poor peoples'
benefits. The PPT framework is not hostile to the market but aims to modify
growth towards pro-poor objectives. Ashley *et al.* (1999: 6) acknowledge that
'a stronger definition of pro-poor growth would be growth that *disproportionately* benefits the poor, but this would exclude many tourism initiatives that
can usefully contribute to poverty elimination'. The PPT Partnership perspective falls within the category of 'reformist' – rather than 'radical' – as evidenced in its pragmatic approach and acknowledgement that marginal
(rather than broad scale) change is expected.

When it comes to corporate interest groups like the World Travel and Tourism
Council (WTTC), pro-poor tourism embodies a very weak sustainability position. Its tourism blueprint calls for governments to 'recognize Travel &
Tourism as a top priority' and, while acknowledging that businesses 'must
balance economics with people, culture and environment', also aims to ensure
the industry's 'long-term growth and prosperity' (WTTC, 2003: para. 6).
'Sustainability' appears to mean the longevity of tourism activity; this single-
sector approach contravenes the holistic perspective sustainable development
demands. There is a critical difference, after all, between sustaining development that contributes to (human and non-human) welfare and sustaining
tourism development per se.

The WTTC's business-as-usual approach of conservative reform within
status quo conditions is shared by the World Tourism Organization. Both
organisations are optimistic about the dynamic abilities of human and
natural capital to withstand industrial activity, as long as it is managed 'appropriately'. What it views as 'appropriate' management is free market economics,
which it believes will allocate resources most efficiently to the benefit of all. As
with the WTTC, the WTO-OMT is heavily promoting its 'Liberalization with a
Human Face' agenda as a way of alleviating poverty (WTO-OMT, 2004b).

The following section will consider the implications of PPT embodying a
weak to very sustainability position – *vis-à-vis* the perceived power of the stakeholder in question – and contemplate the potential outcomes for the poor in
developing countries.

PPT and the Challenge of Global Sustainability

Environmental considerations from a weak to very weak sustainability perspective

Organisations like the World Tourism Organization and the World Travel
and Tourism Council, who embody very weak sustainability perspectives,
view the environment narrowly in economic terms. Creating a market for
environmental services, however, means that rich (rather then poor) people's
preferences dictate how the environment is used (Hamilton, 1997). In developing countries, this often means scarce natural resources are diverted to meet

the profligate needs of (richer) tourists rather than (poorer) locals (Mastny, 2002). Water shortages, for example, already an acute problem in many poverty-stricken tourist destinations, are exacerbated by tourism (Mastny, 2002). This is a grave issue for PPT. The depletion or diversion of community natural resources disproportionately affects the rural poor as their livelihood is critically dependent on these resources (DFID, 2001, 2002).

In Ashley et al.'s (2001) review of six pro-poor tourism case studies, it was acknowledged that little was said about environmental action. At the same time, it is noted that 'the most commonly cited negative impact of tourism relates to degradation of natural resources used by the poor' (Ashley et al., 1999: 15). While it was suggested that 'more might be done in this area' (Ashley et al., 1999: 15), a key concern is whether it will be a case of too little too late, given the ecological vulnerability of the remote destinations upon which PPT tends to focus. As highlighted in Conservation International's report, Tourism and Biodiversity, there is a strong convergence of endangered biodiversity hotspots, marginalised indigenous peoples, fragile economies and expanding tourism development. The report warns that we are currently perched 'at a crossroads in many of these hotspots and wilderness areas, where the last strongholds of biodiversity, the make-or-break world of basic survival for millions of people, and the ever-expanding world of tourism meet' (Christ et al., 2003: v).

Negative environmental impacts create uneven burdens. Wealthy people, for one, have more choices about where they live. They can choose not to live next to toxic waste sites or areas prone to floods and landslides. Affluent communities are also better able to prevent unwanted pollution through 'better access to financial resources, education, skills and ... decision-making structures' (Beder, 1996: 151). Resource scarcity or the privatisation of public goods is less of an issue because the rich can afford to pay higher prices for utilities like water and electricity. The less well-off often have little alternative but to suffer the consequences of bad environmental practices. This leads to a spiral of negative social impacts such as ill-health and disabilities which create further financial burdens (Chambers, 1995).

Placing environmental concerns as secondary has grave implications in a world where global warming is reaching critical stages. Climate change will 'exacerbate existing vulnerabilities and create new ones for the poor', including loss of livelihoods and the deepening of poverty cycles (Logan, 2004). Rich-poor inequalities will widen as impacts 'will fall disproportionately upon developing countries and the poor persons within all countries' (Fogarty, 2004). Tourism's reputation for being a highly polluting and resource-intensive industry with a substantial ecological footprint (Christ et al., 2003; Mastny, 2002) therefore places necessary limits on its appropriateness as a large-scale pro-poor strategy.

Socioeconomic considerations from a weak to very weak sustainability perspective

Tourism is a commercial sector that operates within a global neo-liberal market economy. This market model narrowly defines human beings as consumers and turns 'what are essentially social decisions involving ethical judgments into private economic decisions based on self-interest' (Hamilton, 1997: 42). This model is unable to accommodate the concept of generalised reciprocity or responsibility to society (Rees, 2002). Pro-poor strategies therefore find themselves in a problematic bind. On the one hand, public and private stakeholders are urged to look beyond pure commercial interests and prioritise the needs of those who suffer. Yet economic priorities continue to frame stakeholders as consumers indifferent to factors expressed outside market activity (Rees, 2002). Meanwhile, a (very weak sustainability) belief in infinite resources – or an infinite ability to generate more resources – places the onus of poverty alleviation on the market, a sort of 'rising tide raises all boats' mentality (Rees, 2002). This lends an almost schizophrenic quality to the pro-poor tourism discourse, as it upholds moral arguments for poverty alleviation within a predominantly business-as-usual environment.

Pro-poor tourism places considerable demands on tourism stakeholders. In order to generate net benefits for the poor in the South, tourism enterprises and their various linkages have to consider how best to maximise benefits for the local poor. Strategies and processes have to be financially feasible as well as socially, culturally and environmentally beneficial. Such an approach to tourism, however, is dependent on the willingness of the non-poor to bear any attendant costs – economic, social, cultural and environmental.

Tourism businesses, for example, would be expected to hire and provide appropriate training for local community members. Fair wages may mean higher wages – which need to be paid regardless of tourism cycles and tourist flows. Environmentally-friendly tourist facilities might rely on renewable (but erratic) energy sources which may restrict tourists' water and energy usage. Aviation and transport companies must be willing to ferry tourists to areas where tourist numbers are restricted – this might mean reduced profits if they do not meet economies of scale. A sufficient number of tourists must be willing to bear potentially higher airfares and transport costs. Tourists also have to respect restrictions if they are placed – for example, restrictions on water usage or personal behaviour, such as the desire to touch wildlife. Successful PPT relies, to a large extent, on the altruism of non-poor tourism stakeholders to drive the industry towards increasing benefits and reducing costs for the poor.

Ashley *et al.* (2000: 6) emphasise that 'changing the attitudes of tourists (at both international and national levels) is essential if PPT is to be commercially viable and sustainable'. Recommendations include introducing voluntary codes and certification as well as tourist education programs regarding socio-economic issues. In this regard, Ashley *et al.* (2000: 6) believe that 'valuable lessons can be learned from the environmental sphere'. This is true – but as Duffy (2002) shows, the lesson appears to be that 'ecotourists' often display the same hedonistic, self-indulgent tendencies as mass tourists. In Belize, 'ecotourists' ignored environmental briefings and pilfered wildlife as well as ancient archeological ruins. They displayed a similar fondness for excessive drinking and drug-taking, as well as engagement with the local sex industry (Duffy, 2002).

When there are trade-offs (whether real or perceived) between potential benefits for the poor versus reduction in profits and/or collective and personal restraints on the non-poor, it is highly questionable if altruistic motives will triumph. While there is no denying that tourism enterprises can spring from genuinely altruistic motives, the bottom-line remains that tourism is, essentially, 'a commercial sector driven by business opportunities, not an engine for providing social services to the poor' (DFID, 1999: 2). It therefore seems overly idealistic to assume that self-regulation in the private sector is sufficient (or likely) to meet pro-poor challenges.

Given that altruistic motives alone cannot be relied upon to guide decisions to benefit the poor and/or the environment, one could argue that the onus lies on political commitment to direct tourism development towards this aim. Unfortunately, as Richter (1993: 192) points out, the 'distribution of political power over decision-making in tourism tends to mirror the distribution of political influence more generally'. The likelihood of the Asian Development Bank's ambitious (and highly profitable) Greater Mekong Subregion (GMS) tourism project (ADB 2002) benefiting poor locals, therefore, is questionable. As highlighted in *New Frontiers* (2004):

> The [Mekong River] basin countries include three communist regimes (China, Laos, Vietnam), a military dictatorship in Burma, and an increasingly authoritarian government in Thailand. Those, and the sixth basin country, Cambodia, already get poor to abysmal marks on the environment, corruption, official transparency, and local participation in decision making. (*New Frontiers*, May–June 2004)

Tourism policy in Southeast Asia, Richter (1993: 192) argues, has so far been an 'elite-driven policy', and capital requirements mean 'negotiations will more closely follow private economic advantage than some ideal of balanced development'. Richter (1993: 192) then suggests that 'arguments for investing in areas where a critical mass of services already exists may be much more persuasive than diffusion of economic opportunity'. Pro-poor tourism initiatives that encourage tourism development in poor, peripheral regions – isolated geographically but also socially and politically – have to critically mediate these considerations, not just in southeast Asia but globally. Weak (and particularly very weak) sustainability positions also have to grapple with the reality that genuine (or strong) sustainability requires core fundamental changes. There are real moral dilemmas involved in attempting to meet sustainability challenges in a pragmatic way, which often demands that those in positions of less power work within existing structures in order to have their needs met without conflict.

Tourism in relatively remote and poor areas – as PPT suggests – means integration into the global economy and a whole new set of trade rules, uneven power relations as well as new health and environmental risks (Mastny, 2002; Mowforth & Munt, 2003; Reid, 2003). Pro-poor tourism has to consider if its weak to very weak sustainability position will be able to compete with the forces of a global economy that may offer some beneficial opportunities but will also create permeable borders for the flourishing of illicit networks that thrive in poor countries and prey on the vulnerable (Duffy, 2002).

Tourism 'hotspots' in Southeast Asia such as Thailand, Bali, Cambodia, Vietnam and the Philippines show that crime and tourism are closely inter-linked – rates of exploitation of women and children continue to increase as well as human and wildlife trafficking and illegal logging activities (Beddoe, 2001; Cullen, 2005; ECTWT, 2005; Tourism Investigation & Monitoring Team, 2005). There are also widespread reports of indigenous minorities and rural communities being resettled or displaced to make way for tourist infrastructure. This has occurred from Botswana (Mbaiwa, 2004) to Burma (Burma Campaign UK, 2005), Taiwan (Matsui, 1999) to Tanzania (Mowforth & Munt, 2003).

This is not to suggest that technological advancement and international trade should be limited to wealthy nations. Nor is it the case that tourism is the only industry guilty of gross human rights and environmental violations. The point here is that resources directed towards promoting rapid tourism growth in developing countries appear disproportionate to what is available in combating the problems which tend to arise with it. PPT discourse, at present, does not appear to offer clear directives on how to manage this asymmetry. At the same time, its adherence to status quo conditions calls into question the wisdom of promoting what is widely acknowledged as a highly competitive and centralised industry (Reid, 2003; Pleumarom, 2002; Madely, 1999) to poverty-stricken countries and communities without any established capacity to manage the potentially negative socioeconomic consequences.

According to Pleumarom (1999: para. 8), coordinator of the Bangkok-based Tourism Investigation & Monitoring Team, 'Travel and tourism has emerged as one of the world's most centralised and competitive industries, and hardly any other economic sector illustrates so clearly the global reach of transnational corporations (TNCs)'. A more centralised industry means high levels of foreign ownership, leading to large-scale repatriation of profits away from host economies. Already, many tourist destinations in the South are struggling to retain tourism revenues; the problem of high levels of tourism leakage (i.e. when tourism revenue 'leaks' out of host countries) is well documented (Madeley, 1999; Mastny, 2002; UNEP, 2002).

The tourism and travel industry is highly competitive. Such competitiveness, particularly in a price sensitive market, often leads to price wars and particularly anti-poor practices justified as 'cost-cutting measures'. For tourism employees in developing countries, this may translate to a reduction of wages and benefits as well as large-scale dismissals (Beddoe, 2004; Cooper, 2003; Lyons, 2004). These measures take place within an industry already characterised by poor labour standards and weak regulatory frameworks (Beddoe, 2004).

A recent report by Tourism Concern paints a dire picture of labour standards in the tourism industry. The report, *Labour Standards, Social Responsibility and Tourism*, is based on research undertaken in Bali, Canary Islands, Dominican Republic, Egypt and Mexico. It found that workers, particularly in the hotel industry, face difficult conditions characterised by 'low wages, over-dependency on tips, long working hours, stress, lack of secure contracts, poor training and almost no promotion opportunity' (Beddoe, 2004: 5). Many workers are subcontracted which effectively barred them from staff benefits like maternity leave, severance pay or union membership (Beddoe, 2004).

This not only made them particularly vulnerable to exploitation and abuse (unremunerated overtime was widespread), this form of underemployment does not allow for the accumulation of assets, nor does it provide safety nets or any real escape from the poverty cycle. Many workers also faced discrimination as locals, migrant workers, or women in a gender-stratified tourism industry (Beddoe, 2004; Mbaiwa, 2004). Reports of locals being barred from tourist facilities are rife, particularly in enclave tourism developments (Cooper, 2003).

Often referred to as the world's largest employer, tourism is frequently touted a good pro-poor strategy for its employment generating abilities (Sofield *et al.*, 2004; UNESCAP, 2003; WTO-OMT, 2004a). However, while the tourism industry rates high on job creation, job losses can be equally dramatic. Overall, up to 5 million jobs in tourism would have been lost since 2001, when a crisis in world tourism was triggered by the 11 September terrorist attacks (Beddoe, 2004). Employment losses are most acutely felt by the lower-skilled and socially weaker staff members. The fact that job security is tenuous for large numbers of workers employed in tourism has important implications for pro-poor tourism. Poverty alleviation from a sustainable livelihood approach means reducing vulnerabilities – this includes providing safety nets for the poor during bad times, 'mitigating seasonal stress and enabling them to conserve their livelihood assets' (Chambers, 1995: 196).

Research in Kenya, a key tourist destination in Africa, showed that declines in tourism in the late 1990s resulted in enduring hardship for the poor, particularly in areas where livelihoods were tourism-based (Kareithi, 2003). The physical hardship from sharp declines in household income – there were reported drops of over 70% in total monthly income – were compounded by increased social conflict due to mounting debts (Kareithi, 2003). Poor families were forced to sell assets such as livestock; there was also increased exploitation of the poor as they moved from self-employment to other livelihood options out of desperation. Mounting debts had a crippling effect, further perpetuating poverty cycles.

It was noted that women responded differently to men. The former withdrew from tourism activities much sooner, selecting activities that offered *less* remuneration as long as they were more regular sources of income (Kareithi, 2003). Livelihood stability is therefore more important than mere job or income creation. PPT has to critically consider if tourism development, in the long-term, will jeopardise or restrict the poor's livelihood portfolios (e.g. through its impact on the health of community natural resources and access to such resources), as well as their livelihood capabilities (e.g. through replacing traditional livelihoods yet offering little training or promotional opportunities in the 'formal' sector).

The aggressive push for greater trade liberalisation in tourism needs to be considered within the context of current global economic and socio-political realities, which prioritise corporate interests over that of the poor in destination countries. Currently, the negative impacts discussed are likely to be intensified rather than ameliorated with a rapid expansion and liberalisation of tourism markets (Pleumarom, 1999, 2002, 2003; Williams, 2002). Globally, poverty reduction strategies tend to emphasise the need for more growth, in the absence of redistributive policies (Mestrum, 2003). This is clearly pro-rich rather than pro-poor. So is increasing competition in an unlevel playing field without safeguards for the vulnerable. Moreover, liberalisation in tourism is inextricably linked to liberalisation in other sectors and the combined effect of such interlocking liberalisation will likely be severe environmental and social consequences (Williams, 2002).

Conclusion

Globally, there is a lack of convincing empirical evidence to support the claim that tourism benefits the poor. Despite this, tourism continues to be prioritised as a key development option for struggling economies. Habiba Sarobi, Afghanistan's first female governor, is campaigning for funds to develop Bamiyan as a tourist site (Walsh, 2005). Bamiyan, which lies along the Silk Route, is where the spectacular giant Buddhas once stood, before the extremist Taliban blew them up in 2001. It is an ancient town abundant with cultural riches – as well as land mines. There are no hotels in Bamiyan; there is also no electricity. A trip to Kabul takes eight hours. Developing a viable tourism industry in a war-torn country bereft of adequate infrastructure presents immense challenges. Afghanistan is also situated in a region considered politically unstable and unsafe for travelling. Yet the myth that tourism can solve a country's economic woes – and hence its social, political and environmental problems – is pervasive and continues to seduce many.

On a global scale, PPT advocates must be explicit about the fact that stakeholders include winners and losers working on a vastly uneven playing field. It is important to consider what forms of tourism development are likely to emerge from such an asymmetrical political landscape, despite the best of intentions. Tourism is highly political and the values of powerful stakeholders greatly shape outcomes. In a socio-political climate of shrinking civil liberties and top-down governance styles, tourism policies and plans are less likely to be reflective of a community's social, cultural and environmental concerns than they are of the economic imperatives of those in power. While marginalised communities are, in rhetoric, often encouraged to 'participate' in tourism development, it cannot be assumed that they are able to participate meaningfully. Neither should it be assumed that their participation will lead to an equitable distribution of the benefits. When inequitable relationships underlie the change-making process, this critically influences 'the resources that people can access ... as well as the resources which remain out of reach' (Eversole, 2003: 791).

Moreover, while PPT's focus is mainly on the rural poor, a 2003 United Nations study estimates that the urban population in the developing world is expected to double to 4 billion in 30 years; this means one in every three people will live in urban slums by 2033. Currently, almost 80% of the urban population in the world's 30 least developed nations live in slums (UN-Habitat, 2003). In urban slums, the poor do not have the same comparative advantage that PPT is currently promoting – namely, pristine landscapes, abundant wildlife, indigenous cultural heritage and traditions. For the poor living in urban slums, their comparative advantage tends to be undervalued and weakly organised labour. The long-term prospects of PPT are therefore in question, if mass urban poverty becomes the reality of our future.

Currently, the PPT agenda appears to be heavily dictated by corporate and bureaucratic interests whose focus is garnering political support for tourism as a policy priority. At the United Nations Conference on Trade and Development (UNCTAD) in Brazil, 2004, the World Tourism Organization advocated for tourism expansion in the least developed countries through a 'visionary focus on this win-win sector by all states as a development tool par excellence: the political will at the national and institutional level, to put tourism at the core of policymaking' (WTO-OMT, 2004b: para. 4). Firstly, it is highly questionable if 'win-win' is an accurate description of the tourism industry at present. Secondly, while it is true that the tourism industry needs to adopt a pro-poor focus, this is different to the prescription that tourism is an appropriate poverty alleviation strategy for all countries. A critical distinction also has to be made between policy support for any form of tourism development and tourism enterprises that specifically adopt pro-poor and sustainability principles.

Tourism remains a dynamic phenomenon with often irreversible and interlocking impacts. It is important that tourism not be pursued independently as a surefire pro-poor strategy – all industries should be directed towards pro-poor objectives. Reducing regulatory frameworks at a national, regional or global policy level for a single sector contradicts the systems approach which sustainability demands. (It is akin to making mining or automobile manufacturing a policy priority.)

Influential industry gatekeepers like the World Tourism Organization and the WTTC often credit the tourism industry for being 'resilient' and 'adaptive'. Such reassurances often come after a major shake-up of the industry, to boost investor confidence and counteract accusations of tourism being volatile and vulnerable (WTO-OMT, 2003, 2005b). It is worth asking, however, whose resilience and adaptability tourism's continued and rapid expansion has been dependent on.

It is often socially weaker groups who bear the brunt of financial upheavals. Within these groups, there are further differential impacts, with women and children suffering the most. Vulnerability characterises poverty and poor people's lack of means to counter external shocks (Chambers, 1995) means boom-and-bust cycles are particularly detrimental for them. Affluent people are better able to insulate themselves from the negative consequences of economic turbulence through safety nets such as insurance, savings and accumulated assets. The poor lack such safeguards and thus ensuring livelihood stability is generally pro-poor. A growth-at-all-costs economic model which 'lurches along irresponsibly' (Saul, 1995: 151) is not. The bottom-line is that *any* industry or commercial activity that condones exploitative labour conditions and income instability cannot be considered pro-poor. The focus should be on identifying and addressing the deep-rooted structural inequities within our global development paradigm (tourism included) which exacerbate poverty and constrain pro-poor attempts.

Eliminating poverty should not be regarded as 'charity' – the domain of 'bighearted' pop stars or 'enlightened' bureaucrats. Appealing to altruistic motives may be important in galvanising popular and political support for poverty alleviation initiatives. It must be recognised, however, that this is a limited strategy. As Chambers (1995) highlights, relying on 'mutual interest' arguments to rally support for poverty reduction measures is to risk loss of support from the rich when it appears they have little to gain. Tourism development that generates net benefits for the poor and protects the environment places will place restrictions on human activity and challenge our current rapid expansion development model. In other words, there may be strong moral imperatives but weak profit margins.

In encouraging a move away from 'mutual interest' arguments in poverty alleviation, Chambers (1995: 196) says 'ethical arguments are stronger, surer and better' and recommends actions founded on 'the values of common decency, compassion and altruism'. In tourism, however, altruism plays second fiddle to profits in what is inherently a commercial activity. Pro-poor tourism therefore either needs to make a stronger ethical argument – where actions are founded on altruism as a non-negotiable principle, not mutual material benefits – or else abandon the pretence entirely. Otherwise, there is a real chance that confusion between the two – and hijacking of the 'altruistic' tag as a marketing tool – will discredit the discourse and mislead stakeholders into a false sense of optimism over what can (and cannot) be achieved under this rubric.

Finally, it is important to realise that in PPT discourse, tourism is but a *tool* for poverty alleviation. A tool may be used to perform or facilitate a task but it cannot compensate for ill-conceived plans, lack of capacity and/or co-operation, inappropriate technology transfers and general dysfunction. PPT will not 'cure' corruption and cronyism, nor can it rid a place of patriarchy and racism. As a tool, tourism is overly burdened with ideals it cannot realise, especially on a large scale and with any regularity or consistency. Fortunately for some and unfortunately for many, tourism is also a highly profitable and pleasurable tool, which may go some way in explaining the global reluctance to relieve it of some of its misplaced burdens.

Correspondence

Any correspondence should be directed to Ms Stephanie Chok, School of Social Sciences and Humanities, Murdoch University, South Street, WA 6150, Australia (stephchok@gmail.com); Associate Professor Jim Macbeth, Program Chair, Tourism, School of Social Sciences and Humanities, Murdoch University, South Street, WA 6150, Australia (j.macbeth@murdoch.edu.au) or Associate Professor Carol Warren, Asian Studies, School of Social Sciences and Humanities, Murdoch University, South Street, WA 6150, Australia (c.warren@murdoch.edu.au).

References

Ashley, C. and Haysom, G. (2005) From philanthrophy to a different way of doing business: strategies and challenges in integrating pro-poor approaches into tourism business. Submission to ATLAS Africa Conference, presented in Pretoria, October 2004. Submitted as a paper January 2005, Pro-Poor Tourism Partnerhship. On WWW at http://www.propoortourism.org.uk/Publications%20by%20partnership/propoor_business_ATLASpaper.pdf. Accessed 29.5.05.

Ashley, C., Bennett, O. and Roe, D. (1999) *Sustainable Tourism and Poverty Elimination Study*. Deloitte and Touche, International Institute for Environment and

Development and Overseas Development Institute, London. On WWW at http://www.odi.org.uk/pptourism/dfid_report.pdf. Accessed 29.5.05.

Ashley, C., Boyd, C. and Goodwin, H. (2000) Pro-poor tourism: Putting poverty at the heart of the tourism agenda. *Natural Resource Perspectives*, No 51. On WWW at http://www.odi.org.uk/nrp/51.pdf. Accessed 29.5.05.

Ashley, C., Roe, D. and Goodwin, H. (2001) *Pro-Poor Tourism Strategies: Making Tourism Work for the Poor. A Review of Experience*. Pro-poor Tourism Report No. 1, Overseas Development Institute, International Institute for Environment and Development, London, and Centre for Responsible Tourism, University of Greenwich. On WWW at http://www.propoortourism.org.uk/ppt_report.pdf. Accessed 29.5.05.

Asian Development Bank (ADB) (2002) *Report and Recommendation of the President to the Board of Director on Proposed Loans to the Kingdom of Cambodia, Lao People's Democratic Republic, and Socialist Republic of Viet Nam for the Greater Mekong Subregion: Mekong Tourism Development Project*. Asian Development Bank, Manila. On WWW at http://www.adb.org/Documents/RRPS/CAM/rrp_35282-cam.pdf. Accessed 29.5.05.

Beder, S. (1996) *The Nature of Sustainable Development* (2nd edn). Australia: Scribe Publications.

Beddoe, C. (2001) *The Incidence of Sexual Exploitation of Children in Tourism: A Report Commissioned by the World Tourism Organization*. Madrid, Spain: World Tourism Organization.

Beddoe, C. (2004) *Labour Standards, Social Responsibility and Tourism*. Tourism Concern, London. On WWW at http://www.tourismconcern.org.uk/downloads/pdfs/TC-Union-Final2.pdf. Accessed 11.6.05.

Birkeland, J., Dodds, S. and Hamilton, C. (1997) Values and ethics. In M. Diesendorf and C. Hamilton (eds) *Human Ecology, Human Economy* (pp. 125–147). NSW, Australia: Allen & Unwin.

Burma Campaign UK (2005) Boycott Burma Holidays – How tourism benefits Burma's dictators. On WWW at http://www.burmacampaign.org.uk/tourism.php. Accessed 11.6.05.

Chambers, R. (1998) Us and them: Finding a new paradigm for professionals in sustainable development. In D. Warburton (ed.) *Community and Sustainable Development: Participation in the Future* (pp. 117–147). UK: Earthscan.

Chambers, R. (1995) Poverty and livelihoods: Whose reality counts? *Environment and Urbanization*. 7 (1), 173–204.

Christ, C., Hillel, O., Matus, S. and Sweeting, J. (2003) *Tourism and Biodiversity: Mapping Tourism's Global Footprint*. Conservation International, Washington. On WWW at http://www.unep.org/PDF/Tourism-and-biodiversity.pdf. Accessed 11.6.05.

Cooper, M. (2003) Behind globalization's glitz: In 'the other' Cancun, tourist-industry workers live in poverty and squalor. *The Nation*. On WWW at http://www.thenation.com/doc.mhtml?=i20030922&s=cooper. Accessed 11.6.05.

Cullen, S. (2005) Sex tourism is big money for pimps and politicians. *Contours* (Vol. 15), (p. 12). ECTWT. On WWW at http://www.ecotonline.org/Pages/downloads/Contours%20Vol%2015_No.1_for%20ECOT.pdf. Accessed 29.5.05.

Dale, A. (2001) *At the Edge: Sustainable Development in the 21st Century*. Canada: UBC Press.

Department for International Development (DFID) (1999) Tourism and poverty elimination: Untapped potential. DFID, UK. On WWW at http://www.propoortourism.org.uk/dfid_summary.PDF. Accessed 29.8.04.

Department for International Development (DFID) (2001) *Biodiversity – A Crucial Issue for the World's Poorest*. DFID, UK. On WWW at http://www.dfid.gov.uk/pubs/files/biodiversity.pdf. Accessed 29.5.05.

Department for International Development (DFID) (2002) *Wildlife and Poverty Study*. DFID, UK. On WWW at http://www.dfid.gov.uk/pubs/files/wildlifepovertystudy.pdf. Accessed 29.5.05.

Duffy, R. (2002) *A Trip Too Far: Ecotourism, Politics and Exploitation*. London: Earthscan.

Ecumenical Coalition on Third World Tourism (ECTWT) (2005) *Contours* 15 (1). ECTWT, Hong Kong. On WWW at http://www.ecotonline.org/Pages/downloads/Contours%20Vol%2015_No.1_for%20ECOT.pdf. Accessed 29.5.05.

Eversole, R. (2003) Managing the pitfalls of participatory development: Some insight from Australia. *World Development* 31 (5), 781–795.

Farrell, B. and Twinning-Ward, L. (2005) Seven steps towards sustainability: Tourism in the context of new knowledge. *Journal of Sustainable Tourism*, 13 (2), 109–122.

Fogarty, D. (2004) Asia faces living nightmare from climate change. *Reuters*. On WWW at http://www.planetark.com/dailynewsstory.cfm/newsid/28300/story.htm. Accessed 29.5.05.

Hamilton, C. (1997) Foundations of ecological economics. In M. Diesendorf and C. Hamilton (eds) *Human Ecology, Human Economy* (pp. 35–63). NSW, Australia: Allen & Unwin.

Hunter, C. (1997) Sustainable tourism as an adaptive paradigm. *Annals of Tourism Research* 24 (4), 850–867.

Irwin, A. (2001) *Sociology and the Environment: A Critical Introduction to Society, Nature and Knowledge*. Cambridge: Polity.

Jacobs, M. (1999) Sustainable development as a contested concept. In A. Dodson (ed.) *Fairness and Futurity* (pp. 21–45). Oxford: Oxford University Press.

Kabeer, N. (1994) *Reversed Realities: Gender Hierarchies in Development Thought*. London and New York: Verso.

Kareithi, S. (2003) Coping with declining tourism – Examples from communities in Kenya. PPT Working Paper No. 13, Pro-Poor Tourism Partnership. On WWW at http://www.propoortourism.org.uk/13_Kenya.pdf. Accessed 11.6.05.

Leepreecha, P. (1997) Jungle tours: A government policy in need of review. In K. Kampe and D. McCaskill (eds) *Development or Domestication? Indigenous Peoples of Southeast Asia* (pp. 268–288). Chiang Mai, Thailand: Silkworm Books.

Logan, M. (2004) Guess who extreme weather hits hardest? Inter Press Service News Agency. On WWW at http://ipsnews.net/new_nota.asp?idnews=26104. Accessed 29.5.05.

Lyons, C.H. (2004) What about the workers? *Developments* (pp. 16–17). UK: DFID.

Macbeth, J. (2005) Towards an ethics platform for tourism. *Annals of Tourism Research* 32 (4), 962–984.

Madely, J. (1999) Tourism: The great illusion. In *Big Business, Poor Peoples: The Impact of Transnational Corporations on the World'S Poor* (pp. 128–144). New York: Zed Books.

Mastny, L. (2001) Traveling light: New paths for international tourism. Worldwatch Paper 159, December 2001. Worldwatch Institute, Washington. On WWW at http://www.worldwatch.org/pubs/paper/159/. Accessed 29.8.04.

Mastny, L. (2002) Redirecting international tourism. In L. Starke (ed.) *State of the World 2002* (pp. 101–126). New York: Worldwatch Institute, Worldwatch.

Matsui, Y. (1999) Taiwan and Thailand: The other side of the travel boom. In *Women in the New Asia: From Pain to Power* (pp. 110–120). Victoria, Australia: Spinifex Press.

Mbaiwa, J.E. (2004) The socio-cultural impacts of tourism development in the Okavango Delta, Botswana. *Journal of Tourism and Cultural Change* 2 (3), 163–184.

McMichael, P. (2000) *Development and Social Change: A Global Perspective* (2nd edn). California: Pine Forge Press.

Mestrum, F. (2003) Poverty reduction and sustainable development. *Environment, Development and Sustainability* 5, 41–61.

Mowforth, M. and Munt, I. (2003) *Tourism and Sustainability: Development and New Tourism in the Third World* (2nd edn). New York: Routledge.

New Frontiers (2004) Asia's "last frontier" poised for irrevocable change. *New Frontiers*, 10 (3). On WWW at http://www.twnside.org.sg/tour.htm. Accessed 28.2.05.

Pleumarom, A. (1999) Tourism, globalisation and sustainable development. t.i.m-team. On WWW at http://www.twnside.org.sg/title/anita-cn.htm. Accessed 29.5.05.

Pleumarom, A. (2002) Campaign on Corporate Power in Tourism (COCPIT). t.i.m-team. On WWW at http://www.twnside.org.sg/title/eco1.htm. Accessed 29.5.05.

Pleumarom, A. (2003) Our world is not for sale! The disturbing implications of privatization in the tourism trade. Paper presented at the International Seminar on Tourism: Unfair Practices – Equitable Options, 8–9 December 2003, Hannover, Germany, hosted by DANTE/The Network for Sustainable Tourism Development. On WWW at http://www.twnside.org.sg/title/tourism.doc. Accessed 29.5.05.

Pro-Poor Tourism Partnership (PPTP) (2004a) Defining pro-poor tourism. Pro-poor tourism info-sheets, Sheet No.1. On WWW at http://www.propoortourism.org.uk/info_sheets/1%20info%20sheet.pdf. Accessed 29.5.05.

Pro-Poor Tourism Partnership (PPTP) (2004b)Tourism and poverty reduction – making the links. Pro-Poor Tourism Info-Sheets, Sheet No.3. On WWW at http://www.propoortourism.org.uk/info_sheets/3%20info%20sheet.pdf. Accessed at 29.5.05.

Pro-Poor Tourism Partnership (PPTP) (2004c) Economic data on international tourism's contribution to developing country economies. Pro-Poor Tourism Info-Sheets, Sheet No. 6. On WWW at http://www.propoortourism.org.uk/info_sheets/7%20info%20sheet.pdf. Accessed 29.5.05.

Pro-Poor Tourism Partnership (PPTP) (2004d) Policy instruments supporting pro-poor tourism. Pro-Poor Tourism Info-Sheets, Sheet No. 8. On WWW at http://www.propoortourism.org.uk/info_sheets/8%20info%20sheet.pdf. Accessed 29.5.05.

Prugh, T. and Assadourian, E. (2003) What is sustainability anyway? *Worldwatch* 10–21.

Rees, W. (2002) An ecological economics perspective on sustainability and prospects for ending poverty. *Population and Environment* 24 (1), 15–46.

Reid, D. (2003) *Tourism, Globalization and Development: Responsible Tourism Planning.* London: Pluto Press.

Richter, L. (1993) Tourism policy-making in South-East Asia. In M. Hitchcock, V.T. King and M.J.G. Parnwell (eds) *Tourism in South-East Asia* (pp. 179–199). London: Routledge.

Roe, D. and Urquhart, P. (2004) Pro-poor tourism: Harnessing the world's largest industry for the world's poor; turning the rhetoric into action for sustainable development and poverty reduction. In T. Bigg (ed.) *Survival for a Small Planet – The Sustainable Development Agenda* (pp. 309–325). London: Earthscan.

Saul, J.R. (1995) *The Doubter's Companion: A Dictionary of Aggressive Common Sense.* Australia: Penguin Books.

Sofield, T., Bauer, J., Delacy, T., Lipman, G. and Daugherty, S. (2004) *Sustainable Tourism ~ Elimination Poverty (ST ~ EP): An Overview.* Queensland, Australia: CRC for Sustainable Tourism.

Storey, D., Bulloch, H. and Overton, J. (2005) The poverty consensus: some limitations of the 'poverty agenda'. *Progress in Development Studies* 5 (1), 30–44.

Tourism Investigation & Monitoring Team (t.i.m.-team) (2005) *New Frontiers* newsletters, campaigns and articles regarding justice in tourism. On WWW at http://www.twnside.org.sg/tour.htm. Accessed July 2005 and Aug 2004.

UNEP (2002) Economic impacts of tourism. On WWW at http://www.uneptie.org/pc/tourism/sust-tourism/economic.htm. Accessed 29.5.05.

UNESCAP (2003) *Poverty Alleviation through Sustainable Tourism Development.* UN, New York. On WWW at http://unescap.org/ttdw/Publications/TPTS_pubs/Pub_2265/pub_2265_fulltext.pdf. Accessed 29.5.05.

UN-Habitat (2003) *The Challenge of Slums: Global Report on Human Settlements 2003.* London: Earthscan.

Walsh, D. (2005) A first for Afghan women: The governor. *The Guardian Weekly,* p. 20.

Williams, M. (2002) Tourism liberalization, gender and the GATS. *Economic Literacy Series: General Agreement on Trade in Services.* On WWW at http://www.igtn.org/pdfs/37_GATStourism.pdf. Accessed 21.9.04.

WTO-OMT (2002) *Tourism and Poverty Alleviation.* Madrid, Spain: WTO-OMT.

WTO-OMT (2003) Statement by Mr Francesco Frangialli, Secretary-General of the World Tourism Organization (WTO-OMT), Ministerial Conference, Fifth Session, Cancun, 10–14 September 2003. On WWW at http://www.world-tourism.org/liberalization/menu_trade.htm. Accessed 11.6.05.

WTO-OMT (2004a) *Tourism and Poverty Alleviation: Recommendations for Action.* Madrid, Spain: WTO-OMT.

WTO-OMT (2004b) Tourism can help reduce poverty with fair and progressive liberalization, WTO tells UN Trade & Development Conference (media release). On WWW at http://www.world-tourism.org/newsroom/Releases/2004/june/unctad.htm. Accessed 11.6.05.

WTO-OMT (2005a) *ST-EP (Sustainable Tourism-Eliminating Poverty)*. On WWW at http://
www.world-tourism.org/step/menu.html. Accessed 15.3.05.

WTO-OMT (2005b) WTO Tourcom Conference in Bali promises a new era in tourism and
media relations in Asia. World Tourism Organization, Nusa Dua, Bali, 19 May 2005.
On WWW at http://www.world-tourism.org/newsroom/Releases/2005/May/
tourcom.htm. Accessed 29.5.05.

WTTC (2003) WTTC's blueprint for new tourism calls on government and industry to
make significant long term commitments (media release). On WWW at http://
www.wttc.org/frameset1.htm. Accessed 15.3.05.

WTTC (2005) About WTTC. On WWW at http://www.wttc.org/framesetaboutus.htm.
Accessed 15.3.05.

Growth Versus Equity: The Continuum of Pro-Poor Tourism and Neoliberal Governance

Daniela Schilcher
Tourism Department, University of Otago, Dunedin, New Zealand

This paper proposes a model which integrates tourism in a continuum of poverty alleviation strategies within the antipodes of neo-liberalism and protectionism. It is argued that despite growing evidence in favour of regulative and (re)distributive approaches that in practice come closer to protectionism than neoliberalism, the most influential international organisations, as well as governments worldwide, follow a largely neoliberal laissez-faire approach to poverty alleviation coupled with market-friendly 'pro-poor' supplements. This paper argues that tourism per se fits very well into neoliberal interpretations of poverty alleviation, while it tends to aggravate poverty-enhancing inequalities if allowed to operate in a free market environment. Drawing on evidence from current research into poverty alleviation, it is argued that in order to be pro-poor, growth must deliver disproportionate benefits to the poor to reduce inequalities which have been found to limit the potential for poverty alleviation. Hence, it is necessary to shift policy focus from growth to equity, which calls for strong institutions capable of regulating the tourism industry and distributing assets in order to facilitate 'pro-poor growth'. In this respect, this paper challenges the conventional pro-poor tourism approach with its implicit growth-bias, where strategies are judged as pro-poor if they deliver net benefits to 'the poor' even if 'the rich' benefit disproportionately. However, through a contextualisation with the reality of politico-economic governance, this paper shows that strategies enhancing equity through shifting benefits towards the poor and, importantly, the poorest, are unlikely to be pursued in practice given policy-makers' neoliberal bias and systemic constraints. Hence, only strategies that are largely in sync with a neoliberal ideology and the 'World Bank orthodoxy', such as industry self-regulation or government incentives, have much potential to be implemented on a large-scale basis. More radical approaches such as pro-poor regulation and distribution – the equity side of the continuum – are bound to remain predominantly rhetoric of some United Nations organisations.

doi: 10.2167/cit304.0

Keywords: neoliberalism, pro-poor tourism, inequality, equity, poverty alleviation, tourism policy

Introduction

Referring to the 31st G8 summit held from 6 July to 8 July 2005, former UN Secretary General Kofi Annan praised the wide consensus on the objective to 'make poverty history' (United Nations, 2005). However, academics and international organisations stand divided on how to achieve this objective in practice. While the World Bank and International Monetary Fund (IMF) still largely promote neoliberal laissez-faire strategies with the intention to foster economic growth, others such as the United Nations Development Programme (UNDP)

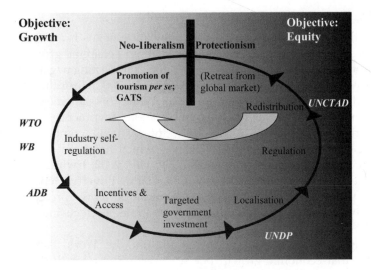

Figure 1 The continuum of poverty-alleviation strategies

and United Nations Conference on Trade and Development (UNCTAD) call for strong institutions to redistribute the unequal gains of growth and access to resources (Culpeper, 2002). In other words, strategies to alleviate poverty are subject to ideological interpretations lying within the (capitalist) extremes of neoliberalism and protectionism. This paper proposes a model which integrates tourism in a continuum of poverty alleviation strategies within these antipodes (Figure 1). On the one hand, it is shown that the further one moves away from the 'neoliberal' side of the continuum, the less likely are the strategies implemented in political practice. On the other hand, promoting tourism *per se* as a tool for poverty alleviation constitutes a neoliberal pro-poor approach which neglects the dimension of equity. Neglect of this dimension, however, implies that poverty among the *poorest* is bound to aggravate (Culpeper, 2002; United Nations, 2000).

This paper takes account of depth and severity of poverty, which relates to different strata among 'the poor', by including the dimension of 'the poorest' who fall far below the poverty line and are most deprived in terms of human capital and power. Hence, the concept is perceived broader than in the widely used 'poverty headcount' which relates to the proportion of the total population falling below the absolute poverty line (United Nations, 2000). Such an approach is necessary given the fact that a certain strategy may reduce the overall headcount of people below the poverty line, yet may simultaneously increase the severity of poverty among 'the poorest'.

Moreover, while poverty has been defined in a variety of ways (e.g. Griffith, 2003; United Nations, 2000; World Bank, 2005a), for the purpose of this paper an inclusive definition is utilised that adds to economic and human development criteria the dimension of power, which perceives poverty as lying in people's vulnerability and risk, as well as deprivation of socio-political voice (Griffith, 2003).

Tourism, Poverty and Economic Growth

While the economic growth-poverty alleviation nexus is a rather contested topic, there appears to be some consensus about economic growth to reduce poverty headcount, which implies that strategies impacting negatively on economic growth should be avoided (e.g. Culpeper, 2002; Griffith, 2003; Klasen, 2001; Rodrik, 2000; United Nations, 2000). While this statement may appear self-explanatory, it has far-reaching implications in practice in that radical protectionism – the withdrawal from international competition through imposing economic barriers (Hill, 2002) – which has been found to inhibit economic growth (Frankel & Roemer, 1999; Hill, 2002; Irwin & Tervio, 2002) does not constitute a viable strategy for alleviating poverty. Hence, on a continuum of pro-poor tourism strategies (Figure 1) full-blown protectionism may be perceived as the unviable antithesis to strategies focusing primarily on economic growth through openness.

Marking the other extreme on the continuum, the 'World Bank orthodoxy' stipulates that economic growth per se benefits the poor through a trickle-down effect (Dollar & Kraay, 2000). Cross-sectioning the data of 65 countries' experiences with economic growth and poverty, Dollar and Kraay (2000) found that the *average* income of the poorest 20% rises one for one with economic growth. In line with such a trickle-down logic, the World Bank used to focus on an acceleration of economic growth in order to reduce poverty without paying any attention to the relative gains accruing from growth (Oyen, 2001). While the neoliberal model of poverty-alleviation will be termed the 'World Bank orthodoxy', it must be acknowledged that the organisation is not ideologically homogenous throughout. Moreover, Bank strategies increasingly recognise the importance of equity (World Bank, 2005a) and domestic policy ownership as illustrated in the substitution of the Bank's controversial neoliberal structural adjustment programmes (SAPs) with so-called Poverty Reduction Strategy Papers (PRSPs). In general, however, the Bank continues to promote neoliberal laissez-faire approaches to economic policy in developing countries aiming at economic liberalisation and openness to stimulate growth (Oyen, 2001).

The tourism industry per se fits very well in such a growth-focused neoliberal approach. On the one hand, despite a high degree of volatility, tourism has been proven to accelerate economic growth particularly in countries and regions deprived of alternative means of economic development, such as small island states and rural areas (Briedenhann & Wickens, 2004; Gössling, 2003a; Harrison, 2003). Indeed, prior to concerns about economic leakage, economic dependency and negative socio-cultural and environmental impacts, tourism was regarded as a panacea for economic development, a mirage that still finds some support in practice (Mowforth & Munt, 1998; Sharpley & Telfer, 2002). On the other hand, tourism is a direct beneficiary of neoliberalism, as it tends to flourish in an open economic environment that facilitates the free movement of capital, labour and consumers. Compared to tourism, few other industries have experienced the same degree of vertical integration and proliferation of multinational enterprises (MNEs) (Go & Pine, 1996; Meethan, 2001), which is further enabled and validated through institutional arrangements such as the General Agreement on Trade in Services (GATS) (Kalisch, 2001; Kamp, 1999). The GATS and its counterpart on Tariffs and Trade, the GATT, are based on the belief that economic liberalisation and market openness will ultimately promote economic growth globally (Kalisch, 2001) – an orthodoxy which finds much support (e.g. Dollar & Kraay, 2003; Frankel & Roemer, 1999; Irwin & Tervio, 2002) but also opposition (Greenaway *et al.*, 2002; Hertel *et al.*, 2003; Klein, 2003). The reason for such disagreement might lie in the scholars' differing approaches: those in favour tend to examine the effects of free(er) trade and capital on growth, while the 'opposition' focuses on the effects of liberalisation (as policy input) (Sumner & Tiwari, 2004). Tourism itself contributes to the incorporation of national economies into the global economy and may even constitute the lead sector in this process (Williams & Shaw, 2002). As Hall (1998: 146) noted in the context of the South Pacific Island states, tourism 'helped draw the Pacific into the global capitalist system', which illustrates the industry's 'perfect fit' with neoliberal development orthodoxy. In fact, at the invitation of the World Tourism Organisation (WTO-OMT) a Declaration on tourism and poverty alleviation was signed by donors, governments and industry leaders, which explicitly called for higher priority of tourism liberalisation in the Doha Development Round, to capitalise on its potential as an export sector and economic driver for small island and poor states (WTO-OMT, 2005). Nation states are, however, only one piece of the puzzle.

On a local level, even small-scale tourist ventures under the banner of 'ecotourism' or 'community based tourism', for instance, may draw previously self-sufficient communities into the global economic system (Russell & Stabile, 2003) not least due to their commercial dependency on (often multinational) tour operators and marketing channels (Britton, 1983; Fisher, 2003). While some 'poor' individuals and communities may in fact be 'willing participants' (Harrison, 2003: 13) in furthering economic globalisation through an incorporation in the global economy via tourism (as part of a 'modernisation' process in general), others strongly aim to resist it due to an incompatibility with existing social structures and belief systems. For instance, de Burlo's (2003: 79) study of rural Vanuatu draws attention to 'tensions over tourism in the past [which] illustrate how tourism breaches island-wide networks of social exchange relations'. Tourism's compatibility with a poverty reduction ideology based on the need to incorporate into the global economic system to accelerate economic growth must hence be recognised.

The Issue of Inequality

While an economic growth-focused orthodoxy relating to poverty alleviation may prove successful for levels of absolute poverty (i.e. poverty headcount), there is growing evidence that neoliberal laissez-faire policies aimed at growth per se may in fact aggravate the severity of poverty through increasing inequality between 'the rich' and 'the poor', and more significantly still, between 'the rich' and 'the relatively poor' on the one hand and 'the poorest' on the other hand (Culpeper, 2002; Griffith, 2003; Talwar, 2004). Within the context of tourism, inequalities may be increased between developed and developing countries due to systemic distortions favouring the 'rich', as argued by authors adopting a dependency theory/political economy (Britton, 1982; Lea, 1988; Mowforth & Munt, 1998; Weaver, 1998) or even feminist view (Enloe, 1990). From a meso perspective, a neoliberal environment is prone to creating tourism industry clusters with lower investment flows directed at less developed regions within a country where poverty levels tend to be highest, such as in rural areas (Briedenhann & Wickens, 2004). Tourism in the Caribbean for example is 'characterized by the juxtaposition of an elite resort-based coast with an impoverished labor-supplying interior' (Weaver, 1988, quoted in Brohman, 1996: 57). At a micro level, inequalities may be aggravated between different strata of people whose livelihoods are connected to the industry, such as between managers of tourist facilities – particularly multinational enterprises – and local workers, or between 'powerful' individuals and other members of a community (Castaneda, 1991; Morgan & Pitchard, 1999; Norkunas, 1993; Reed, 1997). As Richter (1989: 53) noted, tourism is 'particularly well-suited to assuaging elites'.

Drawing on a holistic definition of poverty, inequalities should not only be perceived in terms of economic parameters. The perception of individuals and communities in terms of being empowered or disempowered is equally important. Focusing on local perceptions of the benefits (or otherwise) of tourism development in Pacific communities, Burns (2003) and Berno (2003) illustrate the importance of local ownership and control. However, assuring control, as well as giving 'voice' to the poor as it relates to tourism development is difficult to achieve in practice. On the one hand, as noted above, local 'elites' may prevent the 'poor's' wishes to enter the decision-making arena and may accrue the majority of benefits (Milne & Ateljevic, 2001; Reed, 1997; Richter, 1989). On the other hand, tourism as an 'appropriate avenue' to development and poverty alleviation may be imposed on 'the poor' in a top-down manner. Participative and consultative approaches to community tourism development (see e.g. Murphy, 1985) may in fact constitute little more than fostering consent among members of the community in the interest of industry growth, which is geared more towards reducing resistance than to genuinely empower and 'give voice' (Mowforth & Munt, 1998; Sofield, 2003). As Sofield (2003: 107) noted with regard to a tourism plan drawn up by the WTO-OMT for Sri Lanka, the proposed 'community involvement' was in effect intended to 'assist in minimizing adverse community reaction, rather than genuine community involvement in determining for itself the role of tourism development in its community. It is more concerned, it would appear, with a public relations exercise'. Pro-poor tourism should not be about the industry, but the needs of 'the poor' (however conceptualised in a specific context at the micro level). Hence, in a community context, the poor should be enabled to genuinely decide on their development priorities, even if that means 'no' to tourism development, or tourism in a specific form, which might be judged unsuccessful from a policy maker's or donor's perspective, yet satisfactory in the opinion of 'the poor' themselves (see de Burlo, 2003 for a case study of an indigenous tourism enterprise which defied an economic-rational view of success but enhanced cultural capital).

At the supranational level, the World Bank has introduced a process called 'community driven development' (World Bank, 2005b) which – in theory – aims to empower 'the poor' to decide on their path of development. While constituting an important step towards giving voice to 'the poor', Cheater (1999: 59) dismissed the World Bank's 'new participatory-cum-empowerment development-speak' for being restricted to process and consultation, while the more salient issues of income and assets distribution or macroeconomic decisions about liberalisation and global integration are 'off limits' (Perrons, 2004; Stiglitz, 2002). In this context, Perrons (2004: 328) reminded of the 1968 slogan 'Je participe, Tu participe … Ils décident' [I participate, You participate … They decide]. While there is always space for resistance (Jamal *et al.*, 2003), 'the local' operates within a context of decision-making structures which span all levels up to the global. Despite predictions of the 'death of the nation state' (Guéhenno, 1996; Kratochwil & Ruggie, 1986; Ohmae, 1995) national governments are still the prime decision-making organs despite being somewhat constrained considering their embeddedness in a global economic system (Bennett, 1980; Farazmand, 1999; Kahler & Lake, 2003; Karns & Mingst, 2004), as well as their general adherence to a predominantly neoliberal 'development' ideology (Brand, 2001; Cox, 1996; Gill & Law, 1989; Jessop, 1999). The decisions taken by governments may in fact work against social considerations, and 'the poor' in particular. As Anita Pleumarom, coordinator of the Bangkok-based Tourism Investigation and Monitoring Team pointed out 'a hard look at tourism development in the Mekong subregion leads to the conclusion that the policies pursued by the national tourism authorities and supranational bodies (…) have been those most suitable for promoting the industry rather than for the protection of the environment and the well-being of the local communities' (Pleumarom, quoted in Rajesh, 2004: 1). Without genuine government intervention (and industry regulation) focusing on the well-being of 'the poor', the latter are bound to carry an unproportionate share of the industry's inherent costs of environmental degradation, cultural commodification and social displacement (see Hall & Page, 1999; Mathieson & Wall, 1982; Theobald, 1994; Williams, 2001). As Brohman (1996: 60) noted, 'tourism development can indeed be positive for local communities if their needs and interests are given priority over the goals of the industry *per se*'. In the current economic environment, however, many governments *need* tourism growth – which tends to discriminate against the former.

Economic Restructuring and 'the Poor'

In general, developing countries pursue structural adjustments aimed at increasing competitiveness in a market environment including labour market deregulation, facilitation of foreign direct investment, and a shift from agriculture towards manufacturing and untraditional export sectors including tourism – a strategy that is heavily promoted by donors and international financial institutions (Brohman, 1996; Gibbon, 2004). Multinational tourism enterprises clearly thrive in such an environment (Mowforth & Munt, 1998). Being enabled to repatriate profits, import goods from the economic North to cater for the international visitor market, and employ expatriates for high-skills positions results in high levels of economic leakage and minimises tourism's potential benefit to the host country's local economy – and 'the poor' within it – through linkages and income creation (Britton, 1982, 1983; Mowforth & Munt, 1998). While the pro-poor tourism approach – particularly the WTO-OMT's ST-EP programme – emphasises the potential of tourism per se for creating employment among the poor (WTO-OMT, no date), and MNEs certainly do create jobs, these may be low-skilled, low-wage and coupled with long working hours (Britton, 1982, 1983; Burns, 2003; Mowforth & Munt, 1998; Parliament of Fiji, 2004) – a problem which a policy of labour market deregulation tends to aggravate. Instead of aiming at job creation per se, pro-poor policies should focus on income and working conditions, which would require regulation (e.g. minimum wages; compulsory local training schemes) not deregulation (Culpeper, 2002). This would need to be coupled with uncompromising resource transfers (e.g. skills, land and political 'voice') to increase the poor's ability to either gain 'meaningful' employment (with a higher wage, as well as the possibility for pride in work), participate in entrepreneurial activity, or retain/achieve self-reliance (even if based on a subsistence economy if so chosen by 'the poor' themselves).

Apart from employment generation, it has been argued that tourism may generate benefits for 'the poor' through entrepreneurial activity (Ashley *et al.*, 2000, 2001; Bauer *et al.*, 2004; Cattarinich, 2001; DFID, 1999). However, opportunities for 'the poor' themselves to participate in the tourism industry, for example, in the form of community tourism enterprises or small-scale locally owned businesses, are weakened in a neoliberal environment due to competition from capital-intensive, vertically integrated MNEs, or due to market entry constraints given 'the poor's' limited bargaining power and access to assets such as capital and land without any protective intervention by the state (Kalisch, 2001; Williams, 2001). Poverty reduction through tourism in a neoliberal environment may be perceived as a 'self-help system' where 'the poor' are expected to lift themselves out of poverty through becoming economically active agents. Lesotho for example

> is striving to create a favourable and enabling climate to attract not just foreign capital but to stimulate local entrepreneurship in gainful economic participation particularly through tourism activities. Lesotho to a large extent has demonstrated its commitment and willingness to be 'open for business' by liberalizing its policies and reduce restrictions on attraction of inward investment. (Lesotho Tourism Development Corporation, 2003: 4)

In general, self-help approaches are a constructive supplement to pro-poor strategies targeting the 'poor' and especially 'poorest' in terms of social protection, as self-help reduces aid dependency (and dependency is a source of powerlessness, see Caporaso, 1978; Caporaso & Haggard, 1989). However, those who lack the necessary skills, assets and power (or will, given tourism's potential clash with the social fabric) to start up their own tourism business, do not only fail to benefit from any dubious trickle-down effect of tourism growth, but are also worst affected by structural adjustment programmes and a dismantling of the state's welfare functions (Brohman, 1996; Mowforth & Munt, 1998).

Hence, while poverty headcount may decrease, not only inequalities but also the severity of poverty tends to increase, leaving 'the poorest' even poorer (Talwar, 2004; WIDER, 2004). The failure of the 'trickle-down' logic has also been asserted within the tourism literature, giving rise to calls for government intervention (Briedenhann & Wickens, 2004; Sofield, 2003).

Recent studies make a strong case for reducing inequality not simply on moral grounds but through demonstrating a positive relationship between equity, growth and poverty reduction (WIDER, 2004). Unequal distribution of assets, particularly land, credit and education, decreases productivity and efficiency (Culpeper, 2002; Griffith, 2003; Klasen, 2001; Oxfam, 2000; Talwar, 2004; WIDER, 2004). Hence, *distributive* policies 'that are effective in increasing the incomes and assets of the poor and poorest – such as investment in primary education, rural infrastructure, health and nutrition – are also policies that enhance the productive capacity of the economy in aggregate' (Rodrik, 2000: 1). Moreover, policies directed towards asset redistribution and equitable taxation target inequality and should therefore contribute to improved future growth performance and poverty reduction (Culpeper, 2002). In this sense, there need not be a trade-off between the policy foci of growth and equity; instead, the continuum of poverty alleviation strategies can be bridged and can go full circle (Figure 1).

Political Practice: The Nebuleuse of Neoliberalism

The WTO-OMT is bound to promote the growth of tourism *per se* – now under the new banner of poverty alleviation. In an interesting application of Lukes' (1974) three faces of power, Hall (2005b) points out that the WTO-OMT *needs more tourism* due to its profit-generating activities, which implies policy advice in the form of neoliberal liberalisation and deregelution and renders advice of 'no' or 'minimal' tourism very unlikely. Mowforth and Munt (1998) go as far as to claim that pro-poor tourism constitutes little more than a 'repackaging' of existing approaches so that they fit within the dominant development paradigm. In this vein, the South Pacific Tourism Organisation (SPTO), a regional intergovernmental organisation, increasingly tries to 'sell' tourism to the donor community under the banner of poverty alleviation out of a need to attract funds for its work programme after the cease of long-term European Union (EU) funding (Schilcher, 2007). However, an analysis of the SPTO's past activities has shown that the impact on the 'poor' has been neutral at best (Cleverdon Associates, 2003) if not negative. The SPTO has attracted criticism from its members for neglecting both small-scale operators and less developed (in tourism terms) countries in the region (Cleverdon Associates, 2003; Pacific Magazine, 2001).

In fact, the 'donor community' has been largely opposed to promoting tourism due to concerns about negative impacts and leakage (Keith-Reid, 2004; SPTO official, 2005), making tourism a 'hard sell' (EU Trade Advisor, 2005). Their current embracing of pro-poor tourism appears to be a result of successful lobbying efforts by tourism organisations and industry consortia (see e.g. CHA, 2005; PATA, 2003; SPTO, 2001) who 'sold' tourism under the banner of poverty alleviation, coupled with the fact that tourism fits with

donors' neoliberal approach to poverty alleviation based on economic liberalisation and private-sector driven growth. The EU, for example, approved
another grant to the SPTO under the so-called Pacific Regional Economic
Integration Programme which aims at promoting the African, Caribbean and
Pacific (ACP) states' move towards larger and more unified markets in the
form of free trade areas and trade liberalisation with the overall goal of
poverty alleviation (EC/Pacific ACP, 2003). On the one hand, tourism supports
such an approach. On the other hand, the grant has been predominantly
awarded after severe lobbying (SPTO official, 2005) to give 'SPTO a bit of a
soft landing, not to pull the plug too violently' after long-term funding had
ended (EU Trade Advisor, 2005). Thus, organisations that need more tourism
are bound to emphasise tourism's pro-poor potential to donors while promoting neoliberal approaches in which the industry can flourish. Suggestions to
'make tourism more pro-poor' therefore mostly take the form of voluntary
codes of conduct, declarations and calls for public-private partnership – all
soft law approaches avoiding disruptions to growth and systemic change –
which would require governments or a supranational body to interfere with
market forces (see Richter, 2004).

The academic literature on pro-poor tourism does not aim to expand the
industry, but rather to 'tilt the cake'. In general, governments are recognised
to play an important role in this process, yet merely alongside numerous
other 'stakeholders' (DFID, 1999, http://www.propoor-tourism.org). However,
to what extent are governments willing or able to favour 'the poor' within
policy and action? In practice, redistributive policies targeting the 'poor'
and 'poorest' encounter resistance (Culpeper, 2002). Such practice necessitates
strong political institutions willing and able to regulate and interfere with
market forces and to allocate scarce financial resources and assets to people
below the poverty line. Such policies, however, conflict with the ideology
and practical requirements of neoliberalism, as well as systemic conditions
under globalised markets. Despite a rhetorical discreditation of neo-liberalism
– even within the World Bank group which has replaced its controversial
SAPs with PRSPs – not much has changed in practice.

The 'donor community' and international financial organisations increasingly stress, not least due to substantial criticism of SAP's negative impact
on 'the poor' (see e.g. Farazmand, 1999; Klak & Conway, 1998; Mowforth &
Munt, 1998), that a furthering of economic globalisation through liberalisation,
deregulation and privatisation must be accompanied by the provision of some
sort of 'social protection' and strategies focusing on 'the poor' – the so-called
Augmented Washington Consensus (Beeson & Islam, 2005). However, the new
'consensus', while pointing in a positive direction in terms of acknowledging
neoliberalism's shortcomings, has attracted criticism for being 'an impossibly
broad, undifferentiated agenda' (Rodrik, 2002 quoted in Beeson & Islam,
2005: 207), still prescribing one-size-fits-all neoliberal reforms coupled with
some desirable features of development. How the latter is to be achieved in practice (and financed) remains unknown. The PRSPs have in turn been subject to
criticism for still being donor-driven (Beeson & Islam, 2005). The PRSPs have
to be accepted by international financial institutions to be eligible for conces-
sional aid and debt relief (http://www.imf.org, http://www.unctad.org).

While the 'new' focus has generally been welcomed by NGOs (http://www.oxfam.org.uk) and it is now less obvious to speak of an 'imposition' of policies, the financial institutions' overall neoliberal outlook has remained unchanged (Oyen, 2001).

Within the framework of the World Trade Organisation (WTO), the economic North has in fact called to include enforceable social (and environmental) standards in the international trade regime. However, this encountered strong resistance by countries of the economic South which perceived these to be protectionism in disguise (Singh & Zammit, 2004). In fact, far from constituting an altruistic call for improved social conditions in the South, the US' insistence on universal labour standards, for example, has been interpreted as an intension to protect its domestic labour from the relocation of enterprises to 'low wage' destinations (Singh & Zammit, 2004). Irrespective the motivations behind calls for social protection, 'the poor' would benefit from such a strategy as long as this would not result in economic stagnation. Fear of the latter may induce governments to further dismantle social (and environmental) standards – the so-called 'race to the bottom' (Glyn, 2004; Singh & Zammit, 2004).

While arguments relating to the 'race to the bottom' to increase global competitiveness under globalisation relate largely to manufacturing (Hill, 2002), the tourism industry is subject to the same systemic conditions. As Przeworski and Wallerstein (1988) argued, the structural dependence of the state on capital predetermines the direction of policies to be taken. While such a deterministic structuralist view has been largely discredited (Best & Kellner, 1991), it is undeniable that economic globalisation has somewhat constrained governments' choice options. Within the contemporary system of liberalised markets, many governments of the South have no choice but to elevate tourism to constituting the 'lead sector' in the economy. For many economically marginalised and resource-poor countries tourism appears to be the only hope for 'development', perceived in line with an interpretation focusing on economic growth (Britton, 1983; Hall, 1998; Harrigan, 1974; Milne, 1992; Momsen, 1998; Vellas & Bécherel, 1995). In theory, under liberalised market conditions, a country can only remain competitive if it offers products or services in which it has a comparative advantage (Hill, 2002). For many countries, this sector inevitably needs to be tourism. Given the competitive pressures in a neoliberal environment, scarce government resources are allocated to cash-generating export sectors, such as tourism, which capitalise on their major resources of cheap labour and land. In many developing countries and resource-poor small island states, adherence to the neoliberal principles of liberalisation and deregulation has automatically increased dependency on tourism as one of their few viable export sectors of comparative advantage.

Various studies have illustrated the link between an increasing dominance of the services sector in general, and tourism in particular, and neoliberal economic reform (Brohman, 1996; Mair, 2006; Williams & Montanari, 1995). Case studies on neoliberal reform and the corresponding government promotion of tourism in developing and transition countries include Mexico (Clancey, 1999), Zanzibar (Gössling, 2003b), Turkey (Juda & Richardson, 2001), Peru (Desforges, 2000) and Madagascar (Duffy, 2005). Governments of the South – caught up in economic reform – have been largely 'retreating' from interfering with market mechanisms guiding the industry in order to ensure its growth. The major guiding principles have been economic liberalisation and deregulation, providing a supportive environment for private sector activity (Brohman, 1996). In theory, governments may choose to promote small-scale, locally controlled tourism as opposed to large-scale, capital intensive tourism based on foreign ownership (and control) (Mowforth & Munt, 1998). However, faced with scarcity of domestic capital, many governments have no choice but to deregulate the market in order to promote tourism (Britton, 1983; Hall, 1998), despite its implications on local control and the government's tax base. Hall (1998: 146) noted that due to their limited resource base (including indigenous capital), the island nations of the South Pacific, for example, are 'reliant on foreign powers to provide capital for economic development and the transport links that enable the export of goods and services. In addition, most have relatively little control over their natural resources, and even less power to influence the economic and political direction of the region'. Systemic constraints therefore require developing countries' governments to liberalise tourism's economic environment in order to ensure the sector's growth.

It is important to note that neoliberal reforms with the frequent elevation of tourism to the top of the government's economic 'development' agenda, may have statist elements. As Clancey (1999) noted, the government of Mexico actively interfered with market forces by investing in tourism in order to push the development of the sector. This observation correlates to a number of studies examining Asian countries' (ranging from Thailand to Malaysia, Korea and China) experience with economic reform after the financial crisis (Hewison, 2005; Liew, 2005; Robinson & Hewison, 2005). They found that 'pure' neoliberal reform as envisaged in the IMF's rescue packages has been contested by governments. In most states, the government has not fully retreated but remained a powerful actor guiding economic and social affairs – in alliance with powerful domestic political and economic elites. Ensuring to serve elite interests, governments have rather pursued a 'raisin picking' approach with regard to neoliberal strategies. Drawing on some neoliberal elements, such as the facilitation of foreign direct investment and trade and privatisation of state assets, governments have retained protective elements geared at serving the interests of domestic elites. The outcome, however, has been mostly the same as with unfettered neoliberalism: increasing domestic inequalities. As Liew (2005) noted with regard to China, the ruling party has to forge an alliance with what it considers as the 'advanced elements of the new social strata' whose interests are better served by the country's promotion of a market economy than are those of workers or peasants. In an interesting twist, Thailand, however, is an example where IMF induced post-crisis neo-liberal reforms have resulted in better social protection of 'the poor' (Hewison, 2005). Being threatened by international capital due to neoliberal reforms, domestic business tycoons forged an alliance with an emerging political party to serve their interests in future economic policy. In order to gain votes, the party (under Thaksin Shinawatra who recently stepped back due to an alleged corruption and privatisation scandal (BBC, 2006)) provided village support and health schemes which found much support among the 'poor'.

In most cases, however, where governments adhere to the requirements of a liberalised market environment (and offer tax incentives to attract capital), they face difficulties in mobilising the required tax revenue for providing genuine social protection in terms of education and health for example – which is of paramount importance to the 'poor' and 'poorest' (Badillo *et al.*, 2001; Farthing & Kohl, 2004; Rodrik, 1997a, 1997b; Shastri Institute, 2004). Even the 'rich' OECD countries struggle to maintain their welfare systems, and many have reduced the role of the state to a bare minimum (Birdsall, 1999). As already noted, governments of the North, as well as international financial institutions (including the World bank and IMF) call for 'social protection' in the South alongside a continuation of economic neoliberalism. However, it is unclear how this is supposed to be financed (Deacon, 2000). The World Bank and IMF propose some bare minimum provision and to privatise the majority of public social services (see Deacon, 2000; World Bank, 2001). In this sense, economic neoliberalism remains unchallenged.

Tourism certainly fits well with such an approach, in that the task of poverty alleviation is delegated to the private sector. Governments and donors laying much hope in tourism per se for poverty alleviation seem to kill two birds with one stone: the focus on economic growth through tourism as an export sector – and the related foreign exchange earnings – can be retained, while at the same time the cost intensive task of universal welfare provision is substituted with a private-sector-led self-help system. Supranational organisations such as the World Bank or IMF frequently constitute key drivers behind this process. Gössling's (2003b) case study of Zanzibar, for example, illustrates how the World Bank has put the country's socialist government on the neo-liberal track and influenced tourism development to the detriment of government commitment to 'the poor' and resulting in the latter's increased powerlessness (see also Duffy, 2005; Mowforth & Munt, 1998).

Developing countries' governments hardly have a choice but to support export promotion to service their debt to international financial institutions like the World Bank or Asian Development Bank and to fill their ever-growing trade deficits – the logical consequence of which is an increased economic importance of the tourism sector. As a consequence, even governments that have so far promoted local empowerment and control to benefit the 'poor' largely reversed their stance due to systemic pressure. For example, Mowforth and Munt's (1998: 311) study of Costa Rica draws attention to 'the link between the burden of international debt and government capitulation to the pressure of transnational companies to develop large-scale tourism projects'. Moreover, the before mentioned difficulty of developing countries' governments to raise the necessary tax revenue for pro-poor social spending (Rodrik, 1997a, 1997b) often requires the uptake of further loans (Béjar, 2001), the debt burden in turn requiring an additional promotion of tourism. Other countries such as India (Shastri Institute, 2004), Bolivia (Farthing & Kohl, 2004) or Ecuador (Badillo *et al.*, 2001) have simply opted to significantly reduce their spending on 'the poor'.

From a trade perspective, the replacement of trade preferences with reciprocal trade agreements is likely to further exacerbate developing countries' dependence on tourism as the lead sector in the economy. For instance, the

African, Caribbean and Pacific (ACP) countries are currently negotiating so-called Economic Partnership Agreements (EPAs) with the European Union that will replace the preferential trade regime the ACP had enjoyed for decades under the Lomé Conventions. EPAs will not only demand reciprocal market access, which will increase competitive pressures on the ACP, they will also go hand in hand with an elimination of the export price stabilisation scheme STABEX under the new Cotonou Agreement and the preferential 'sugar protocol'. This will have the effect that entire sectors like Fiji's or the Caribbean's sugar industry are likely to collapse, which then in turn would increase the dependency on tourism (EU Development Committee, 2006). It is hardly surprising that both, the Caribbean and Pacific EPA negotiating machineries call for tourism to be included in a trade agreement, laying much hope in the EPA's 'development dimension' (EU Trade Advisor, 2005; Zeller, 2005). The latter basically constitutes aid for 'trade facilitation' and structural adjustment – which Pacific and Caribbean negotiators (as well as private sector lobby groups (see CHA, 2005)) hope to channel into the tourism sector. As the South Pacific Tourism Organisation (SPTO, 2001: 20) put it 'recent and new trade agreements (...) have precipitated withdrawal of trade preferences that many of the SP [South Pacific] islands depended on in the past. Tourism, which had never been subject to trade preference, is becoming more important as a sector to the region'. Government support to tourism per se as sector of comparative advantage is hence required in a liberal market environment.

Support to tourism in turn requires a laissez-faire approach to encourage investment through labour market deregulation and tax incentives (often coupled with 'statist' investment in infrastructure) as, for example, in Fiji (Chand, 2000), Mexico (Clancey, 1999) or Zanzibar (Gössling, 2003b). Such a policy stance may, however, displace distributive pro-poor policies, degrade social standards and minimise 'the poor's control over development'. Hence, the bridging of the continuum from equity to growth is compromised. Statements arguing for tourism as a 'tool for poverty alleviation' must hence be treated with much caution. Based on the previous discussion, tourism per se as both driver and beneficiary of neoliberalism with its inherent bias towards inequality is prone to enhance rather than solve the problem of poverty. It follows from a pro-poor perspective that:

(1) Tourism should only be promoted if it does not replace distributive policies with a focus on reducing inequalities and benefiting the 'poorest', such as wide-ranging social protection, labour standards, equitable taxation and redistribution of assets, investment in education and health, and facilitation of local ownership and control over 'development' (Badillo *et al.*, 2001; Farthing & Kohl, 2004; Rodrik, 1997a, 1997b, 2000; Shastri Institute, 2004). To this ends, both 'poor' countries (meso level) and the 'poor' within countries (micro level) need to be empowered to exercise choice, rather than being subject to one-size-fits-all approaches stipulating tourism as a route to poverty alleviation.
(2) The tourism industry must be 'moulded' so that 'the poor' and 'poorest' receive a proportionately higher share of tourism's benefits than people above the poverty line in order to reduce poverty-enhancing inequalities.

It has already been demonstrated that governments largely follow the logic of neoliberalism which frequently implies the promotion of tourism as key export sector. As Mair (2006: 1) suggested: 'As capital cements its latest form through the withdrawal of the state and the extension of the consumption, service-based economy, tourism is naturalised as an appropriate policy response'. Despite some encouraging attempts to empower communities in development decision-making even by the World Bank (World Bank, 2005b), 'the poor' are usually denied voice in the process, as well as most benefits due to elite politics (Mansuri & Rao, 2002) and a remaining element of top-down decision-making (Patel, 2000). Equally important, the local is embedded within the national – governments' need for tourism growth (due to their embeddedness in the global economy) implies that the path of tourism development impacting on the local is to some extent pre-determined – a neoliberal path focusing on growth. Hence, requirement (1) does not correspond to the reality of politico-economic governance, which only leaves option (2) as a compromise.

Making Tourism More Pro-Poor

A variety of strategies intended to 'make tourism more pro-poor' have been put forward. These include the provision of training to the poor, local sourcing, micro-credits, improving access to the industry and decision-making, supporting community initiatives, directing investment into impoverished regions, and mitigating negative impacts away from the poor (Ashley et al., 2000, 2001; Bauer et al., 2004; Cattarinich, 2001; DFID, 1999). However, most of these strategies are prone to failure (in terms of truly fighting poverty) as they are based on the view that tourism is pro-poor 'as long as poor people reap net benefits [. . . and] even if richer people benefit more than poorer people' (Ashley et al., 2001: 2), a position supported by the World Bank orthodoxy. Movement beyond poverty head-count reduction strategies requires the recognition that pro-poor implies 'the poor' benefiting more than the 'non-poor' (UNDP, 2004); a concept grounded in the importance of equity to poverty alleviation. Strategies designed to close the gap between the 'rich' and the 'poor' and 'poorest' require a political will to interfere with market forces, which, as has been demonstrated in the previous section, is generally lacking.

Strategies to 'make tourism more pro-poor' that do have general political support are those in proximity to the extreme of neoliberalism on the continuum (Figure 1). With a policy bias towards growth, tourism may be rendered marginally 'more pro-poor' yet increase inequalities due to disproportionate benefits accruing to the 'rich'. Appealing to corporate social responsibility (CSR) and codes of conduct constitutes the ultimate neoliberal 'pro-poor tourism' strategy. In this scenario, governments refrain completely from interfering with market forces in order to stimulate 'growth for poverty alleviation', hence shifting responsibility for being 'pro-poor' to the private sector. As Richter (2004: 14) noted with regard to the 'mantra of globalisation', 'as private economic interests grow vis a vis the nation's, the ability of the government weakens as it seeks to protect itself from privatization of activities once deemed too important to the public to be in private hands'. Such a strategy finds support among international organizations such as the World Tourism Organisation (WTO-OMT, no date) and Asian Development Bank (Viravaidya, 2002), governments (see SPTO, 2005) and academics (Ashley *et al.*, 2001; Roe *et al.*, 2002). For example, in an appeal directed at Fiji's primarily foreign-owned tourism enterprises, Fijian politician Mick Beddoes claimed that 'the state no longer has the resources to resolve this problem [of poverty alleviation] and it was now everyone's problem. The industry could directly help 12,500 families or about 50,000 people if it shifts its current habit of buying food from abroad to buying at least 50% of local food' (SPTO, 2005: 1). That such a strategy can only ever generate marginal benefits to the 'poor' and particularly 'poorest' is self-evident given the total reliance on poverty headcount reduction through growth.

Moreover, a strategy of shifting responsibility for poverty reduction to the private sector may show some success in single cases in terms of 'making tourism more pro-poor' (see e.g. Cattarinich, 2001), but will not allow 'the poor' and 'poorest' to capture disproportionate benefits. 'Business is about business' (Fernweh, 2004; Ite, 2005) and hence tourism enterprises can only ever marginally contribute to increased rates of equity within the margins of commercial reality. Unsurprisingly, the rate of (supranational) soft law – such as codes of conduct – that were actually implemented remains low (Davidson & Maitland, 1997; Santana, 2001; Timothy, 2001, 2003). Soft law approaches to pro-poor tourism may be compared those on 'sustainable tourism' or 'ethics in tourism', in which the majority of tourism enterprises does not fare particularly well (Fennell & Malloy, 1999). While the private sector may voluntarily take on a supportive role in social development (if it makes business sense, see Roe *et al.*, 2002), it remains the government's main charge to represent society and ensure equitable distribution among the various stakeholders (Ite, 2005), which equally encounters resistance. As Richter (2004: 14–15) succinctly pointed out with regard to the WTO-OMT's codes of conduct and Declarations (focusing on sustainability), 'these pronouncements illustrate a rhetorical regard for host communities but for implementation of its goals the WTO must depend on the tourist industry and interested governments – neither group having established a record for self-policing or a desire for increased regulation ... [each of these issues] cries out for regulation, supranational agreements, an international court and a variety of controls totally ad odds with the current political climate in the most powerful nations'.

Of similar growth-bias are 'pro-poor' government incentives such as tax incentives to businesses investing in areas lacking alternative forms of economic development (the major rational of which would be job, not income creation), or state subsidies for in-house training programmes to improve the local skills base. Countries ranging from Panama (Shirley & Associates, 1994) to the Philippines (Philippines Department of Tourism, no date) and French Polynesia (Pacific Magazine, 2005) offer wide-ranging incentives to tourism businesses willing to invest in rural areas or outer islands respectively. However, in this scenario the industry is left to the rules of demand and supply, and commercial reality dictates whether or not businesses draw upon 'pro-poor' incentives provided by the state (Ite, 2005).

Moreover, business incentives run directly against distributive policies focusing on equity, as government resources are directly allocated to the private sector instead of the 'poor' (through upgrading tourism infrastructure for instance) and undermine the state's tax base necessary for social spending (Badillo, 2001; Farthing & Kohl, 2004; Rodrik, 1997; Shastri Institute, 2004). Moreover, the minimum investment requirements are typically excessive of any amount indigenous entrepreneurs (let alone 'the poor') could afford (see e.g. Pacific Magazine, 2005; Philippines Department of Tourism, no date, Shirley & Associates, 1994), hence necessitating reliance on the discredited 'trickle down' effect through possible job creation or stimulation of the informal sector. Incentives offered by the government of Fiji apply to foreign investors as they do to local ones – the government introduced a policy of non-discrimination in line with GATS – and there are no restrictions on the repatriation of profits (FTIB, 2005) despite leakage levels in excess of 60% (Levett & McNally, 2003) not least due to a high dependency on foreign capital (Forsyth, 1997). Of 132 tourism projects implemented between 1988 and 2000, 94% were foreign owned including joint ventures, leaving a mere 6% with local ownership status (Narayan & Prasad, 2003).

Moving away from neoliberalism towards 'equity' on the continuum (Figure 1), government investment in rural infrastructure for tourism for example may specifically target the 'poor'. However, this strategy not only builds on the growth-model through enhancing economic opportunities for both, 'the poor' and 'the rich' in a self-help system, but it also displaces scarce government resources targeting primary education and health among others. Apart from offering investment incentives (FTIB, 2005), the government of Fiji, for example, has made major investments in tourism infrastructure in recent years to cater for developers' needs (Vaile, 2002) despite growing levels of poverty (ADB, 2004). Yet, the public budget allocated only an additional 1.3% in expenditures on poverty reduction, a significant decrease in real terms. Government spending on social welfare, housing and microfinance – the redistributive function of the state – also dropped considerably (ADB, 2004). Moreover, government promotion of tourism in impoverished regions may in fact enhance inequalities if the major beneficiaries constitute the economic elite and the government instead of 'the poor', despite any 'pro-poor' rhetoric emphasising backward linkages (see e.g. Torres & Momsen, 2005 for a case study of Quintana Roo, Mexico).

Uncompromising pro-poor tourism implying that 'the poor' reap unproportionately higher benefits than 'the rich' would necessarily take the form of local ownership and compulsory local sourcing in an environment where 'the poor' have been granted access to the assets of land, credit and skills (UNDP, 2004) – strategies targeting 'equity' on the continuum (Figure 1) (see Crosby, 2002 for a case study of a local community attempting to use community-owned and controlled tourism development as a means of achieving independence form the local elite. However, the project failed: see Bennett, 2005). These strategies generally run counter to the *nebuleuse* of neoliberalism, as well as systemic constraints under economic globalisation (Cox, 1996). Not only do governments follow a largely neoliberal logic of less market intervention to stimulate growth and investment, but they are also 'locked into' neoliberal regimes such as the GATT and GATS. Regulation and distributive strategies are virtually prevented not only through ideas – in a Gramscian sense (Gramsci, 1971) the hegemony of a neoliberal ideology – but also institutions (Falk, 1995; Massicotte, 1999; Murphy, 1994; Ougaard, 1999). As the example of Fiji demonstrates, positive discrimination in favour of local ownership or labour runs counter the requirements of GATS and a liberalised environment in general, moving political practice towards neoliberal growth on the continuum. Local ownership and control, for example, are bound to be compromised.

Apart from Costa Rica (Mowforth & Munt, 1998) and Madagascar (Duffy, 2005), Samoa constitutes a further example of a developing country compromising 'the poor's' control over their 'development' due to neoliberal practice. Tourism in Samoa has long been of an unusually pro-poor nature due to the government's ambiguity about the industry out of a fear of any negative cultural impacts (Scheyvens, 2002). More than 90% of Samoa's tourism businesses are locally owned with only one of four hotels with more than 50 beds in foreign ownership, and local sourcing is high given the prevalence of *aiga potopoto-* (extended family-) owned enterprises that directly support the local economy (Scheyvens, 2002; Twining-Ward & Twining-Ward, 1998). In recent years, however, the Samoan government has embarked on an aggressive course of promoting foreign direct investment and standardisation in tourism in an attempt to gear the industry towards mid- to top-end market segments (Government of Samoa, 2001; Pacific Islands Trade and Investment Commission, 2003); thus, investment laws have been liberalised accordingly. This change in track has been supported by international organisations such as the Asian Development Bank and the European Union-funded South Pacific Tourism Organisation – the latter having developed a tourism plan for Samoa explicitly recommending a liberalised investment regime (TCSP, 1992), and the former having supported wide-ranging structural adjustment policies in the 1990s and recommending the establishment of a 'name brand' resort (ADB, 2000). Moreover, as a member of the ACP group, as well as a member-to-be of the WTO, Samoa is increasingly facing pressures to boost export performance in a liberalised environment due to the dismantling of trade preferences. The country has strongly benefited under the now obsolete STABEX scheme (EU, 2005), and an impact assessment has shown that the forthcoming EPAs are likely to have a negative impact on the country's finances (Scollay, 2001). A boost of tourism – one of Samoa's few competitive sectors – is therefore unavoidable.

While Samoa's high rate of local ownership in tourism could even provide for a competitive industry when combined with a strategy of localisation and place marketing, the increasingly neoliberal environment demands tourism to become a lead sector for economic growth – and the government has indeed identified tourism as such (Government of Samoa, 2005). Where tourism used to be tolerated rather than promoted, it has been promoted to one of nine economic lead sectors in 2002 (Government of Samoa, 2002), and one of only six in 2005 (Government of Samoa, 2005). The required boost can only occur via further relaxation of regulations relating to the industry itself in order to attract foreign investment capital (the local economy could not support much of an expansion), such as the elimination of local contents requirements and the facilitation of a repatriation of profits and employment of expatriate workers – a trend that is clearly evident in current government policy (Government of Samoa, 2001, 2002, 2005; Pacific Islands Trade and Investment Commission, 2003). While potential growth may reduce the poverty headcount, these strategies are likely to reduce the true pro-poor potential of tourism due to increasing inequalities.

Conclusion

It may not be surprising that on its website the World Tourism Organisation introduces its programme on sustainable tourism for poverty alleviation (implying a promotion, not just 'moulding' of the industry) under the general heading of trade liberalisation (WTO-OMT, no date). The ideology of neoliberalism is too widespread and 'locked in' despite the Augmented Washington Consensus to allow for uncompromising strategies targeting the 'poor' and 'poorest' through a focus on equity. Instead, the World Bank ortho-doxy of economic growth reducing poverty headcount is widely embraced, which implies a general promotion of tourism per se. This promotion, however, displaces redistributive strategies and reinforces inequalities if allowed to operate without interference in market forces. The *nebuleuse* of neoliberalism prevents government intervention targeting equity within tourism, which rea-listically restricts 'pro-poor tourism' strategies to those in sync with the growth mentality (the left-hand side of the continuum). This, however, will at best only reduce poverty headcount, whereas it is likely to further aggravate the severity and depth of poverty.

To genuinely target poverty requires a focus on equity – not neglecting 'the poorest' – instead of growth (while still preventing negative growth), which necessitates both ideological and systemic change. International organisations, governments and academics need to allow access to the policy arena to ideas and strategies challenging neoliberalism. Such ideological change would need to be accompanied by a change in the international system so that devel-oping countries are granted greater decision-making power in institutions such as the World Trade Organisation, the World Bank and IMF. Flexibility and genuine policy-ownership allowing for individual responses to poverty are key. One-size-fits-all approaches – such as the promotion of tourism per se – are entirely unsuitable for the multi-dimensional problem of poverty.

It has been argued that 'the poor' must reap disproportionate benefits from tourism in order to make it truly pro-poor. The question remains whether there is scope to translate such a proposition into practice. It would be naïve and unconstructive to rely on some mass versus alternative tourism dichotomy (see e.g. Khan, 1997) given the interrelatedness of both types (Weaver, 1999). Moreover, as already noted, the alternative types of 'ecotourism' or 'commu-nity based tourism' may be equally prone to increasing inequalities due to elite politics. Significantly, governments' need for an increase in tourism (earn-ings) need not necessarily take the form of a promotion of conventional 'mass tourism' but may include economic rational concepts such as carrying capacity considerations to save the environment for 'high quality' tourism (with a higher yield and even more based on neoliberal approaches to attract capital) (see e.g. Jamal *et al.*, 2003; Mowforth & Munt, 1998). Ilha Grande, Brazil, is an example of the less privileged and 'poor' striving for a mass type of tourism (based on local ownership attracting the 'mass' backpackers market), while the political and economic elite seeks to restrict numbers (Wunder, 2003).

Irrespective the 'type' of tourism, the major question relating to equity is who ultimately benefits ('cui bono'). A radical view on equity goes well beyond 'sustainable tourism' prescriptions which, while incorporating the element of inter- (and to some extent intra-) generational equity (see e.g. Jamal *et al.*, 2003) set the needs of host communities (the social element) on equal footing with the environment and industry needs. The radical view would require the host (given the fact that 'the poor' are recipients, not generators of travel flows; Mowforth & Munt, 1998) to reap the majority of benefits – economic, cultural, environmental, political, however defined by 'the poor' themselves. Pro-poor strategies focusing on equity need to incorporate dimensions apart from economic criteria – political or cultural capital for instance may be valued equally, if not more, to economic criteria by different strata among 'the poor' (see e.g. de Burlo, 2003). *If* tourism development is desired, than it has to be accompanied by uncompromising transfers of assets to 'the poor', such as land rights and skills (long-terms training programmes) (see Crosby, 2002; Bennett, 2005 for a community tourism project that had much potential, yet failed due to the lack of resource transfers).

Rather than promoting tourism (in whichever form) as a cure for poverty, policy-makers, donors and researchers should (re-)discover local knowledge (Jamal *et al.*, 2003) instead of merely using the rhetoric under the umbrella of alternative or sustainable development. As poverty is a multi-dimensional phenomenon, different (poor) people define both the problem per se, as well as the aspired solutions in different ways (see e.g. de Burlo, 2003). While community-driven development approaches are certainly an inspiring step into this direction, ways need to be explored of how to prevent local elites from appropriating the majority of benefits. While some tourism researchers have identified the problem (Milne & Ateljevic, 2001; Norkunas, 1993; Reed, 1997; Richter, 1989), there is a need to examine how it can be resolved (while Reed (1997) would contest that it can be resolved at all).

Even more significantly, there is a need to find ways to bridge the implicit micro–macro dichotomy. This dichotomy within pro-poor approaches is similar to sustainable (tourism) development approaches which define both problem and solutions from a macro (global) perspective incorporating the desirability of fostering (inter- and intra-generational) equity while failing to address the concept's application at the micro level (Jamal, 2005) within a governance system spanning all levels from the local up to the global. How may the poor's development choices – if given voice through localised approaches – be accommodated if they run counter governmental or systemic requirements? For example, the options of 'no tourism' or 'community owned tourism' may not correspond to politico-economic reality. In order to allow for free choice at the local level, national governments need to be freed from systemic constraints. While certain constraints, such as limited resource endowments preventing certain development options, are unsurpassable, others are not. First of all, there is the possibility of taxing global capital transactions (Tobin Tax), the gains of which might be used to support developing countries in the provision of wide-ranging social protection, or to pay right into development initiatives chosen by communities in order to reduce dependency on foreign capital. Coupled with debt relief and more flexible rules of special and differential treatment within the framework of the WTO, these measures would take a great burden off many countries that are currently forced to rely on tourism growth by any means.

Instead of adding to the list of desirable attributes of 'pro-poor' tourism, the author would therefore like to draw attention to the urgent need for future research. Rather than focusing on 'best practice' in terms of adding to the list of individual pro-poor projects and case studies (the positive impact of some individual projects – frequently fulfilling the criteria of local ownership, skills and resource transfer and linkages – has certainly been demonstrated; see e.g. Cattarinich, 2001), research should focus on practical solutions to the question of empowerment of the poor – both at a national and local level. How can governments of developing countries escape the need for tourism growth within the current economic environment? How may developing countries' need for foreign capital to ensure growth be aligned with the poor's need for control over development and retention of benefits (and are there ways of regulating foreign investment to render the alleged trickle-down effects of skills and technology transfers less speculative)? Given policy flexibility at the national level, routes facilitating empowerment of the 'poor' at the local level must be examined. How can 'elite capture' of decision-making power and benefits be avoided in a local setting? Focus must truly shift to the 'poor', which can only occur if one departs from blue-print approaches and allows for individual responses to the multi-dimensional issue of poverty – including the possibility that in some cases tourism, irrespective the 'type', may not be 'pro-poor' after all.

Acknowledgements

I am grateful to my PhD supervisors Professor Colin Michael Hall and Dr Neil Carr, Tourism Department, University of Otago, as well as my friend and fellow PhD student Andrea Valentin for reviewing this manuscript and providing invaluable suggestions.

Correspondence

Any correspondence should be directed to Daniela Schilcher, University of Otago, Tourism Department, Commerce Building, PO Box 56, Dunedin, New Zealand (schda333@student.otago.ac.nz).

References

ADB (2000) *Samoa 2000*. Pacific Studies Series, Manila: Asian Development Bank.
ADB (2004) Asian Development Outlook 2004: *II. Economic Trends and Prospects in Developing Asia*. Asian Development Bank. On WWW at http://www.adb.org/Documents/Books/ADO/2004/fij.asp. Accessed 24.8.05.

Ashley, C., Boyd, C. and Goodwin, H. (2000) Pro-poor tourism: Putting poverty at the heart of the tourism agenda. *Natural Resource Perspectives* 51. On WWW at http://www.odi.org.uk/nrp/51.html. Accessed 12.8.05.

Ashley, C., Roe, D. and Goodwin, H. (2001) *Pro-Poor Tourism Strategies: Making Tourism Work for the Poor*. Pro-Poor Tourism report no. 1, Nottingham: The Russell Press.

Badillo, D., Garnier, L., Vargas, J.E. and Carrera, F. (2001) Liberalisation, poverty-led growth and child rights: Ecuador from 1980 to 2000. In G.A. Cornia (ed.) *Harnessing Globalisation for Children*. Florence: UNICEF.

Bauer, J., Sofield, T., De Lacy, T., Lipman, G. and Daugherty, S. (2004) *Sustainable Tourism Eliminating Poverty (STEP): An Overview*. On WWW at http://www.world-tourism.org/step/ST ~ EP%20CRC.pdf. Accessed 25.8.05.

BBC (2006) *Thai Protesters Issue Ultimatum*. BBC News 28 February 2006 On WWW at http://news.bbc.co.uk. Accessed 1.3.06.

Beeson, M. and Islam, I. (2005) Neo-liberalism and East Asia: Resisting the Washington Consensus. *Journal of Development Studies* 41 (2), 197–219.

Béjar, H. (2001) *Globalisation, Consolidated Poverty and Increased Inequality*. New York: UNPAN.

Bennett, A.L. (1980) *International Organizations* (2nd edn). Englewood Cliffs: Prentice-Hall.

Bennett, O. (2005) Report on the contribution of Oliver Bennett. UNDP launch of the *Strategic Framework for Development of Tourism in Northern & Central Montenegro*. New York: UNDP.

Berno, T. (2003) Local control and sustainability of tourism in the Cook Islands. In D. Harrison (ed.) *Pacific Island Tourism* (pp. 94–109). New York, Sydney, Tokyo: Cognizant Communication Corporation.

Best, S. and Kellner, D. (1991) *Postmodern Theory: Critical Interrogations*. New York: The Guilford Press.

Birdsall, N. (1999) Globalisation and the developing countries: The inequality risk. Paper presented at *Overseas Development Council Conference Making Globalization Work*. Washington: International Trade Centre, 18 March 1999.

Brand, U. (2001) Ordnung und Gestaltung. Global Governance als hegemonialer Diskurs postfordistischer Politik? In M. Berndt and D. Sack (eds) *Global Governance? Voraussetzungen und Formen demokratischer Beteiligung im Zeichen der Globalisierung* (pp. 93–110). Wiesbaden: Westdeutscher Verlag.

Briedenhann, J. and Wickens, E. (2004) Tourism routes as a tool for the economic development of rural areas – Vibrant hope or impossible dream? *Tourism Management* 25 (1), 71–79.

Britton, S.G. (1982) The political economy of tourism in the third world. *Annals of Tourism Research* 9 (3), 331–358.

Britton, S.G. (1983) *Tourism and Underdevelopment in Fiji*. Canberra: Australian National University Press.

Brohman, J. (1996) New directions in tourism for Third World development. *Annals of Tourism Research* 23 (1), 48–70.

Burns, G.L. (2003) Indigenous responses to tourism in Fiji: What is happening? In D. Harrison (ed.) *Pacific Island Tourism* (pp. 82–93). New York, Sydney, Tokyo: Cognizant Communication Corporation.

Caporaso, J.A. (1978) Dependence, dependency and power in the global system: A structural and behavioral analysis. *International Organization* 32 (1), 13–43.

Caporaso, J.A. and Haggard, S. (1989) Power in the international political economy. In R.J. Stoll and M.D. Ward (eds) *Power in World Politics* (pp. 99–120). Boulder and London: Lynne Rienner.

Castaneda, Q.E. (1991) An Archaeology of Chichen Itza: Discourse, power and resistance in a Maya tourist site. PhD thesis, University of Albany.

Cattarinich, X. (2001) *Pro-Poor Tourism Initiatives in Developing Countries: Analysis of Secondary Case Studies*. PPT working paper no. 8. On WWW at http://www.propoor tourism.org.uk/initiatives_cs.pdf. Accessed 21.3.05.

CHA (2005) *The Caribbean Hotel Association Advocacy Programme*. On WWW at http://www.caribbeanhotels.org/Select/advocacy.htm. Accessed 21.10.05.

Chand, G. (2000) Labour market deregulation in Fiji. In A.H. Akram-Lodhi (ed.) *Confronting Fiji Futures* (pp. 152–177). Canberra: Asia Pacific Press.

Cheater, A. (1999) *The Anthropology of Power: Empowerment and Disempowerment in Changing Structures*. London and New York: Routledge.

Clancey, M.J. (1999) Tourism and development: Evidence from Mexico. *Annals of Tourism Research* 26 (1), 1–20.

Cleverdon Assiciates (2003) *Pacific Regional Tourism Development Programme Final Evaluation*. Final report prepared for Pacific Island Forum Secretariat, October 2003. Suva: Forum Secretariat.

Cox, R.W. (1996) Structural issues of global governance: issue for Europe. In R.W. Cox and T. Sinclair (eds) *Approaches to World Order* (pp. 237–240). Cambridge: Cambridge University Press.

Crosby, A. (2002) Archaeology and vanua development in Fiji. *World Archaeology* 34 (2), 363–378.

Culpeper, R. (2002) *Approaches to Globalization and Inequality in the International System*. Geneva: United Nations Research Institute for Social Development.

Davidson, R. and Maitland, R. (1997) *Tourism Destinations*. London: Hodder and Stoughton.

Deacon, B. (2000) *Globalization and Social Policy: The Threat to Equitable Welfare*. Geneva: UNRISD.

de Burlo, C.R. (2003) Tourism, conservation, and the cultural environment in rural Vanuatu. In D. Harrison (ed.) *Pacific Island Tourism* (pp. 69–81). New York, Sydney, Tokyo: Cognizant Communication Corporation.

Desforges, L. (2000) State tourism institutions and neoliberal development: A case study of Peru. *Tourism Geographies* 2 (2), 177–192.

DFID (1999) *Tourism and Poverty Elimination: Untapped Potential*. Department for International Development (UK) Briefing Paper. London: DFID.

Dollar, D. and Kraay, A. (2000) *Growth is Good for the Poor*. Preliminary paper, Development Research Group. Washington: The World Bank.

Dollar, D. and Kraay, A. (2003) Institutions, trade and growth. *Journal of Monetary Economics* 50 (1), 133–162.

Duffy, R. (2005) Global environmental governance and the politics of ecotourism in Madagascar. Paper presented at the Conference on *The Politics of Mobilities: Ecotourism in North-South Relations*. Lancaster: Lancaster University Conference Centre, 14–15 January, 2005.

EC/Pacific ACP (2003) *Financing Agreement Between the European Commission and the Pacific ACP Countries, Pacific ACP Regional Economic Integration Programme (REG/7718/000) EDF IX*. Brussels and Suva: EC/PACP.

Enloe, C. (1990) *Bananas, Beaches and Bases: Making Feminist Sense of International Politics*. Berkeley: University of California.

EU (2005) *EU Relations with Samoa*. On WWW at http://europa.eu.int/comm/development/body/country/country_home_en.cfm?cid = ws&status = new. Accessed 22.1.06.

EU Development Committee (2006) *Hearing on the Development Impact of the Economic Partnership Agreements (EPAs)*. Brussels, 31 January 2006.

EU Trade Advisor (2005) Personal interview with an EU trade advisor. EC Delegation to the Pacific, 16 November 2005.

Falk, R. (1995) *On Humane Governance: Toward a New Global Politics*. Pennsylvania: Pennsylvania University Press.

Farazmand, A. (1999) Globalization and public administration. *Public Administration Review* 59 (6), 509–522.

Farthing, L. and Kohl, B. (2004) Shock to the system: A growing indigenous people's movement in Bolivia. *Committee on US-Latin American Relations Newsletter*. Winter 2004–2005. On WWW at http://www.rso.cornell.edu/cuslar/newsletter/newsletter.html. Accessed 29.1.06.

Fennell, D.A. and Malloy, D.C. (1999) Measuring the ethical nature of tourism operators. *Annals of Tourism Research* 26 (4), 928–943.

Fernweh (2004) *Tourism Interventions.* Freiburg: Fernweh.

Fisher, D. (2003) Tourism and change in local economic behaviour. In D. Harrison (ed.) *Pacific Island Tourism* (pp. 58–68). New York, Sydney, Tokyo: Cognizant Communication Corporation.

Frankel, J. and Roemer, D. (1999) Does trade cause growth? *American Economic Review* 89 (3), 379–399.

Forsyth, D. (1997) The economy of Fiji. In B. Lal and T.R. Vakatora (eds) *Fiji in Transition* (Vol. 1) (pp. 178–185). Suva, Fiji: University of South Pacific.

FTIB (2005) *Government Policies.* Fiji Trade and Investment Board. On WWW at http://www.ftib.org.fj/show/contents/reasons_invest/govt_policies.htm. Accessed 28.8.05.

Gibbon, P. (2004) *The Commodity Question: New Thinking on Old Problems.* Copenhagen: Danish Institute for International Studies.

Gill, S.R. and Law, D. (1989) Global hegemony and the structural power of capital. *International Studies Quarterly* 33 (4), 475–499.

Glyn, A. (2004) The assessment: How far has globalization gone? *Oxford Review of Economic Policy* 20 (1), 1–14.

Go, F.M. and Pine, R. (1996) Globalization in the hotel industry. In R. Kotas, R. Teare, J. Logie, C. Jayawardena and J. Bowen (eds) *The International Hospitality Business* (pp. 96–106). London: Cassell/HCIMA.

Gössling, S. (2003a) Tourism and development in tropical islands: Political ecology perspectives. In S. Gössling (ed.) *Tourism and Development in Tropical Islands: Political Ecology Perspectives* (pp. 1–37). Cheltenham and Northampton: Edward Elgar Publishing.

Gössling, S. (2003b) The political ecology of tourism in Zanzibar. In S. Gössling (ed.) *Tourism and Development in Tropical Islands: Political Ecology Perspectives* (pp. 178–202). Cheltenham and Northampton: Edward Elgar Publishing.

Government of Samoa (2001) *National Investment Policy Statement 2001/2002.* Apia: Government of Samoa.

Government of Samoa (2002) *Strategy for the Development of Samoa 2002–2004 'Opportunities for All'.* Apia: Ministry of Finance.

Government of Samoa (2005) *Strategy for the Development of Samoa 2005–2007 'Enhancing People's Choices'.* Apia: Ministry of Finance.

Gramsci, A. (1971) Selections from the prison notebooks. In Q. Hoare and G.N. Smith (eds) London: Lawrence & Wishart.

Greenaway, D., Morgan, W. and Wright, P. (2002) Trade liberalisation and growth in developing countries. *Journal of Development Economics* 67 (1), 229–244.

Griffith, M. (2003) *Pro Poor Growth.* London: CAFOD.

Guéhenno, J. (1996) *The End of the Nation State.* Minneapolis: University of Minnesota Press.

Hall, C.M. (1998) Making the Pacific: Globalization, modernity and myth. In G. Ringer (ed.) *Destinations: Cultural Landscapes of Tourism* (pp. 140–153). London: Routledge.

Hall, C.M. and Page, S.J. (1999) *The Geography of Tourism and Recreation.* London: Routledge.

Harrigan, N. (1974) The legacy of Caribbean history and tourism. *Annals of Tourism Research* 2 (1), 13–25.

Harrison, D. (2003) Themes in Pacific Island tourism. In D. Harrison (ed.) *Pacific Island Tourism* (pp. 1–23). New York, Sydney, Tokyo: Cognizant Communication Corporation.

Hertel, T., Ivanic, M., Preckel, P. and Cranfield, J. (2003) Trade liberalisation and the structure of poverty in developing countries. Paper prepared for *Globalisation, Agricultural Development and Rural Livelihoods.* New York: Cornell University, 11–12 April 2003.

Hewison, K. (2005) Neo-liberalism and domestic capital: The political outcomes of the economic crisis in Thailand. *Journal of Development Studies* 41 (2), 310–330.

Hill, C.W.L. (2002) *International Business: Competing in the Global Marketplace.* New York: McGraw-Hill.

Irwin, D. and Tervio, M. (2002) Does trade raise income: Evidence from the twentieth century. *Journal of International Economics* 58 (1), 1–18.

Ite, U.E. (2005) Poverty reduction in resource-rich developing countries: What have multinational corporations got to do with it? *Journal of International Development* 17 (7), 913–929.

Jamal, T. (2005) Virtue ethics and sustainable tourism pedagogy: Phronesis, principles and practice. *Journal of Sustainable Tourism* 12 (6), 530–554.

Jamal, T., Everett, J. and Dann, G.M. (2003) Ecological rationalization and performative resistance in natural area destinations. *Tourist Studies* 3 (2), 143–169.

Jessop, B. (1999) Reflections on globalisation and its (il)logic(s). In K. Olds, P. Dicken, P.F. Kelly, L. Kong and H. Wai-chung Yeung (eds) *Globalisation and the Asia-Pacific. Contested Territories* (pp. 19–38). London: Routledge.

Juda, N. and Richardson, S. (2001) Preliminary assessment of the environmental and social effects of liberalisation in tourism services. *WWF International Discussion Paper*, Gland: WWF.

Kahler, M. and Lake, D.A. (2003) Globalization and governance. In M. Kahler and D.A. Lake (eds) *Governance in a Global Economy. Political Authority in Transition* (pp. 1–30). Princeton: Princeton University Press.

Kalisch, A. (2001) GATS and the tourism industry. *Fair Trade in Tourism* 2 (Winter 2001/ Spring 2002). London: Tourism Concern. On WWW at http://www.tourismconcern. org.uk. Accessed 5.9.04.

Kamp, C. (1999) GATS undermines sustainable development in tourism. *Working Towards Earth Summit III – Outreach* 4 (9).

Karns, M.P. and Mingst, K.A. (2004) *International Organizations. The Politics and Processes of Global Governance*. Boulder and London: Lynne Rienner Publishers.

Keith-Reid, R. (2004) Aid donors cautious: They don't want to fund projects that benefit big hotel businesses. *Pacific Magazine*, June 2004. On WWW at http://www. pacificislands.cc. Accessed 12.10.04.

Khan, M.M. (1997) Tourism development and dependency theory: Mass tourism vs. ecotourism. *Annals of Tourism Research* 24 (4), 988–991.

Klak, T. and Conway, D. (1998) From neoliberalism to sustainable development? In T. Klak (ed.) *Globalization and Neoliberalism. The Caribbean Context*. Lanham: Rowman & Littlefield Publishers, Inc.

Klasen, S. (2001) *In Search of the Holy Grail: How to Achieve Pro-Poor Growth?* (pp. 257–277). Munich: University of Munich.

Klein, M. (2003) Capital account openness and the varieties of growth experience. *NBER Working Paper No. 9500*. Cambridge, USA: NBER.

Kratochwil, F. and Ruggie, J.G. (1986) International organization: A state of the art on an art of the state. *International Organization* 40 (4), 753–775.

Lea, J. (1988) *Tourism and Development in the Third World*. London: Routledge.

Lesotho Tourism Development Corporation (2003) *Promoting Responsible and Sustainable Economic Development through Tourism*. On WWW at http://www.ltdc.org.ls/Profile/ brochure.doc. Accessed 1.2.06.

Levett, R. and McNally, R. (2003) *A Strategic Environmental Assessment of Fiji's Tourism Development Plan*. Godalming: WWF.

Liew, L.H. (2005) China's engagement with neoliberalism: Path dependency, geography and party self-reinvention. *Journal of Development Studies* 41 (2), 331–352.

Lukes, S. (1974) *Power: A Radical View*. London and Basingstoke: The Macmillan Press Ltd.

Mair, H. (2006) Global restructuring and local responses: Investigating rural tourism policy in two Canadian communities. *Current Issues in Tourism* 9 (1), 1–45.

Mansuri, G. and Rao, V. (2002) *Community-Based and -Driven Development: A Critical Review*. On WWW at http://www.cultureandpublicaction.org/conference/commentaries.htm. Accessed 12.10.05.

Massicotte, M. (1999) Global governance and the global political economy: Three texts in search of a synthesis. *Global Governance* 5 (1), 127–148.

Mathieson, A. and Wall, G. (1982) *Tourism Economic, Physical and Social Impacts*. Harlow: Longman.

Meethan, K. (2001) *Tourism in Global Society. Place, Culture, Consumption*. Basingstoke: Pelgrave.

Milne, S. (1992) Tourism and development in South Pacific microstates. *Annals of Tourism Research* 19 (2), 191–212.

Milne, S. and Ateljevic, I. (2001) Tourism, economic development and the global-local nexus: Theory embracing complexity. *Tourism Geographies* 3 (4), 369–393.

Momsen, J.H. (1998) Caribbean tourism and agriculture: New linkages in the global era? In T. Klak (ed.) *Globalization and Neoliberalism* (pp. 115–133). *The Caribbean Context*. Lanham: Rowman & Littlefield Publishers, Inc.

Morgan, N.J. and Pritchard, A. (1999) *Power and Politics at the Seaside: The Development of Devon's Resorts in the Twentieth Century*. Exeter: University of Exeter Press.

Mowforth, M. and Munt, M. (1998) *Tourism and Sustainability: New Tourism in the Third World*. London: Routledge.

Murphy, C.N. (1994) *International Organization and Industrial Change*. New York: Oxford University Press.

Murphy, P. (1985) *Tourism: A Community Approach*. New York and London: Methuen.

Narayan, P.K. and Prasad, B.C. (2003) Fiji's sugar, tourism and garment industries: A survey of performance, problems and potentials. *Fijian Studies* 1 (1), 3–28.

Norkunas, M.K. (1993) *The Politics of Memory: Tourism, History, and Ethnicity in Monterey, California*. Albany: State University of New York Press.

Ohmae, K. (1995) *The End of the Nation State. The Rise of Regional Economies. How New Engines of Prosperity are Reshaping Global Markets*. New York: The Free Press.

Ougaard, M. (1999) *Approaching the Global Polity*. Centre for the Study of Globalisation and Regionalisation (CSGR) Working Paper No. 42/99. On WWW at http:// papers.ssrn.com. Accessed 18.11.04.

Oxfam (2000) *Growth with Equity is Good for the Poor*. Oxford: Oxfam.

Oyen, E. (2001) *A Critical Review of the World Development Report 2000/2001: Attacking Poverty*. On WWW at http://www.acdi-cida.gc.ca. Accessed 12.1.05.

Pacific Islands Trade and Investment Commission (2003) *Encouraging Tourism Growth – Samoa*. On WWW at http://www.pitic.org.au/pdfdocs/publications/publi-13914–200601.pdf. Accessed 20.9.904.

Pacific Magazine (2001) *Political Backing to Go After the Money*. Pacific Magazine September 2001. On WWW at http://www.pacificmagazine.net. Accessed 21.10.04.

Pacific Magazine (2005) *French Polynesia: Tourism Minister wants more Tourism Tax Exemptions*. Pacific Magazine, 23 December 2005. On WWW at http://www.pacific islands.cc. Accessed 15.1.06.

Parliament of Fiji (2004) *Parliamentary Debates – The Senate*. Suva: Daily Hansard, 25 February 2004.

PATA (2003) *News@PATA*. On WWW at http://www.pata.org/patasite/index.php?id=365. Accessed 13.11.05.

Patel, S. (2000) Stitching coats that fit. *Viewpoint* 6 (4); United Nations Centre for Human Settlements. On WWW at http://www.unhabitat.org. Accessed 12.1.06.

Perrons, D. (2004) *Globalisation and Social Change. People and Places in a Divided World*. London and New York: Routledge.

Philippines Department of Tourism (no date) *Laws & Incentives*. On WWW at http:// www.tourism.gov.ph/dot/laws_and_incentives.asp. Accessed 2.2.06.

Przeworski, A. and Wallerstein, M. (1988) Structural dependence of the state on capital. *American Political Science Review* 82, 11–29.

Rajesh, N. (2004) ADB's tourism plans for the Mekong region poses risks not benefits. *ASED Themes*. On WWW at http://www.ased.org/artman/publish/article_556.shtml. Accessed 12.5.05.

Reed, M.G. (1997) Power relations and community-based tourism planning. *Annals of Tourism Research* 24 (3), 566–591.

Robinson, R. and Hewison, K. (2005) Introduction: East Asia and the trials of neoliberalism. *Journal of Development Studies* 41 (2), 183–196.

Richter, L.K. (1989) *The Politics of Tourism in Asia*. Honolulu: University of Hawaii Press.

Richter, L.K. (2004) Democracy and tourism: Nature of an untidy relationship. Paper presented at the *Tourism, Politics and Democracy Conference*, Centre for Tourism Policy Studies, Eastbourne, 9–10 September 2004.

Rodrik, D. (1997a) Trade, social insurance, and the limits to globalization. NBER working paper 5905. Cambridge, USA: NBER.

Rodrik, D. (1997b) *Has Globalization Gone Too Far?* Washington: Institute for International Economies.

Rodrik, D. (2000) *Growth and Poverty Reduction: What are the Real Questions?* Harvard: Harvard University.

Roe, D., Goodwin, H. and Ashley, C. (2002) *Pro-Poor Tourism Briefing No. 2*, March 2002. On WWW at http://www.odi.org.uk/RPEG/PPT/busbrief.pdf. Accessed 20.8.05.

Russell, D. and Stabile, J. (2003) Ecotourism in practice: Trekking the Highlands of Makira Island, Solomon Islands. In D. Harrison (ed.) *Pacific Island Tourism* (pp. 38–57). New York, Sydney, Tokyo: Cognizant Communication Corporation.

Santana, G. (2001) Tourism in the Southern Common Market: MERCOSUL. In D. Harrison (ed.) *Tourism and the Less Developed World: Issues and Case Studies* (pp. 77–91). Wallingford and New York: CABI Publishing.

Scheyvens, R. (2002) *Growth and Benefits of Budget Beach Fale Tourism in Samoa*. On WWW at http://www.devnet.org.nz/conf2002/ papers/Scheyvens_Regina.pdf. Accessed 12.1.05.

Schilcher, D. (2007) Supranational governance of tourism: aid, trade and power relations between the European Union and South Pacific island States. PhD thesis, University of Otago, Dunedin, NZ.

Scollay, R. (2001) Regional trade agreements and developing countries: The case of the Pacific Islands. Proposed Free Trade Agreement. *Policy Studies in International Trade and Commodity Series No. 10*. New York and Geneva: UNCTAD.

Sharpley, R. and Telfer, D. (2002) *Tourism and Development: Concepts and Issues*. Clevedon: Channel View Publications.

Shastri Institute (2004) *Social Sector Expenditure and the Poor Under the New Economic Policy*. Calgary: University of Calgary.

Sheyvens, R. (2004) Five star hotels the Samoan way. *Just Change* 1, 7.

Shirley and Associates (1994) *Legislation for Development Incentives for Tourism in the Republic of Panama*. On WWW at http://www.shirleylaw.com. Accessed 15.1.06.

Singh, A. and Zammit, A. (2004) Labour standards and the 'race to the bottom': Rethinking globalization and workers rights from developmental and solidaristic perspectives. *Oxford Review of Economic Policy* 20 (1), 85–104.

Sofield, T.H.B. (2003) *Empowerment for Sustainable Tourism Development*. Amsterdam and New York: Pergamon.

SPTO (2001) *South Pacific Tourism Organisation: Organisation Profile*. On WWW at http://www.southpacificislands.org/spto/SPTO_Profile.pdf. Accessed 12.2.05.

SPTO (2005) *SPTO Weekly Newsletter*, Issue 32, 12 August 2005. On WWW at http://www.tcsp.com/spto/export/sites/SPTO/news/press/NewsLetter_Aug_2005_82.shtml. Accessed 2.9.05.

SPTO Official (2005) Personal interview with a SPTO official, Suva, 15 November 2005.

Stiglitz, J.E. (2002) *Globalisation and its Discontents*. New York and London: W.W. Norton.

Sumner, A. and Tiwari, M. (2004) Poverty reduction: Has research answered the big policy questions? Issues paper prepared for *DSA Poverty Study Group Re-launch Meeting*. London: Church House, 6 November 2004. On WWW at http://www.devstud.org.uk. Accessed 12.1.06.

Talwar, N. (2004) The inequality challenge: Perspectives on growth, poverty and inequality. *UN Chronicle* 2, 73.

TCSP (1992) *Western Samoa Tourism Development Plan 1992–2001*. Suva: Tourism Council of the South Pacific.

Theobald, W. (ed.) (1994) *Global Tourism. The Next Decade*. Oxford: Butterworth-Heinemann.

Timothy, D.J. (2001) *Tourism and Political Boundaries*. London: Routledge.

Timothy, D.J. (2003) Supranationalist alliances and tourism: Insights from ASEAN and SAARC. *Current Issues in Tourism* 6 (3), 250–266.

Torres, R. and Momsen, J. (2005) Planned tourism development in Quintana Roo, Mexico: Engine for regional development or prescription for inequitable growth? *Current Issues in Tourism* 8 (4), 259–285.

Twining-Ward, L. and Twining-Ward, T. (1998) Tourism development in Samoa: Context and constraints. *Pacific Tourism Review* 2, 261–271.

UNDP (2004) *Pro-Poor Growth: Concepts and Measurement with Country Case Studies*. Brasilia: UNDP International Poverty Centre.

United Nations (2000) *A Better World for All*. New York: UN.

United Nations (2005) *Press Release SG/T/2453*. On WWW at http://www.un.org/News/Press/docs/2005/sgt2453.doc.htm. Accessed 12.1.06.

Vaile, M. (2002) Fiji: Open and ready for business. Speech held at the *Australia-Fiji and Fiji-Australia Business Councils' 15th Australia Fiji Business Forum*, 13 October 2002. On WWW at http://www.trademinister.gov.au/speeches/2002/021013_mvt_fijibusiness.html. Accessed. 22.10.05.

Vellas, F. and Bécherel, L. (1995) *International Tourism*. Basingstoke: Macmillan Press Ltd.

Viravaidya, M. (2002) *The Privatisation of Poverty Alleviation*. On WWW at http://www.adb.org/Documents/Books/Defining_Agenda_Poverty_Reduction/Vol_1/chapter_14.pdf. Accessed 1.9.05.

Weaver, D.B. (1998) Peripheries of the periphery: Tourism in Tobago and Barbuda. *Annals of Tourism Research* 25 (2), 292–313.

Weaver, D.B. (1999) Magnitude of ecotourism in Costa Rica and Kenya. *Annals of Tourism Research* 26 (4), 792–816.

WIDER (2004) *Wider Perspectives on Growth, Inequality and Poverty*. On WWW at http://www.wider.uni.edu. Accessed 25.10.05.

Williams, A.M. and Montanari, A. (eds) (1995) *European Tourism: Regions, Spaces and Restructuring*. Chichester: Wiley.

Williams, A.M. and Shaw, G. (2002) *Critical Issues in Tourism. A Geographical Perspective* (2nd edn). Oxford: Blackwell Publishers Ltd.

Williams, M. (2001) The political economy of tourism liberalization, gender and the GATS. Working paper *IGTN-Secretariat*. On WWW at http://www.genderandtrade.net/GATS/GATSTourismArticle.pdf. Accessed 5.9.04.

World Bank (2001) Improving safety nets vital for making globalization work for world's poor. *News Release No. 2001/194/S*. On WWW at http://web.worldbank.org. Accessed 21.10.05.

World Bank (2005a) *World Development Report 2006: Equity and Development*. Washington: The World Bank.

World Bank (2005b) Community driven development. On WWW at http://web.worldbank.org/WBSITE/EXTERNAL/TOPICS/EXTSOCIALDEVELOPMENT/EXTCDD/0,,menuPK:430167~pagePK:149018~piPK:149093~theSitePK:430161,00.html. Accessed 12.2.06.

WTO-OMT (2005) Use tourism in war on poverty. *News Release*. On WWW at http://www.world-tourism.org. Accessed 12.1.06.

WTO-OMT (no date) *Tourism and Poverty Alleviation*. On WWW at http://www.world-tourism.org/liberalization/menu_poverty.htm. Accessed 15.1.06.

Wunder, S. (2003) Native tourism, natural forests and local incomes on Ilha Grande, Brazil. In S. Gössling (ed.) *Tourism and Development in Tropical Islands: Political Ecology Perspectives* (pp. 148–177). Cheltenham, UK, and Northampton, USA: Edward Elgar Publishing.

Zeller, J. (2005) CARIBBEAN: Regional sustainable tourism policy framework to assist in developing or enhancing existing national strategies. *Tourism Newswire*, December 2005. On WWW at http://www.sidsnet.org/archives/tourism-newswire/2005/msg00173.html. Accessed 12.1.06.

Web addresses

http://www.imf.org/external/np/esafhipc/1999/.
http://www.oxfam.org.uk/what_we_do/issues/democracy_rights/bp51_prsp.htm.
http://www.propoor-tourism.org.
http://www.unctad.org/Templates/webflyer.asp.

Lao Tourism and Poverty Alleviation: Community-Based Tourism and the Private Sector

David Harrison
International Institute for Tourism, Culture and Development, London Metropolitan University, London, UK; and Overseas Development Institute, London, UK

Steven Schipani
Lao Tourism National Tourism Administration, Vientiane, Lao PDR

Tourism as a tool for development was first mooted in the 1970s. Recently, focus has been on the role of ecotourism, pro-poor tourism and community-based tourism (CBT). This has been so in Lao People's Democratic Republic, where international tourism is a vital source of foreign exchange and employment and an important feature of the government's poverty-alleviation strategy. The Asian Development Bank (ADB) finances many infrastructural projects facilitating tourist movement in the Lower Mekong Basin, and with the Lao Government and the Netherlands Development Agency (SNV) is a key player in donor-assisted, community-based tourism (DACBT). The development of DACBT in Lao PDR is discussed in some detail, especially the Nam Ha Ecotourism Project, and is compared briefly with the role of the private sector in tourism development in Southern Lao PDR. It is concluded that while DACBT projects can indeed alleviate poverty and develop financial and cultural capital, private sector tourism enterprises also have an important role in poverty alleviation, and it should not be assumed that DACBT is the only – or necessarily the most efficient – form of pro-poor tourism.

doi: 10.2167/cit310.0

Keywords: Lao PDR, development, community-based tourism, pro-poor tourism, private sector tourism

Tourism as 'Development'

The study of tourism's role as a tool for development is not new. From the 1960s, at least, academic approaches to tourism phenomena have included what might be described as a 'development' stream (de Kadt, 1979a; Peters, 1969; Smith, 1978a). This is seen in the earliest of contributions. Focusing on less developed countries and regions (LDCs), de Kadt recognised tourism could create jobs, develop backward linkages with agriculture and other economic sectors, create opportunities for young people and women, encourage local entrepreneurial activity, and improve the quality of life of the poor through funding basic utilities, training and education. He also noted a tendency for expatriates to obtain the best-paid jobs, and for tourism to exacerbate economic and other inequalities, and emphasised that the extent to which tourism would benefit residents in tourist destinations depended considerably on local conditions and was certainly not inevitable (de Kadt, 1979b: 11–12).

De Kadt did not focus specifically on poverty, but clearly saw it as a feature of development, noting that in the 'development thinking' of the time, there was a

> realization that growth alone may not suffice to overcome poverty within a reasonable time, and that the distribution of the material benefits of development among the poorest countries and the poorest population groups within individual countries requires special attention. (de Kadt, 1979c: xii)

Several contributors to de Kadt's volume considered the impact of tourism on the poor. Wilson, for example, noted that tourism had brought few benefits to the urban and rural poor of the Seychelles (1979: 229), and Andronicou that – as with capitalism generally – the economic benefits from tourism were not distributed equally to all Cypriots (1979: 258). By contrast, Groupe Huit suggested that the poor of Tunisia *did* benefit, especially through employment at the construction stage of tourism development (1979: 291).

The overall impression of tourism's economic benefits is similarly mixed in Smith's edited volume. Summarising the views of her contributors, she suggests the extent to which tourism brought economic benefits to different sectors of the population depended on 'the type of tourism, the expectations of the tourists, and the host's ability to provide appropriate facilities and destination activities', and, she continued, 'the effects of tourism can be assessed along a continuum from a highly positive relationship that benefits all, to a highly disruptive, negative interaction fraught with conflict' (Smith, 1978b: 4).

During the 1980s and 1990s, tourism studies broadened across a wide range of academic interests and disciplines. There was a general move to a more empirical 'knowledge-based' orientation (Jafari, 1989) and, among planners, to a wider, more holistic planning process (Hall *et al.*, 1997: 18–22). Simplistic models of modernisation and underdevelopment were rejected for a more comprehensive globalisation framework (Harrison, 2001; Mowforth & Munt, 2003; Scheyvens, 2002; Telfer, 2002); environmentalist perspectives joined economic, social and cultural analysis; top-down development was (largely) rejected (theoretically) in favour of bottom-up development and local participation, and locally-owned, small-scale tourism enterprises were preferred (at least by academics) to transnational companies and mass tourism (Rodenburg, 1980). As a consequence, sustainable tourism development, especially ecotourism, became the preferred future of tourism in LDCs (Boo, 1990; Cater & Lowman, 1994; Fennell, 1999; Honey, 1999; Weaver, 1998).

During this period, too, some did investigate tourism's impacts on the poor, often as part of wider anthropological tourism studies (e.g. Chambers, 2000: 32–39; Freitag, 1994; van den Berghe, 1994: 50–52), and other researchers spent many years investigating such phenomena, as indicated, for example, by Momsen's continued interest in tourism's linkages to the agricultural sector in the Caribbean (Momsen, 1972, 1986; Torres & Henshall Momsen, 2004).

The 1980s and 1990s saw the increasing popularisation of variants of sustainable tourism development, including ecotourism (with 2001 being the 'year of ecotourism') and other forms of alternative tourism, but just as the notion of sustainable development has itself been criticised (Adams, 1990), so too has its application to tourism. Ecotourism and other forms of 'alternative' or 'sustainable' tourism were said to be 'the thin end of the wedge' (Butler, 1992), to lack the potential to replace or improve on mass tourism, and to have negative impacts of their own (Butler, 1999; Cohen, 1989; Duffy, 2002), perhaps even leading to mass tourism (Wheeller, 1993). In addition, it has been argued that 'sustainability' is difficult to measure or apply in practice (Harrison, 1996) and that it has often been 'hijacked to give moral rectitude and "green" credentials to tourist activities' (Mowforth & Munt, 2003: 80). Of special relevance to those with an interest in 'pro-poor tourism', it has been suggested that claims that sustainable tourism development, especially ecotourism, specifically benefits local people (Fennell, 2001: 407) have yet to be substantiated. 'Relatively little quantitative analysis of ecotourism's success in achieving conservation and development objectives has been reported' (Lindberg *et al.*, 1996: 544), and inputs from the informal sector are especially difficult to measure (Timothy & Wall, 1997: 323–325). Referring explicitly to community-based tourism (CBT), one critic has commented that 'the literature is full of claims but short on data and quantitative analysis' (Kiss, 2004: 234).

Indeed, studies demonstrating how economic benefits are *distributed* (from any type of tourism) are rare and, where assessments *have* been made, conclusions are contradictory. Some have argued that large-scale tourism can bring economic benefits, that leakages are low, and that it is an important tool in poverty alleviation for LDCs (Butcher, 2003; Page, 1999: 62–63, 89–90), while others claim local benefits are few and leakages high (Walpole & Goodwin, 2000: 571–572). In fact, whether the focus is on mass (mainstream) tourism or small-scale ecotourism or community-based tourism, economic data are rarely available and extremely hard to collect, either for such apparently precise measures as the tourist income multiplier (Archer, 1996) or of the overall economic and other benefits achieved by the many aid agencies working at community level.

In recent years, academic studies of tourism and development have been enriched by a much more specific focus on the benefits that tourism might bring to the poor. Such approaches, often instigated by practitioners outside the academic mainstream, have brought a distinctive, empirical and more economic orientation to the study of tourism and development. The term 'pro-poor tourism' emerged in 1999 in a report by de Loitte Touche to the UK's Department for International Development (DFID), which then funded a series of research projects into ways which tourism could enhance the livelihoods of the poor (DFID, 1999, 2004). The Pro-poor Tourism Partnership[1] defined pro-poor tourism as 'tourism that generates net benefits for the poor' (Ashley *et al.*, 2001: 2) and implemented a series of case studies designed to test experimental methods of poverty alleviation by stimulating local involvement, partnerships and procurement (Ashley, 2000). More particularly, drawing on experiences in Southern Africa, Uganda, the Gambia, Nepal, Ecuador, the Caribbean and the Czech Republic, case studies explored the benefits (and limitations) of partnerships involving the private sector and communities and community-based tourism enterprises (including non-government organisations). They show that companies can derive business advantages from closer links with communities which, for their part, receive enhanced economic benefits through direct employment, or (with training) by providing goods and other services the company needs in the course of its normal trading relationships (Ashley *et al.*, 2001; Pro-Poor Tourism Partnership, 2006)

The above pro-poor tourism publications were supplemented and influenced by initiatives from numerous other organisations. Many national aid agencies, for instance, have devoted resources to 'community-based tourism'. The Canadian Agency for International Development (CAID), for instance, funded the Bali Sustainable Development Project (Nash, 1996: 139); the New Zealand Agency for International Development (NZAID), formerly New Zealand Official Development Assistance (NZODA), financed ecotourism projects in Fiji (Ministry of Foreign Affairs and Trade, 1995), and AusAid, the Australian Development Agency, also has an interest in tourism development in the South Pacific.

Researchers from the Partnership also contributed to discussions in the World Tourism Organisation, which since 2001 has promoted its own 'Sustainable Tourism: Eliminating Poverty (ST-EP)' initiative (Denman & Denman, 2004; WTO, 2002). Other UN organisations, too, have become involved. Both the United Nations Commission on Sustainable Development (UNCSD) and the United Nations Environmental Programme (UNEP) have highlighted the role of tourism in poverty alleviation (Gerosa, 2003: 18), as has the United Nations Economic and Social Commission on Asia and the Pacific (ESCAP).

Defining 'poverty' extremely broadly, and moving from the very specific projects of the Pro-Poor Tourism Partnership, ESCAP, in effect, returned to tourism as a development 'tool'. Following a seminar on tourism and poverty alleviation, held in 2003, it issued a massive manual, aimed primarily at government officials, with practical information to enable the planning and management of sustainable tourism, and details of 'techniques for achieving pro poor tourism' (Jamieson, 2003: 1). It later published a series of country studies, and examples of good practice in pro-poor tourism, also presented at the 2003 seminar (ESCAP, 2005).

The main point to note here is that while interest in tourism as a tool for 'development' started in the 1970s, the concentration on its role in alleviating poverty emerged only in the late 1990s and, since then, 'pro-poor tourism' has quickly become a recognised, worthwhile and more self-consciously *moral* approach to tourism, especially when practised by community-based organisations under the broader rubric of 'sustainable tourism'.

Despite, or perhaps because of, their current popularity, 'pro-poor tourism' approaches have not been without their critics. Noting that pro-poor tourism initiatives have emerged from very different kinds of organisations, with very different ideological orientations, Scheyvens suggests that at least in some cases they have been prompted by a 'neo-liberal' (rather than a 'critical' or 'alternative') agenda, which focuses on trade liberalisation, market-led growth and private sector development (Scheyvens, 2004: 8). Furthermore, she asserts (on her own admission, with very little evidence) that in such instances they have *not* benefited the poor. By contrast, in Bhutan and

Samoa, local factors, including indigenous ownership and control of the tourism sector, have led to economic benefits being distributed more widely (Scheyvens, 2004: 10–12).

A similar position is taken by Mowforth and Munt. They suggest, first, that pro-poor tourism initiatives (of the kind advocated by the UK Pro-Poor Tourism Partnership) inevitably take place in developing countries that are economically disempowered in the world economic system. Quoting Ashley *et al.* (2001), they remark that most 'critical decisions that affect this sector are made outside the country or by a few powerful local interests' (Mowforth & Munt, 2003: 271). Second, in so far as pro-poor initiatives *are* successful–and they note the uncertainties in many reports and case studies – pro-poor tourism does not necessarily eliminate or alleviate absolute poverty. Rather, it is 'principally a measure for making some sections of poorer communities "better-off" and reducing the vulnerability of poorer groups to shocks (such as hunger)' (Mowforth & Munt, 2003: 272).

Third, if it *does* have any effect, pro-poor tourism is likely to result in 'geographically uneven and unequal ... development' and 'may well display sharp regional and social disparities' (Mowforth & Munt, 2003: 272). Indeed, any support for pro-poor initiatives is simply repackaging familiar themes in development 'paradigms' and exacerbates existing power inequalities:

> In addition, it will prove necessary in the long run to consider the cumulative effect of supporting (through multilateral and bilateral aid programmes focused on economic growth) the expansion of capitalist relations and the manner in which this may undercut 'sustainable livelihoods' and exacerbate, rather than alleviate, poverty. (Mowforth & Munt, 2003: 273)

This is the nub of their complaint: pro-poor tourist initiatives take place within a capitalist context and, in effect, help support the system.

When faced with this kind of criticism – itself a crude repackaging of a perspective frequently stated in the 1970s and 1980s – a limited number of responses are possible. First, one can simply agree or disagree with what is, in essence, an ideological position. Secondly, attempts can be made (with the support of much unassailable historical evidence) to show that capitalist 'development' can indeed bring benefits and, thirdly, it can be argued that, in the absence of any current socialist role models (a situation not universally deplored), the only choices today centre on the *kinds* of capitalist development that ought to be promoted. After all, as was noted in a similar debate more than two decades ago, no-one has ever asserted that capitalism leads directly to equality, or that it has ever been 'nice' (Smith, 1983: 74).

Clearly, there is still a view that tourism, even ecotourism, does *not* bring about development and is, instead, a form of imperialism or colonialism (Johnston, 2006: 66; Nash, 1977, 1996: 28–32). However, notwithstanding this debate, many LDCs, supported by international organisations and aid agencies, continue to promote tourism as a tool for development and poverty alleviation. In the remainder of this paper, the focus will be on one country, the Lao People's Democratic Republic (PDR), where such policies are prominent, to examine how they are promoted, and to see what light, if any, can be shed on the general debate over tourism's role as a development tool. In this context, it will be argued that the distinction between 'pro-poor, community based tourism' and tourism enterprises operating in the private sector, both in Lao PDR and elsewhere, may need to be re-assessed, as donor-supported, community-based tourism projects may be sustainable only in partnership with the private sector, while the pro-poor credentials of tourism enterprises in the private sector are frequently under-rated.

Lao PDR: The Background

The landlocked southeast Asian country of Lao PDR (commonly known as Laos) has a population of about 6.2 million, of which (depending on the criteria of categorising them) nearly two-thirds are ethnic minorities, that is, not in the Lao-Tai linguistic group (Chazée, 2002: 14).

It emerged in the 1970s from a long period of war and civil unrest, prompted largely by the involvement of outside powers in its affairs. In 1893, it became a French Protectorate, was briefly occupied by Japan during the second World War, and later gained limited autonomy by the French in 1949. In 1953 it became fully independent, only then to enter a protracted civil war, which largely reflected big power interests in the region. In the north east, the communist Pathet Lao was supported by the Viet Minh, and to the south the anti-communist government forces were supported primarily by the USA.

Laos was secretly but massively drawn into the Vietnam/American war. During this 'secret war', US forces were supported by Thai and Hmong recruits, and US pilots carried out bombing missions from bases in Thailand and Viet Nam, assisted by non-uniformed military personnel and 'advisors' based in western Laos. The Ho Chi Minh trail in Laos and North Viet Nam were subjected to sustained bombing. In the East, the Pathet Lao were trained by and fought with the North Vietnamese army, which had tens of thousands of troops stationed in Laos, and proved more than a match for the US forces, despite the latter's superior weaponry (Hamilton-Merritt, 1999; Warner, 1997).

A ceasefire was agreed in 1973 and was followed by two years of coalition government. However, in 1975 the Pathet Lao gained control, removed the monarchy, and formed the Lao People's Democratic Republic. From then until the mid-1980s, Pathet Lao government was based largely on communist principles. Since 1986, however, especially after the collapse of the Soviet Union, there has been a sustained attempt to move from a command economy to a more capitalist, market-orientated system. One-party government continues, with only a slow emergence of a more open democratic system, but despite occasional domestic unrest up to 2000, the stability of the region has been reflected in Lao PDR and, with considerable international assistance, the poverty that is widespread throughout the country is being addressed.

Since the mid-1990s, the government has set itself the target of eradicating poverty, reducing its dependence on overseas development assistance, and moving out of the category of 'less developed country' by 2020 (Lao People's Democratic Republic, 2004: 1–4). Substantial poverty reduction has undoubtedly occurred, partly because of increased social stability, but also because government policy and substantial overseas aid have had some success. From 1991 to 2000, for instance, real Gross Domestic Product grew at an annual average of 6.3%, and those living in poverty declined overall from 46% of the population in 1992 to 33% in 2002–2003. Most social indicators confirm the trend (Asian Development Bank, 1999a: 3; World Bank, 2005: 4–6).

Much remains to be done. There are stark differences across and within Provinces (especially between north and south), between urban and rural areas, and across ethnic minorities (World Bank, 2005: 4–6). And although in 2003 the United Nations Development Programme upgraded Lao PDR to a medium developed country, poverty is still prevalent and the country relies heavily on overseas aid. In 2003, overseas development assistance amounted to more than 14% of GDP, and Lao PDR remained lower on the Human Development index (133) than neighbours Thailand (73), China (85), Viet Nam (108), Cambodia (130) and even Burma (Myanmar) (129) (United Nations Development Programme, 2005: 238–239, 282).

The Development of Tourism in Lao PDR

International tourists have been welcomed in Lao PDR only since 1989 (Hall, 2000: 183), and the country's first national tourism plan was published in 1990 (Lao PDR, 1990). At that time, the emphasis was on small, tightly-controlled groups of package tourists. However, in 1995 tourism became a priority for economic development (Schipani, 2002: 18) and the second *National Tourism Development Plan*, published in 1998, (Lao PDR, UNDP and WTO, 1998: 24), emphasised the value of four major types of tourism: conventional sightseers, special interest tourists – for example, eco- and adventure tourists – cross border tourists and domestic tourists (thus including, in effect, most categories of international tourist). All were valued as a source of foreign exchange, and it was thought that together they would bring benefits that would spread across the population and help conserve the natural and built environment (Lao PDR, UNDP and WTO, 1998: 37). The policy succeeded, and the 1999 the *National Tourism Marketing Plan* reported that tourism was the country's most important export (Lao PDR, UNDP and WTO, 1999: 6).

By the opening years of the 20th century, there was further recognition of tourism's potential to alleviate poverty but, closely mirroring the priorities espoused by the Asian Development Bank, as indicated later in this paper, the focus seemed to shift to smaller-scale tourism. As the Government's *National Growth and Poverty Eradication Strategy* (NGPES) was to note:

> Tourism is now a major contributor to national income (7%–9% of GDP) and employment. Tourism is a labour intensive industry and contributes to poverty reduction. The Lao PDR's tourism strategy favours pro-poor, community-based tourism development, the enhancement of specific tourism-related infrastructure improvements, and sub-regional tourism co-operation. (Lao PDR, 2004: 104)

A year later there was a return to a wider, broad-brush approach in the *National Tourism Strategy for Lao PDR*. It was to emphasise the role of properly planned tourism in reducing poverty and promoting national development, and the appeal to tourists of ethnic minority groups and traditional cultures. It also noted the wide range of archaeological and religious sites, and recommended promotion of the country's arts, crafts and its numerous natural attractions to visitors (Allcock, 2004: 12–13, 18, 43).

Finally, yet another year later, a *separate* strategy was put forward for ecotourism, where it was defined as a 'tourism activity based in rural areas that is geared towards: conservation of natural and cultural resources, local socio-economic development, and visitor understanding of, and appreciation for, the places they are visiting' (National Tourism Authority of Lao PDR, 2005: 8).

There was evidently some ambivalence as to the kind of tourist most favoured in Lao development plans, and it is questionable how far increased tourist arrivals can be attributed to these plans, rather than political and social stability and the increasing popularity of southeast Asia as a regional destination. However, while early statistics of tourist arrivals to Lao PDR were unreliable and varied considerably according to their source, recent national data are more consistent and the trends are evident. Although punctuated by the impact of terrorist attacks in the USA (2001), the war in Iraq and, more regionally, by terrorist attacks in Indonesia and the SARS epidemic in Asia (2003), since the early 1990s tourist numbers have increased markedly,

Table 1 International tourism in Lao PDR

Year	Day visitors*	Overnight visitors*	Total visitors
1990	n/a	14,000	n/a
1991	n/a	38,000	n/a
1992	n/a	88,000	92,000
1993	67,000	36,000	103,000
1994	110,000	36,000	146,000
1995	286,000	60,000	346,000
1996	310,000	93,000	403,000
1997	270,000	193,000	463,000
1998	300,000	200,000	500,000
1999	355,000	259,000	614,000
2000	546,000	191,000	737,000
2001	501,000	173,000	674,000
2002	521,000	215,000	736,000
2003	440,000	196,000	636,000
2004	658,332	236,484	894,806
2005	807,550	287,765	1,095,315

Source: World Tourism Organisation, 1996: 96; 1999: 104; 2001: 103; and 2005: 103; Lao National Tourism Administration, 2006.
*Those categorised by the World Tourism Organisation as 'day visitors' are regional tourists who enter the country by road, and in fact they may stay one or two nights. By contrast, those classified as 'overnight visitors' are mainly from outside the region.

as indicated in Table 1. In 2005, there were more than 1 million international arrivals in Lao PDR, an increase exceeding 50% on the 2000 figure, and the total revenue generated by tourism in 2005 is estimated to have been more than US $146 million, undoubtedly making tourism the country's main source of foreign exchange (Lao National Tourism Administration, 2006: 18).

Most visitors (82%) are nationals from within the region, overwhelmingly from other ASEAN countries. This includes those categorised by the World Tourism Organisation as 'day visitors' coming by road (who may, in fact, stay one or two nights), and 'overnight visitors', mainly from outside the region, as indicated in Table 1. However, significant numbers of relatively high-spending tourists were from Europe (1%) and the Americas (5.5%) (Lao National Tourism Administration, 2006: 6). Recognising the value of these small but growing markets, government has prioritised Japan and Australia (with Thailand) in Asia, France, the UK and Germany in Europe, and the USA and Canada in the Americas (Lao National Tourism Administration, 2006: 14).

Much of Lao PDR has only very basic tourism infrastructure, and tourism development is concentrated in the Municipality and Province of Vientiane, at the UNESCO World Heritage Sites Luang Prabang Town and Vat Phou in Champassak, and in Savannakhet City (Lao PDR's second largest), with Savannakhet province serving as a major entry point for visitors from Viet Nam and Thailand. As indicated in Table 2, in 2005 Vientiane Municipality (21%), Vientiane Province (11%), Luang Prabang (15%), Champassak (12%) and Savannakhet (6%) together accounted for 65% of all accommodation establishments in Lao PDR, while the Vientiane-Luang Prabang corridor alone, which includes Vang Vieng, accounted for about half all establishments (Lao National Tourism Administration, 2006: 18–19).

The Organisation of Tourism in Lao PDR

Numerous stakeholders have an interest in tourism in Lao PDR. However, at the time of writing, the main institutional actors are the Asian Development Bank, UNESCO, SNV (the Netherlands development organisation), and the Lao government, primarily through the Lao National Tourism Administration (formerly the National Tourism Authority of Lao PDR). Their respective roles, discussed in detail in a forthcoming publication (Harrison & Schipani, forthcoming) are briefly outlined here to situate the ensuing discussion on the place of ecotourism, community-based tourism and the private sector in Lao tourism. However, as indicated below, their initiatives in tourism have been especially influenced by the Nam Ha Ecotourism Project, one of the earliest ecotourism projects in the country, and certainly the largest, best organised and most important, considered by government and donors alike as the role model for ecotourism throughout the Lower Mekong Basin.

The Nam Ha Ecotourism Project

The Nam Ha Ecotourism Project (NHEP) was started in 1999 in the town of Luang Namtha, in Luang Namtha Province. Funds were provided by the New Zealand Official Development Assistance Programme (NZODA), now the New

Table 2 Concentration of tourism in Lao PDR, 2005: Selected indices

Province	Visitors	No. of hotels and guest houses	Percent of total	No. of rooms	Occupancy rate (%)	Average no. of rooms
Attapeu	13,740	12	1.1	190	50	16
Bokeo	89,027	24	2.2	309	67	13
Bolikhamxay	63,579	26	2.4	435	65	17
Champassak	99,044	126	11.6	1,616	29	13
Houaphanh	3,175	39	3.6	338	29	9
Khammouane	13,633	18	1.6	394	43	22
Luang Namtha	49,258	50	4.6	536	57	11
Luang Prabang	133,569	163	15.0	1,722	70	11
Oudomxay	54,721	63	5.8	703	52	11
Phongsaly	9,452	36	3.3	273	29	8
Saravanh	8,000	22	2.0	230	42	10
Savannakhet	133,569	67	6.2	1,257	60	19
Sayabouli	15,914	47	4.3	431	37	9
Sekong	6,526	17	1.6	172	37	10
Vientiane Muncipality	653,212	224	20.6	4,891	64	22
Vientiane Province	92,657	115	10.6	1,807	52	16
Xieng Khouang	24,174	32	2.9	441	40	14
Saysomboun	n/a	7	0.6	83	n/a	12
Total	—	1088	100.0	15,828	—	15

Source: Lao National Tourism Administration, 2006: 18–19.

Zealand Agency for International Development (NZAID), the Japanese Government, through the International Finance Corporation's Trust Funds Programme, and additional technical assistance by UNESCO and other agencies, as indicated in Figure 1. The aim was to develop a series of treks to ethnic minority villages, with trained local guides, to provide income to the villagers and facilitate conservation efforts within a National Protected Area (NPA).

At the time of writing, the Project is into its second phase (2005–2008). It now operates under the supervision of the Luang Namtha Provincial Tourism Office, and several treks to Akha, Tai Daeng, Khamu and Lahu villages are on offer, ranging from less strenuous one-day forest walks to more challenging two- or three-day treks, which include overnight stays in the villages. Over recent months, it has worked increasingly with Green Discovery, the tour operator in Lao PDR most involved with community-based ecotourism products.

As well as running the treks, the NHEP cooperates with the public sector in developing links with the private sector, strengthening natural resource and

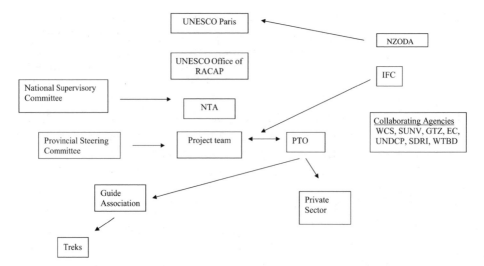

Figure 1 The organisational structure of the Nam Ha Ecotourism Project

protected area management in the Nam Ha NPA, and helping formulate a tourism master plan for Luang Namtha Province.

Financial assistance from NZAID was crucial to the continuation of the NHEP. Indeed, with an overall commitment of up to US $1 million a year until 2010, New Zealand has recently emerged as one Lao PDR's main pro-poor tourism donors. As part of its Lao country strategy, it is supporting not only the NHEP, but also a similar community-based ecotourism programme in Xieng Khouang Province, to begin in mid-2006. In addition, both Nam Ha Phase II and the Xieng Khouang Heritage Tourism Programme utilise technical assistance and monitoring sourced through the Office of the UNESCO Regional Advisor for Culture in Asia and the Pacific (RACAP).

The Asian Development Bank

The Asian Deveolpment Bank (ADB) is a major presence in the Greater Mekong region and in 2002 funded a feasibility study of priority tourism infra-structure projects in Lao PDR, Cambodia and Viet Nam (ADB, 1999b). Committed to developing tourism throughout the region as a means of poverty reduction (ADB, 2002a, 2002b: 24), it has pledged up to US $30 million in low interest loans and technical assistance to the Mekong Tourism Development Project (MTDP), the overall aims of which are as follows:

> The Project's goal is to reduce poverty through increasing economic growth and employment opportunities, increasing foreign exchange earnings, and promoting the conservation of the natural and cultural heri-tage. The specific objective of the Project is to promote sustainable tourism development in the lower Mekong River Basin through infrastructure improvements, increased community and private sector participation, and sub-regional cooperation. The Project is targeted to improve high pri-ority tourism-related infrastructure in the lower Mekong basin, promote

pro-poor, community-based, sustainable tourism in rural areas, and strengthen sub-regional cooperation. It will mitigate environmental degradation from unplanned and unsustainable development, develop human resources, and promote cooperation between private and public sectors within the sub-region through the establishment of national tourism boards. (ADB, 2002c: 7)

About a third of the funds allocated by ADB to the MTDP have been allocated to Lao PDR (ADB, 2002a: 12) and, as in Cambodia and Viet Nam, will be directed to four distinct spheres of activity, over a five-year period. The first emphasis is on loans to improve tourism-related infrastructure, and primarily involves building or improving roads and airports. Currently, three projects are under way, in the Provinces of Luang Namtha, Khammouane, and Luang Prabang.

The second focus is on the development of pro-poor, community-based tourism, and for this purpose ADB has a team of four international and four national consultants working closely with local project implementation units (PIUs), which are comprised of staff from provincial tourism offices in Luang Namtha, Luang Prabang, Champassak and Khammouane. These PIUs cooperate with private and public sector agencies, oversee guide training and awareness programmes, and ensure, where appropriate, that women and ethnic minorities are empowered to participate in tourism activities. ADB is also planning to extend its support for 'pro-poor demonstration projects' in other remote, poor provinces (ADB, 2005: 45).

The third emphasis is on strengthening regional cooperation, improving cross-border tourism facilities and harmonising standards, and developing human resources in the Lower Mekong region, while the final sphere of activity is providing institutional support to implement the three major project components.

SNV (The Netherlands development organisation)

Over the last few years, the ADB has worked increasingly closely with SNV, an independent NGO which has traditionally received most of its income from the Dutch government. It has been in Lao PDR since 2000, initially operating as SUNV (through a cooperative programme with United Nations Volunteers), and is especially committed to providing technical advisers for the development of community-based ecotourism in rural areas. It supported the Nam Ha Ecotourism Project by providing a Handicraft Production and Marketing Adviser, and acknowledged Nam Ha's status as a role model in the *National Ecotourism Strategy and Action Plan*, which it prepared for the Lao National Tourism Administration (National Tourism Authority of Lao PDR, 2005: 6).

SNV focuses primarily on small-scale, community-based tourism in parts of Lao PDR not currently on the main tourist trail – notably Luang Prabang, Houaphanh, Savannakhet and Khammouane – and also cooperates with central government in developing national tourism policies (SNV, 2006). In Luang Prabang, for instance, its advisers work with the provincial authority in trying to extend the benefits of tourism, currently concentrated in the World Heritage city of Luang Prabang, to outlying villages in the Province.

In Houaphanh they helped the PTO formulate a tourism development plan, and are assisting in improving information and services at the network of caves once used by the Pathet Lao as command centres during the Indo-China wars. In Savannakhet, SNV advisers are developing treks to three protected areas in conjunction with villagers and local guides, and similar activities are occurring in Khammouane, as part of the Mekong Tourism Development Project.

All such activities are designed to increase earning opportunities for the rural poor, diversify their sources of income, build local management capacity and expertise in tourism (e.g. in guiding and heritage conservation), and empower local communities. They are complemented by technical assistance provided by SNV to the Lao National Tourism Administration in Vientiane, which promotes the National Ecotourism Strategy (National Tourism Authority of Lao PDR, 2004), and the work of the newly-formed inter-ministerial Ecotourism Technical Cooperation Group, which also receives technical assistance and further support from SNV and Mekong Tourism Development Project advisers. SNV also helped to establish the Lao Sustainable Tourism Network, and in May 2006 launched a three-year programme, funded by the European Union, to improve the marketing and promotion capabilities of the Lao Association of Travel Agents (LATA), strengthen the organisation's management, and institute mechanisms for information-exchange between tour operators and the LNTA. Such examples, along with its cooperation with UNWTO (through the STEP Programme), in disseminating the new Lao Tourism Law (approved by the Lao Parliament on 9 November 2005), show how SNV assists the LNTA in cooperating more closely with the private sector.

Except for its involvement in Savannakhet and Houaphanh, most activities carried out by SNV's international and national advisers in Lao PDR are funded by ADB through the Lao Government, an arrangement that emerged during the first phase of the ADB-financed Mekong Tourism Development Project.

SNV and ADB are not the only international organisations working in Lao tourism. Several other ecotourism projects, based on similar principles and with similar aims, are promoted by other aid agencies. These include a CUSO initiative (a Canadian volunteer organisation), working in Attapeu Province, DED (the German Development Service) in Phou Khao Khouay National Park, near Vientiane and also in Udomxay Province, GTZ (German Development Agency) and Vientiane Travel and Tour, its private sector partner, developing an ecotourism programme for eight Akha villages in the Muang Sing area of Luang Namtha, and small European Union projects in Vieng Phoukha District, Luang Namtha and in Pongsali Province (www.ecotourismlaos.com, accessed 3 March 2006). However, most of these are very small in scale and still at the development stage. At the time of writing, ADB and SNV have leading roles in the development and trajectory of tourism in Lao PDR – in so far as it is oriented towards rural, pro-poor community-based tourism.

The Lao National Tourism Administration

In 2005, the National Tourism Authority of Lao PDR was renamed the Lao National Tourism Administration (LNTA) and upgraded to ministerial level

within the Prime Minister's Office. It is the main government agency responsible for regulating tourism in the Lao PDR, and formally cooperates with
numerous other stakeholders, many of which are also in the public sector
(Allcock, 2004: 67–68). It has branch offices in Vientiane and all 16 provinces,
and has several important roles: first, tourism planning and cooperation;
second, licensing and legal affairs; third, marketing and promotion and
finally, training.

First, in coordinating tourism planning, with assistance from the aid
agencies, the LNTA develops the National Tourism Strategy and produces
master plans for tourism development in the provinces and at specific sites.
SNV's part in preparing the National Ecotourism Strategy and Action Plan
has already been acknowledged, and the current National Tourism Strategy
and Action Plan was formulated with national and international technical
assistance from ADB's Mekong Tourism Development Project.

Second, the LNTA licenses tour companies, tour guides, tourist accommodation and restaurants, and sets appropriate standards, guidelines and codes
of conduct for them. It publishes a compulsory code of conduct for tour
guides and is in the process of setting up a hotel rating system based on
good practice elsewhere in the ASEAN region.

Third, most marketing and general promotion of the Lao tourism industry is
carried out by LNTA, which produces informational materials and participates
in conferences and exhibitions. It also maintains tourist information centres
across the country and two websites (www.tourismlaos.gov.la and www.eco-
tourismlaos.com). More specific tourism products and services are marketed
and promoted directly by the private sector, that is tour companies, hotels
and restaurants, which produce their own advertisements and brochures and
develop and maintain their own websites.

Finally, although some hoteliers and inbound tour operators train their staff,
most training is carried out by government and its NGO partners. The latter are
normally responsible for training guides at provincial and village levels, but
LNTA trains and registers national tour guides, running an annual course in
Vientiane. It also periodically conducts hotel and restaurant management training sessions for the private sector, and runs short tourism management courses
for government employees and the private sector. At local level, it assists disadvantaged and poor groups (particularly women) in obtaining employment
in the hospitality, guiding and handicraft sub-sectors.

The private sector

It was stated earlier that there seems an ambiguity concerning the type of
tourists the country's authorities wish to attract. Furthermore, while ADB's
support for infrastructural development and sub-regional cooperation is
clearly designed to facilitate the movement of all kinds of tourist, and takes
up the bulk of its funds (ADB, 2002a: 12), much of its technical support is explicitly directed towards community-based tourism in rural areas. Similarly, the
publications and promotional literature emanating from ADB, SNV and the
LNTA also have a strong focus on rural tourism, reflecting the fact that its technical advisers are usually specialists in community-based tourism. And while
one of the two official websites focuses specifically on the ethnic minorities

and cultural attractions of Lao PDR, the other is devoted exclusively to ecotourism (www.tourismlaos.gov.la and www.ecotourismlaos.com).

It is arguable, then, those who organise and promote Lao tourism are concentrating on what has come to be known as pro-poor, community-based tourism. However, when attention turns to what is happening in the Lao economy, a very different picture emerges. It transpires that one of the key features of economic change since 1986, when a market-oriented economy was introduced, has been the rapid expansion of small, locally-owned businesses. Indeed, by 1996,

> ... (t)here were 146,000 micro/small enterprises employing the equivalent of 259,000 full-time workers and accounting for 6% to 9% of GDP. This is over ten times the 22,000 that were employed by larger enterprises. Indeed, the micro/small enterprise sector accounted for 86% of rural and 13% of urban employment ...

> 90% of these are family businesses which tend to be multiple enterprises. However, they provide supplementary rather than principal household income. 63% are female-owned and account for 56% of total employment in this sector. (Enterprise Development Consultants Co. Ltd, 2002)

A decade later, the importance of small/micro business is even more pronounced, and the tourism sector provides a specific example of the more general phenomenon, at least in the provision of accommodation, food and beverages. In 1998, for example, there were only 307 accommodation establishments in the country, whereas by 2005 there were 1088 (Table 2). And we are certainly not talking about 'big business', for the average number of rooms was a mere 15, and exceeded 20 only in Khammouane and Vientiane Municipality. Even in Luang Prabang, with the second biggest concentration of establishments in the country, the average was only 11 rooms (Lao National Tourism Administration, 2006: 18–19). The message these figures convey is evident: in all of Lao PDR's main tourism centres, in the accommodation sector (and in restaurants), small/micro businesses are the norm.

Despite criticisms to the contrary (Guttal, 2006), this private sector expansion has been achieved with relatively little support, either from government or from the international aid agencies. Indeed, although SNV, ADB and the Government are formally committed to working with the private sector, LNTA's linkages with tourism businesses remain tenuous, and it might be argued that, at least initially, aid agencies and Government have looked at the private sector with a degree of suspicion For their part, private sector tour operators and tourism-related businesses used to complain at a lack of visible outputs and tangible support from LNTA, especially in marketing and promotion, and regulatory or training activities. It is indeed the case that, while the ADB's Mekong Tourism Development Project is primarily focused on infrastructure projects, product and human resource development, it is also committed to developing tourism through the establishment of a Lao Tourism Promotion and Marketing Board, which is intended to increase participation by the private sector and give it a stronger voice on issues related to tourism policy. However, by the time of writing, such a Board had not materialised in Lao PDR (or Viet Nam or Cambodia).

It is remarkable, too, that despite the lack of formal mechanisms for obtaining credit, poor infrastructure and relatively untrained human resources, the vast majority of small and micro enterprises in the accommodation and restaurant sector are financed by *local* capital. Foreign investors are conspicuous by their absence. This might be explained by the relatively late conversion of government to a market orientation, but the ILO study quoted above also indicates that, in 1996, 'the existing legal and policy framework favours large enterprises' (Enterprise Development Consultants Co. Ltd, 2002). More recently, through legislation enacted by the Government in 2004, international investors were offered even more favourable terms, including the possibility of 100% foreign ownership and tax holidays up to seven years, followed by very low profit taxes thereafter (Lao PDR, 2004, 2006). However, at the time of writing, despite the country's immense potential for tourism, there has been little FDI in its historical, cultural and natural attractions, and such incentives seem to have been ineffective.

Lao Tourism and Poverty Alleviation

At the beginning of this paper, note was made of the emergence in the 1970s of an interest in tourism as a development tool, and the move, at the end of the 1990s, to a closer examination of ways in which it could be specifically targeted to alleviate poverty. This led to an account of how tourism has developed in Lao PDR, and a brief description of the main institutional agencies involved in it. Ideally, what should now follow is a detailed comparison of the role of rural, aid-led, community-based, pro-poor tourism (assuming for the present the last two categories are synonymous) with the relatively unplanned, expansion of small tourism-orientated businesses in the private sector. Unfortunately, though, direct comparisons are extremely difficult to make, primarily because detailed data are not available. If the aid agencies *do* carry out full economic costing of their projects, they are not usually accessible to the general public, and in Lao PDR, at any rate, no sustained research on private sector involvement has been carried out. However, enough data are available in sufficient quantity and quality to raise several pertinent issues about the development of tourism in Lao PDR, to inform the debate about the nature of pro-poor tourism more generally, and to suggest priorities for future research.

The Nam Ha Ecotourism Project

In October 2002, three years after the NHEP started, its external reviewers were unequivocal that it had been 'a tremendous success in providing a model of how tourism might be used for development in rural and largely subsistent villages and as a mechanism for promoting forest conservation' (Lyttleton & Allcock, 2002: 5), and also claimed it 'established a first-class working model for ecotourism activities in areas of great cultural and natural richness' (Lyttleton & Allcock, 2002: 6). In its first three years, after extensive preparation, a total of 89 guides had been trained, of whom 69 were from the town of Luang Namtha and 20 from the villages. The Nam Ha Ecoguide Service (NHEGS), a local inbound tour service created with technical assistance from the project, was operating three treks and a one-day boat trip, involving eight ethnic minority villages (with a combined population of about 2000), and had provided accommodation, food and other service to more than 2800 tourists from 38 countries.

Over the same period, the trekking operations earned the NHEGS a gross revenue of US $70,000, of which about 18% went directly into the villages, which also earned money from selling handicrafts and other services, for example, massages (Lyttleton & Allcock, 2002: 17–21, 41–45). As the authors of the external review point out, 'the per cent of income relative to alternative forms of income varies but in one Akha village it is as high as 40%' (Lyttleton & Allcock, 2002: 42). There is a similar variation in how (and to whom) the funds going to the villages are distributed but, during the first phase, 8% of all income from treks was placed in Village Development Funds, designed to benefit the community as a whole (Lyttleton & Allcock, 2002: 44–45).

Over the following years, the treks continued, as indicated in Table 3, and the NHEP has undoubtedly been recognised in Lao PDR, and indeed throughout southeast Asia, as a successful example of community-based, pro-poor tourism. It also seems, from the little evidence available, that villagers assisted by the project are equally satisfied with its performance, and the reviewers of the Project's first phase note that the Akha villagers they visited 'felt that the tourists dramatically improved their income' (Lyttleton & Allcock, 2002: 42). Indeed:

> In each of the Nam Ha target villages, cash income has been increased markedly by the visits of tourists and the established framework ensures that this income is, to date, reasonably well distributed among the villagers. The villagers are enormously happy to have the tourists visit and feel little in the way of negative impact of their presence. At the same time, the tourist treks have contributed positively to an increased awareness of forest conservation and the means to enact improved conservation practices. (Lyttleton & Allcock, 2002: 5)

This sounds impressive. However, it *also* has to be emphasised that it has been extremely well resourced. As the external reviewers noted, at the end of the first phase:

> The project has had at its disposal the (virtually) full time presence of 3 foreign TAs, an additional presence of 3 part-time foreign volunteers, and the full-time secondment of 3 NTA [National Tourism Authority] personnel with substantial tourism management skills. If one considers the limited number of target villages (no more than 8 in Luang Namtha) it almost equates to 1 TA per village. Clearly this is simplifying the job requirements, but it is unlikely there is a development project in the world that has maintained this level of expertise relative to the number of target communities. While this has directly led to the high level of project achievements, it is impossible that this level of assistance (per target site) be sustained. (Lyttleton & Allcock, 2002: 47)

The reviewers' conclusions seem to be supported by the data. From 2001 until the end of 2005, as indicated in Table 3, the NHEGS operated 1331 tours, catered for 6801 tourists and brought in gross revenue of US $137,794. Of this, $9485 went into village funds, and benefits also accrued to the

Table 3 Income earned by the Nam Ha Ecoguide Service 2001–2005 (US dollars)*

Year	No. tours	No. tourists	Gross revenues	Direct tour expenses	PTO 5% tourism promotion fund	Trek permit	Tax	Village fund	Overheads and profit
2001	201	944	17,795	11,655	889	984	427	1626	3,125
2002	430	2366	47,837	31,093	2362	2647	1185	4850	7,244
2003	165	718	14,755	11,308	748	789	212	306	2,855
2004	270	1366	25,662	18,769	1171	1148	291	870	2,482
2005	265	1407	31,745	21,927	1326	864	545	1833	3,573
Total	1331	6801	137,794	94,752	6496	6432	2660	9485	19,279

*Discrepancies in the columns are in the original.
Source: Lao National Tourism Administration, 2006.

Provincial Tourism Office and to central Government through taxes and pay-
ments for trekking permits. However, as indicated in Table 4, donor support
has been and continues to be considerable. From 1999, when the treks first
started, until 2002, the Project received nearly US $500,000 and from 2005
through to 2008, it is to receive more than $100,000 a year from NZAID.
Indeed, by 2008 the NHEP will have received more than US $860,000 from
international aid agencies.

When examined on a strict profit and loss basis, there is a clear discrepancy in
the amount received from donors and that obtained from the treks. However,
simply comparing the amounts provided by donors with the net profits
received from the treks (even if such detailed figures were consistently
available) is perhaps too simplistic. Other factors need also to be considered.
First, the villages targeted as partners in NHEP were especially poor, and
any economic benefits made an immediate difference. Secondly, one of the
reasons participating villages were selected was to reduce the degree of
opium consumption in the villages, and their reliance on opium as a source
of income. In so far as the Project succeeded in these objectives (and there is
evidence that it did), the *economic* significance is difficult to quantify.

Thirdly, it is also necessary to consider how donors' funds are invested in
other activities, for example: equipment and training (tour guides, managers
and villagers); constructing infrastructure in the villages to contain fresh water
and accommodate tourists, and building the Nam Ha Tourist Information
Centre in Luang Namtha; monitoring the impacts of the treks in the villages;
promoting conservation in the region, and producing advertising materials.
Such activities (and there are many others) are carried out with a view to the
longer term, and while they are necessary in the accumulation of financial
and cultural capital, it is not possible to really incorporate them in a simple
balance sheet.

Fourthly, the NHEP also contributes to the prosperity of Luang Namtha
Province. In 1999, for example, visitors to Luang Namtha simply stayed in
the town overnight and then moved on. However, with the development of
NHEP, they are now likely to go trekking for up to three days, also spending
an additional day or two in the town and bringing further income to the
town's guest houses and restaurants.

The Nam Ha Project and the Asian Development Bank

In 2002, when the ADB was considering further support for community-
based tourism in Lao PDR, the Nam Ha Project was seen as a model
for future tourism CBT projects in the rest of Lao PDR and further afield,
including Cambodia and Viet Nam. Consequently, as part of the Bank's
Mekong Tourism Development Programme's pro-poor, community-based
tourism component, up to US $400,000 per province is being made available
to Luang Namtha, Luang Prabang, Khammouane and Champassak over the
period 2003–2007, an average of $100,000 a year. These projects are now start-
ing to be operational. For the year March 2005 until February 2006, for instance,
as indicated in Table 5, the 14 new village-based tourism products in the provinces of Luang Namtha, Luang Prabang, Khammouane and Champassak,
developed by the Lao National Tourism Administration with ADB financial

Table 4 Donor support for the Nam Ha Ecotourism Project 1999–2002 and 2005–2008 (US dollars)

Year	NZODA (NZAID)*	Japan IFC	Other agencies** WCS, GTZ, EC, UNDCP, SDRI, WTBD; SNV	Financial return from treks etc.	Achievements
1999–2000	158,400		26,700 (plus technical advisers for specific short-term projects and sundry items).	2001–end of 2005: 137,794 (gross), including 9485 to villages. Also income from handicraft sales, massages etc.	1331 tours and 6801 tourists Treks and boat trips Income to poor villages 90 + guides trained Investment in infrastructure and cultural capital for future
2000–2001	93,159	106,698			
2001–2002	96,884				
Sub-total	348,442	106,698	26,700		
2005–2006	128,481				
2006–2007	152,686				
2007–2008	127,826				
Total	$757,346	$106,698	$26,700		

Source: Lao National Tourism Administration, 2006.
*Figures include 13% to UNESCO in support costs.
**Wildlife Conservation Society (WCS), GTZ (German Aid Agency), European Commission (EC), UNDCP (United Nations Drug Control Programme), Sustainable Development Research institute (SRDI), Where There Be Dragons (WTBD); SNV (Netherlands Development Organisation).
Source: Lyttleton and Allcock (2002: 53–56), UNESCO (2005).

Table 5 Financial summary for LNTA/ADB new CBT products: March 2005–February 2006 (US dollars)

	No. villages/estimated no. of significant beneficiaries	No. tours	No. tourists	Total revenue	Village revenue	Permits
Luang Namtha						
(1) Pu Sam Yord Journey	4/65	89	549	21,119	9406	247
(2) Nam Ha Camp	2/40	15	76	3965	1346	228
(3) Akha Trail-Nam Mye Caves	4/65	11	37	1821	901	109
Luang Prabang						
(4) Chomphet Trek	4/65	25	92	4235	420	0
(5) Kiew Kan Trek	4/65	23	96	2991	1844	0
(6) Kwang Si Walk	2/40	47	215	4098	1864	68
Khammouane						
(7) Phou Hin Poun 2-day Trek	3/45	14	78	3502	1092	78
(8) Buddha Cave 1-day Trek	1/10	23	74	1120	312	5
(9) Kong Lor-Natan Homestay	2/40	24	172	2313	2615	121
(10) Konglor Boat Trip	1/20		343	3430	3430	0
Champassak						
(11) Don Daeng Island	1/16	29	171	1300	1207	0
(12) Xe Pian Forest Excursion	2/40	15	78	2677	1094	121
(13) Kiet Ngong Elephant Rides	1/20	1476	2525	14,397	14,177	0
(14) Pu Khong Mountain-Don Ko	1/20	13	50	1227	841	38
Total 14 products	32/551	1804	4556	68,194	40,548	1014

Source: Lao National Tourism Administration, 2006.

support, brought in a gross revenue of US $68,194 and contributed US $40,548 to the 32 villages directly involved, with an estimated 551 people deriving a significant portion of their livelihood from tourism-related activities. These figures are the result of the first year of operation for most of the tour products, many of which are located in remote areas far from the main tourism circuits and thus require sustained marketing and promotion before they can become established destinations.

When the examination of benefits brought by these projects is widened to include those accruing to private sector tour operators operating with technical and financial support from the ADB and the NHEP, not only in ADB-supported villages but also on other sites, other economic benefits become apparent. As indicated in Table 6, in only one year, the four provinces generated some US $474,596 in gross revenue, of which nearly half was realised at the village level, and a considerable (but unquantifiable) percentage of this income might be attributed to direct and indirect support from the Mekong Tourism Development Project.

Before concluding this section, a caveat should perhaps be mentioned. While commercial banks are likely to expect returns on their investments after a period of around 10 years, the ADB allows for loan repayments over 30 years, at a low rate of interest and with a significant interest-free period. This

Table 6 Financial summary for destinations and tour operators receiving support from the LNTA-ADB Mekong Tourism Development Project. March 2005–February 2006

Destination and tour operator support	No. tours	No. tourists	Total revenue	Village revenue	Permits/ tickets
Luang Namtha					
(1) Green Discovery Co.	191	756	18,108	10,184	366
(2) Nam Ha Ecoguide Service	270	1366	25,662	18,796	1148
(3) Muang Sing Ecoguide Service	160	567	12,941	8195	0
(4) Vieng Phoukha Ecoguides & Caves	79	238	6885	2272	125
Luang Prabang					
(5) Muang Ngoi Kao Village	0	7800	195,000	97,500	0
Khammouane					
(6) Buddha Cave in Na Kang Xang Village	0	40,000	48,000	40,000	8000
Champassak					
(7) Ban Mai Singsampanh Market	0	14,000	168,000	84,000	0
Total	700	64,727	474,596	260,947	9639

Source: Lao National Tourism Administration, 2006.

suggests that different criteria of success are being used by the ADB and in the private banking system.

It is also the case that much of the training and HR development in Lao tourism is supported by NHEP and other ADB-supported projects. Not only do they bring immediate economic benefits to the villages where they operate, but also they generate income and employment in the region, raise awareness of cultural and environmental conservation among local people and policy makers, put management systems in place to protect the value and integrity of destinations, and offer training and capacity-building to many people who, without the projects, would be measurably poorer. They also develop models that can then be adopted by private sector players, several of whom are now cooperating with donor-supported projected in Lao PDR, as indicated in Table 7. Such activities may generally be regarded as laudable, but they are almost impossible to quantify.

Despite these caveats, however, when the sums provided by international donors to CBT products in Lao PDR are compared with the short-term financial returns from these projects, the former clearly outweigh the latter. And even if the medium- and longer-term benefits are also taken into account, it could be argued that the contribution of the projects to the financial and cultural

Table 7 Relationship of private sector to selected community-based tourism projects in Lao PDR

Institution	Area of operation	Partnerships with tour operators	Private sector
LNTA	Throughout Lao PDR		Small-scale, locally-owned guest houses and accommodation
NZAID	NHEP: Luang Namtha & Muang Sing; Xieng Khoang	Green Discovery and Diethelm Travel	Non-specialist owners often also with rice lands
ADB & SNV	MTDP: Luang Namtha, Luang Prabang, Khammouane, Champassak	Lao Youth partners with MTDP in Meuang Ngoi, Luang Prabang	Subject to government regulation and licensing
GTZ	Muang Sing	Exotissimo	Profit orientated
CUSO	Attapeu		Major driver of Lao tourism
DED	Phou Khao Khoay National Park (Vientiane Province) & Udomxay Province		
EC	Vieng Phouka (Luang Namtha) & Pongsali Prov		

LNTA = Lao National Tourism Administration; NZAID = New Zealand Aid Agency; ADB = Asian Development Bank; SNV = Netherlands Development Organisation; GTZ = German Aid Agency; CUSO = Canadian aid NGO; DED = German Development Service; EC = European Commission capital of the Lao tourism industry, while potentially great, is (again) likely to remain unquantifiable.

Two other important questions remain. The first concerns whether or not international funds invested in these projects could have been spent more profitably to achieve the same aims and objectives, and the second the extent to which the long-term potential of these projects, effectively permeating and transforming the rest of Lao tourism, will actually be realised. In response to the first question, it has to be said that we simply do not know. And the response to the second is that we do not *yet* know. When we *do*, it will be with the benefit of hindsight.

The private sector

It was indicated earlier that since 1986 there has been a rapid expansion of small, locally-owned businesses in Lao PDR, especially in tourism, to the extent that Lao tourism is characterised by the emergence of many small-scale, locally owned hotels, guest houses and restaurants, often in urban areas, with an average of only 15 rooms (Lao National Tourism Administration, 2006: 18–19). Furthermore, this expansion has been achieved with little support, either from government or from the international aid agencies, and with very little planning. Whereas CBT ventures in Lao PDR resulted from a deliberate targeting of communities by international agencies, private sector development has occurred because individuals saw entrepreneurial opportunities in tourism and took them.

In this section, a brief account will be given of the development of tourism on the island of Don Det, in the Siphandon ('Four Thousand Island') region of Champassak, near to the Cambodian border.[2] As indicated earlier (Table 2), Champassak is one of the provinces most visited by tourists, and many independent tourists visiting the province pass through the Siphandon region en route to or from Cambodia, in couples or singly, often staying a few days in the peaceful Mekong villages, accurately stated by the *Lonely Planet*, 'to offer fascinating glimpses of tranquil river-oriented village life' in communities reported to be 'self-sufficient, growing most of their own rice, sugar cane, coconut and vegetables, harvesting fish from the Mekong and weaving textiles as needed' (Cummings, 2002: 305).

In July 2004, the island of Don Det had a total population of about 880 people, living in two villages, namely Don Det Ok (East) and Don Det Tok (West). The island's tourism started in 1997, when an outsider from the District Centre, Khone Island, built the first guest house. Since then, tourism increased rapidly. In 2002, the island had 19 guest houses, and by 2004 there were 34. Most were concentrated in the village of Don Det Tok, which had a population of 404 people, living in 83 households, as indicated in Table 8.

Whether or not villagers of Don Det Tok are considered 'poor' depends largely on definition. According to the Head Man, who used his own assessment criteria rather than the official income criteria (which until recently defined any rural household with an average income of less than US $8.20 per person per month as poor), 17 households (c. 20%) were poor. However, many of the village houses would be considered by the authorities to be 'temporary' (another criterion of poverty), 75 households (90%) had no toilets and few houses were supplied with fresh water. And when interviewed, more than two thirds of the respondents described *themselves* as poor, usually because they were not self-sufficient in rice (which applied to nearly half the sample), but also for a wide variety of other reasons, ranging from being alone to not having a secure or predictable income.

Table 8 Don Det Tok village, on the island of Don Det, Champassak: July, 2004

	Don Det Tok
Total households	83 (404 pop)
Sample number of households	55 (66%)
Sample household population	292
Average household size	5.3
Nuclear family	23
Extended family	20
Other	12
Total adults born outside Don Khon/Don Det	27 (9.2%)**
Household with at least one in tourism	21 (38%)
At least one person involved in handicrafts	–
Total people in handicrafts	–
Income source	
Agriculture 1	36 (65%)
Agriculture 2	12
Agriculture 3	1
Fishing 1	5 (9%)
Fishing 2	32
Fishing 3	7
Livestock 1	1
Livestock 2	1
Livestock 3	24
Tourism 1	12 (22%)
Tourism 2	6 (11%)
Tourism 3	1
Tourism 4	2
Other 1	3
Other 2	1
Other 3	–
Have own land? No (excluding garden)	13
Sharecropping?	8

(Continued)

Table 8   Continued

	Don Det Tok
Yes	42
Paddy	42
Other	–
Enough rice: yes	29 (52.7%)
No	26 (47.3%)
Self-assessed as poor: yes	37 (67.3%)
No	17
Don't know	1

*One household did not produce enough rice but ran a shop and did not claim to be poor.
**In 21 households.
Source: Author's survey, July, 2004.

From interviews with guest house owner of Don Det, it was clear that sources of finance for guest houses and restaurants vary, but inheritance or the sale of livestock or other assets (perhaps themselves inherited) were commonly mentioned. In 2002, one young guest house operator reported that his father had financed the construction of a five-room guest house and restaurant by selling a buffalo and three cows (at the time of writing, equivalent to US $2000), while another owner said the money that financed his guest house and restaurant came from the sale of three buffalo. Both were well on the way to recouping the initial cost, and other guest house and restaurant owners similarly reported that initial investments were recouped after only a few years.[3]

With few exceptions, buildings were made from local materials, with a basic frame of wood and/or bamboo, walls of woven reeds, and thatched roofs (occasionally on a wooden or corrugated metal base). Nearly all the guest houses in the sample were locally owned and owner operated. Although almost half the owners were not from Don Det, all but one of these were from adjacent islands, with family or affinal kin in Don Det. The remaining owner was from Vientiane Province. Most guest houses in the sample were small, with an average of 5.5 rooms, and nearly all had restaurants (as indicated in Table 9), invariably run by women in the family, who reportedly had independent control of the profits from the enterprise.

Details of the households sampled in Don Det Tok, and their major sources of income, are provided in Table 8. For present purposes, the most relevant points relate to the role of tourism in the village. While 65% of the sampled households indicated that their main source of income was agriculture, in 38% of the sample at least one adult member was involved in catering for tourists, in 22% tourism was their main source of income, and another 11% reported that tourism (and not fishing, as might have been expected) was their second source of income. No household reported any earning from handicrafts, and in fact no weaving was noted in the village.

Within the village, earnings from tourism came from a variety of sources, including accommodation and restaurants, boat trips to other islands (and to view the Irawaddy dolphins of the Mekong River, along the Lao and

Table 9 Summary of sample survey of guest houses of Don Det (July 2004)

	*Don Det** guest houses*
Total	34*
Size of sample	19
Number of rooms	105
Average number of rooms	5.5
Restaurant: Yes	14
No	5
All food obtained locally	–
Some food obtained locally	12
No food obtained locally	2
Owner born in Don Det?	10
Owner born outside Don Det?**	9***
Total with some family labour	1
Number with no family labour	2
Number with only family labour	16
Total workers born in Don Det island	35
Total workers born outside Don Det Island**	–
Total workers	20***
Average number of staff?	3

*In July 2004, nine guest houses in Don Det were closed.
**Of these owners and workers, all but one had come from nearby islands.
Source: Author's survey, July 2004.

Cambodia border), tubing, where large inflated inner tubes are provided for tourists to use to float along the river, and the rental of bicycles and small motor bikes. Tourists could also visit a waterfall, travelling by a small shuttle bus, which charged about 60 cents for the journey.

How important was tourism to the village of Don Det Tok? The estimates may be crude but are nevertheless instructive. According to one owner of a six-room guest house, in a good year he might make US $1200 on accommodation, with much more than double that amount in the restaurant (which was agreed to be the main source of profit). At the normal nightly rate of US $1.00 a room, this would give him an occupancy rate of 55%, which compares with that of 58% given for Champassak province in 2005 (Lao National Tourism Administration, 2006: 17).

From interviews with tourists, and examinations of visitors' books in the guest houses, it was clear that most tourists stayed for at least three nights in the village. The data in Table 10 are likely to be an underestimate, but indicate that tourists visiting Don Det in 2004 or 2005, nearly all relatively 'high spenders' from outside South East Asia, probably spent about US $450,000. A high percentage of this expenditure would have remained in the village, as 12 of the 14 restaurants indicated that they obtained at least some of their

Table 10 Estimate of annual tourist expenditure on the island of Don Det

Annual tourist expenditure	Total ($ US)
34 guest houses with average of 5.5 rooms and 55% occupancy: 37,540 tourists at $1.00 a day	37,540
Restaurants: food and beverages at $8.00 a day for 37,540 tourist days*	300,320
Sundries at $3.00 a day for 37,540 tourist days (bicycle hire, boat trips, tubing etc.)	112,630
Estimated total expenditure	450,950

*Lunch or dinner at a restaurant in Don Det Tok costs about $3.00, and with the addition of Lao beer the estimate of $8.00 a day for food and beverages is likely to be an under-estimate.

supplies locally (e.g. vegetables, fish and some poultry) in Don Det, either from their own kitchen gardens or neighbours, and most of the remainder came from Ban Nakasang, a market town a short journey by boat from the village. And while 36% of the workers in the guest houses were born outside Don Det, as indicated in Table 8, they were living in Don Det with other kin, including family members who owned and ran guest houses.

Other details can be mentioned only in passing. The boat owners of Don Det have formed a boat Association, and operate boats for tourists on a rota basis. Part of the Association's monthly proceeds is paid to Don Khong District in tax ($12.00), while $18.00 stays in the Village Fund, and is used for community projects (for example, painting the local primary school and providing it with fans). Indeed, possession of a large boat and an outboard motor is a great asset, as on a good day in the high season a boatman might earn more than $45.00 from tourism. It will be less in the low season, but is still considerably more than the average monthly earnings of many people. Guest Houses must also pay a monthly tax ($1.80) to the District, as must the restaurants ($1.50).

From this brief account of one small island in the Siphandon region of Champassak, it should be clear that tourism is a valuable source of income to many of the 880 residents, and will contribute about US $460,000 annually to the economy of Don Det. Such success was built on previous prosperity, for those who invested in guest houses and restaurants possessed the capital necessary to make the investment, and the research prompted some discussion in the villages as to whether or not tourism benefited the poor. Most villagers interviewed had no doubt that even though the poor were not specifically targeted, they benefited from having a bigger market for their crops and, less often, employment opportunities in the guest houses, as well as opportunities (if they cared to take them) to be sharecroppers on land owned by more well-to-do farmers.

Some redistribution mechanisms were in place, for example, the Village Fund, and there were reportedly plans to institute a rice bank to assist the poor when they were short of food. In July 2004, this had yet to materialise, and when carrying out the household sample it was clear that some households were distinctly poorer than others, usually because they had no land of their own (or land that was unproductive).

Issues concerning the distribution of income from tourism also arose when comparing villages. Don Det clearly benefited from tourism, but other islands adjacent to it did not. In July 2004, for instance, Don Det's two villages had a population of 880 in 149 households, and boasted a total of 34 guest houses. By contrast, the village of Ban Hang Khon, on the adjacent island of Don Khon, had a population of 250 people in 45 households, but no guest houses or restaurants, even though tourists would occasionally pass through the village to view the Irawaddy dolphins. It was recognisably poorer than the villages of Don Det, which was probably both a cause and a consequence of its failure to develop tourism.

Conclusion

In the first part of this paper, a brief history of approaches to tourism as a tool for 'development' was given, and it was shown that, in recent years, the focus

Table 11 Characteristics of Nam Ha ecotourism model and the private sector

	NHEP model	*Private sector*
(1)	Targeted at the poor, but not necessarily the poorest, especially ethnic minorities	Not specifically targeted at the poor
(2)	Protocapitalist: initial risks born by aid agencies (surrogate entrepreneurs?)	Protocapitalist. Non-specialist entrepreneurs with local capital and family labour
(3)	Planned activities in 'consultation' with and to 'empower' villagers. Bottom up?	Laissez-faire, without formal planning or consultation re 'empowerment'
(4)	Contributes to spread of cash economy in subsistence (usually rural) areas	Expands cash economy, especially in urban areas
(5)	Attempts to contribute to spread benefits through Village Development Funds	No planned distribution of benefits but may usually occur through village funds
(6)	Variable relationship to market demand	Develops in specific response to market demand
(7)	Benefits from infrastructural improvements (roads, airports etc.)	Also benefits from infrastructural improvements
(8)	Training from outside agencies with long-term impact (cultural capital etc.)	Little or no training received from outside agencies or from within private sector
(9)	Linked to conservation of biodiversity in region	No *specific* links with conservation of biodiversity (but depends on indigenous technical knowledge)
(10)	Relies largely on private sector to provide tourists	Supplies tourists to treks but also benefits from extended stays
(11)	Unquantified multiplier effects in locality	Unquantified multiplier effects in locality
(12)	Caters for a minority of tourists	Caters for the majority of tourists

has moved from mainstream tourism (which was often subjected to severe criticism) to such 'alternative' forms of tourism as ecotourism and pro-poor community-based tourism (CBT). Then followed a discussion of international tourism in Lao PDR, which in recent years has come to rely on tourism as a tool for development, and where government, the Asian Development Bank and international aid agencies have together placed the emphasis (and considerable funds) on pro-poor CBT, with the Nam Ha Ecotourism Project (NHEP) in Luang Namtha as the prototype for projects elsewhere, while at the same time leaving the private sector, essentially small-scale, locally-owned guest houses and hotels, to cater for most international visitors to Lao PDR.

In the third section of the paper, the financing and impact of the NHEP was briefly examined, before attention was shifted to the role of the private sector in developing tourism in the Siphandon region of Champassak. It now remains to briefly contrast these two forms of tourism development, as found in Lao PDR, arrive at some tentative conclusions, and suggest future research possibilities. And while, clearly, the comparison arises from the Lao PDR context, the findings may well be more generalisable. The NHEP indeed provides a model for the development of ecotourism in Lao PDR and other parts of SE Asia, but in its aims, objectives, organisation and reliance on donor assistance it has much in common with donor-assisted, community-based tourism projects elsewhere.

As indicated in Table 11, it is possible to compare the two models of tourism development under 12 related categories.

(1) The NHEP model is said to specifically target the poorest members of the community, frequently ethnic minorities, and a key overall aim is to improve their standard of living. By contrast, the private sector does not specifically target anyone. This difference may be less stark than appears at first sight, for poverty is not the only criterion for developing tourism. The targeted community, or its environment, must be perceived to have some kind of value as an attraction and, in any case, tourists are unlikely to be taken to totally inaccessible, dangerous or unhealthy destinations. By contrast, while the private sector does not specifically target the poor, tour operators are aware of the tourist value of ethnic minorities and their cultures and attempt, perhaps insensitively, to meet tourist demand. In this respect, as in others, the private sector could learn from CBT.

(2) Both forms of tourism might be described as 'protocapitalist'. In the NHEP model, initial development costs are born by international donors, who become, in effect, surrogate entrepreneurs. However, unless at some point they involve 'responsible' partners from the private sector, projects are unlikely to survive. For their part, at any early stage of their business development, as in the Siphandon region, guest house owners are also protocapitalists. They may realise capital by selling livestock, which play a major role in the subsistence sector, but they mostly employ unwaged family labour and have yet to engage in product development.

(3) In such CBT projects as the NHEP, activities are deliberately planned in consultation with community members, with the aim of 'empowering' them. The extent to which such a process is really 'bottom up' rather than 'top down' must be an empirical question, but 'targeting'

communities may (at least) involve a degree of persuasion, which may continue well into the project, and there is frequently a marked element of 'consciousness raising'. By contrast, in the private sector there may be little planning and community consultation, but tourism development does not occur in a social or political vacuum, and formal and/or informal sanctions may be brought to bear on those straying too far from communal norms and values. In fact, to suggest that such projects as NHEP are 'community-based', and that small-scale tourism, as encountered in the Siphandon region, is not, is to draw an artificial and ultimately misleading distinction. The guest houses of Don Det and their owners are an integral part of the community, and the community in which they operate is no more or less cohesive a social entity than villages in Luang Namtha. As a consequence, rather then polarising CBT (as promoted by international aid agencies) and private sector tourism, it might be more accurate to refer to donor-assisted, community-based tourism (DACBT) and to acknowledge that many private sector enterprises (and even such institutions as guest house associations) may be strongly rooted in communities.

(4)   DACBT projects undoubtedly contribute to the spread of the cash economy in rural areas, which may hitherto have been characterised by subsistence economies, though tourism is unlikely to be the first source of cash in these communities. Private sector development is also likely to expand the cash economy, though (as in Lao PDR, e.g. in Luang Prabang and Vang Vieng) it is likely to be more active in urban areas and is thus operating in an established cash economy.

(5)   In DACBT, sustained efforts are usually made to ensure the economic benefits from tourism are spread more or less equally through communities. The *success* of such efforts is not always apparent, and much depends on the nature of the communities being developed. This is also the case in the private sector. In Lao PDR, for instance, both DACBT and the private sector may use (or at least *attempt* to use) Village Funds as a redistribution mechanism, but the state can also become involved in redistribution through taxation and expenditure. Private sector development need not automatically lead to stark inequalities, though (arguably) some inequality will be inevitable if entrepreneurs are to make a profit (and thus sustain their businesses).

(6)   As the NHEP and ADB-assisted projects demonstrate, communities may initially be involved in tourism without much reference to market demand. Sooner rather than later, however, destinations and treks have to be marketed. Even the most worthy project is unsustainable if it is too far from the main tourist routes, not marketed, or charged at too high a price. By contrast, the private sector – the guest houses in Don Det, for example – develops to *meet* market demand, though it, too, will in turn seek to influence demand through marketing (if the necessary funds can be found). This means that quite early on in the development of a DACBT product, the private sector will have to be involved. This seems to have been one of the lessons emerging from the NHEP experience.

(7)   Both DACBT and the private sector benefit from infrastructural development. In this respect, ADB's loans to governments to construct and

upgrade roads, airports and river jetties favours all tourism sectors (and commercial and industrial development generally). They may also facilitate unforeseen and less desirable activities, e.g. rural–urban migration, trafficking and prostitution.

(8)   As the NHEP approach indicates, advocates of DACBT emphasise the value of capacity-building and human resource development, and there has already been some cooperation with the private sector, for example inbound tour operators. By contrast, the guest house owners in Siphandon seem to have learned from experience and (as far as is known) receive little training in operating tourism enterprises or developing their products. In this sphere of activity, as in others, there is scope for further collaboration across sectors.

(9)   In matters of conservation and environmental awareness generally, the private sector might learn from DACBT, which is often developed with a keen awareness of the value of the natural context and the damage that tourism might do. For instance, guest house owners of Don Det could improve their tourist product by offering guided boat tours, focusing on the flora and fauna of the region, and learning how to explain their culture to visitors. Nevertheless, one should not neglect the role of indigenous technical knowledge. In the past, for instance, villages in the Siphandon region have cooperated to prevent over-exploitation of fish stocks (Baird, 1999) and there is no reason to suppose they will be less sensitive to the impacts of tourism.

(10)   DACBT and the private sector need each other. Most tourists to Lao PDR do not visit with the sole purpose of trekking in Luang Natha with the NHEP, which relies on mainstream tourism to provide it with clients. It is part of their vacation experience, which in Lao PDR is also likely to include visits to Vientiane and Luang Prabang. However, the guest house owners of Luang Namtha also need the NHEP. It makes their destination more attractive, encourages visitors to extend their stay, and thus brings them additional business.

(11)   There is probably more information on the NHEP, its historical development and its impacts, than on similar projects elsewhere, but as yet there is little information on the direct, indirect and induced economic effects it has had on its targeted villages, or the surrounding region. This is also the case for small-scale, locally-financed private sector tourism development of the kind found in the Siphandon region of Champassak. More broadly, in tourism research generally there is considerable discussion of the tourist income multiplier, but few efforts, if any, have been made to calculate it for either DACBT projects or locally-owned enterprises. What *can* be said, however, is that such projects as the NHEP rely greatly on technical advice from outside consultants, a substantial proportion of whose income is likely to leave the area, as will also a high percentage of donor funds spent on computers, four-wheel drives and other expensive imports.

(12)   Finally, despite the burgeoning literature on 'alternative' tourism, ecotourism and community-based tourism, such projects cater for a minority of tourists, and will continue to do so. By contrast, the private

sector in Lao PDR, even though relatively undeveloped, undoubtedly caters for the tourist majority – and will continue to do so.

All these issues require further research. This examination of two quite specific forms of tourism development in Lao PDR highlights similarities and differences in a particular tourism context, some of which may well be found elsewhere. The intention is *not* to suggest that 'development' is achieved more by one type of tourism than another, but rather to indicate that the 'pro-poor' tourism label need not be applied exclusively to such donor-assisted, community-based projects as the Nam Ha Ecotourism Project. As has been expressed elsewhere (Harrison & Schipani, forthcoming), instead of automatically assuming that tourism enterprises in the private sector are unwelcome and inferior competitors of 'alternative' donor-assisted, community-based tourism projects, they might be considered as potential partners in tourism development, with their own expertise and links to the community, and with an entitlement to at least some of the financial and technical support provided, on a regular basis, by international aid agencies.

It is even possible that, in some circumstance, a 100-bed hotel employing 250 people and directly supporting hundreds of households may be the most appropriate option. At other times it may not. The general point is that dollar for dollar, pound for pound, we need a more realistic, research-based consideration of the role of the private sector in alleviating poverty and (to reintroduce a forgotten term) in bringing 'development' to tourism destination areas.

Acknowledgements

Steven Schipani wishes to acknowledge the support he has received from the Asian Development Bank and the Lao National Tourism Administration, and David Harrison that of his colleagues at the International Institute for Culture, Tourism and Development at London Metropolitan University and at the Overseas Development Institute in London.

Correspondence

Any correspondence should be directed to David Harrison, International Institute for Culture, Tourism and Development, London Metropolitan University, 277–281 Holloway Road, London, N7 8HN, UK (d.harrison@ londonmet.ac.uk) or Overseas Development Institute, 111 Westminster Bridge Road, London, SE1 7JD, UK (d.harrison@odi.org.uk).

Notes

1. Partners are Caroline Ashley (Overseas Development Institute, London), Harold Goodwin (Centre for Responsible Tourism, University of Greenwich, London) and Dilys Roe (Institute for Environment and Development, London).
2. Research in this region, and elsewhere in Lao PDR, was carried out in two phases by David Harrison, a co-author of this paper, first in June 2002 (as a consultant for the Asian Development Bank) and then in July and August of 2004, as part of an ASEAN-EU Universities Network Programme, 'Building Research Capacity for Pro-poor Tourism'. Funded from 2003 until 2005 by the European Commission, this project involved five partner organisations from Europe and South East Asia: the International Institute for Culture, Tourism and Development, at London Metropolitan University, the University of Liege (Belgium), the University of Social

Science (Viet Nam), Udayana University (Bali, Indonesia) and the National University of Laos. Data on tourism and poverty alleviation were obtained in Lao PDR in July and August 2004, and special thanks are due to Dr Sengdeuane Wayakone, of the National University of Laos, and Dr I Nyoman Adiputra, of Udayana Univiersity, who also participated in the Lao part of the research project. Further information on the project can be obtained from www.iictd.org.

3. The owner of a five-room guest house with an attached restaurant, and 55% occupancy over a year, could expect to receive a gross income of about $9000 ($1004 for the accommodation, at $1.00 a night per room) and about $8000 for food. The initial investment of about $2000 should be recouped within a few years.

References

Adams, W.M. (1990) *Green Development: Environment and Sustainability in the Third World*. London: Allen and Unwin.

Allcock, A. (2004) *National Tourism Strategy for Lao PDR: 2005 to 2015*. Vientiane: National Tourism Authority of Lao PDR.

Andronicou, A. (1979) Tourism in Cyprus. In E. de Kadt (ed.) *Tourism: Passport to Development?* (pp. 237–264). Oxford: Oxford University Press.

Archer, B. (1996) Economic impact analysis. *Annals of Tourism Research* 23 (3), 704–707.

Ashley, C. (2000) *Pro-Poor Tourism: Putting Poverty at the Heart of the Tourism Agenda*. Overseas Development Institute Paper 51, London.

Ashley, C., Roe, D. and Goodwin, H. (2001) *Pro-Poor Tourism Strategies: Making Tourism Work for the Poor – A Review of Experience*. London: Overseas Development Institute, International Institute for Environment and Development, and Centre for Responsible Tourism.

Asian Development Bank (ADB) (1999a) *Social Sector Profiles: Lao PDR. Strategic Forward Look*. Manila: ADB.

Asian Development Bank (ADB) (1999b) Regional Technical Assistance 5893: Mekong/Lancang River Tourism Infrastructure Development Project.

Asian Development Bank (ADB) (2002a) Report and Recommendation of the President to the Board of Directors on Proposed Loans to the Kingdom of Cambodia, Lao People's Democratic Republic, and Socialist Republic of Viet Nam for the Greater Mekong Subregion: Mekong Tourism Development Project. Manila: ADB.

Asian Development Bank (ADB) (2002b) *Building on Success: A Strategic Framework for the Next Ten Years of the Greater Mekong Subregion Economic Cooperation Program*. Manila: ADB.

Asian Development Bank (ADB) (2002c) *Memorandum of Understanding Between the Government of Lao PDR and the Asian Development Bank for the Mekong Tourism Development Project*. Vientiane.

Asian Development Bank (ADB) (2005) *The Greater Mekong Subregion Tourism Sector Strategy*. Manila: ADB.

Baird, I. (1999) Environmental Protection and Community Development in Siphandone Wetland, Champassak Province, Lao PDR: Towards sustainable co-management of Mekong River Inland Aquatic Resources, including fisheries, in southern Lao PDR. Champassak Province: CESVI/Centre for Protected Areas and Watershed Management, Department of Forestry.

Boo, E. (1990) *Ecotourism: The Potentials and Pitfalls*: (Vols 1 and 2). Washington: World Wildlife Fund/USAID.

Butcher, J. (2003) *The Moralisation of Tourism: Sun, Sand . . . And Saving the World?* London: Routledge.

Butler, R. (1992) Alternative tourism: The thin end of the wedge. In V.L. Smith and W.R. Eadington (eds) *Tourism Alternatives: Potentials and Problems in the Development of Tourism* (pp. 31–46). Philadelphia: University of Pennsylvania Press.

Butler, R. (1999) Sustainable tourism: A state-of-the-art review. *Tourism Geographies* 1 (1), 7–25.

Cater, E. and Lowman, G. (1994) *Ecotourism: A Sustainable Option*. Chichester: Wiley.

Chambers, E. (2000) *Native Tours: The Anthropology of Travel and Tourism.* Illinois: Waveland Press.

Chazée, L. (2002) *The Peoples of Laos: Rural and Ethnic Diversities.* Bangkok: White Lotus Press.

Cohen, E. (1989) Alternative tourism: A critique. In T.V. Singh, H.L. Theuns and G.M. Go (eds) *Towards Appropriate Tourism: The Case of Developing Countries* (pp. 251–269). Frankfurt: Peter Lang.

Cummings, J. (2002) *Laos.* London: Lonely Planet.

de Kadt, E. (ed.) (1979a) *Tourism: Passport to Development?* Oxford: Oxford University Press.

de Kadt, E. (1979b) The issues addressed. In E. de Kadt (ed.) *Tourism: Passport to Development?* (pp. 3–67). Oxford: Oxford University Press.

de Kadt, E. (1979c) Preface. In E. de Kadt (ed.) *Tourism: Passport to Development?* (pp. ix–xvi). Oxford: Oxford University Press.

Denman, R. and Denman, J. (2004) *Tourism and Poverty Alleviation: Recommendations for Action.* Madrid: WTO.

Department for International Development (DFID) (1999) *Tourism and Poverty Elimination: Untapped Potential.* UK: DFID.

Department for International Development (DFID) (2004) *Tourism and Poverty Elimination: Untapped Potential.* UK: DFID.

Duffy, R. (2002) *A Trip too Far: Ecotourism Politics and Exploitation.* London: Earthscan.

Enterprise Development Consultants Co. Ltd. (2002) *Generating Employment through Micro and Small Enterprise and Co-operatives in Lao, PDR.* Geneva: International Labour Organisation.

UN Economic and Social Commission for Asia and the Pacific (ESCAP) (2005) The contribution of tourism to pooverty alleviation. *ESCAP Tourism Review No. 25.* United Nations.

Fennell, D.A. (1999) *Ecotourism: An Introduction.* London: Routledge.

Fennell, D.A. (2001) A content analysis of ecotourism definitions. *Current Issues in Tourism* 4 (5), 403–421.

Freitag, T.G. (1994) Enclave tourism development: For whom the benefits roll? *Annals of Tourism Research* 21 (3), 538–554.

Gerosa, V. (2003) Tourism: A viable option for pro-poor growth in Africa? *Expert Group Meeting,* Munyonyo Speke Resort, Kampala, Uganda, 23–24 June.

Groupe Huit (1979) The sociocultural effects of tourism in Tunisia: A case study of Sousse. In E. de Kadt (ed.) *Tourism: Passport to Development?* (pp. 285–304). Oxford: Oxford University Press.

Guttal, S. (2006) Marketing the Mekong: The Asian Development Bank and the Greater Mekong Sub-region Economic Cooperation Program. Jubilee South. On WWW at www.jubileesouth.org/news/EpZyVyEAZFESZsvoiN.shtml. Accessed 1.1.06.

Hall, C.M. (2000) Tourism in Cambodia, Laos and Myanmar: From terrorism to tourism? In C.M. Hall and S. Page (eds) *Tourism in South and South East Asia: Issues and Cases* (pp. 178–194). Oxford: Butterworth-Heinemann.

Hall, C.M., Jenkins, J. and Kearsley, G. (1997) *Tourism Planning and Policy in Australia and New Zealand.* Sydney: Irwin.

Hamilton-Merritt, J. (1999) *Tragic Mountains: The Hmong, the Americans, and the Secret Wars for Laos, 1942–1992.* Bloomington: Indiana University Press.

Harrison, D. (1996) Sustainability and tourism: Reflections from a muddy pool. In B. Briguglio, R. Butler, D. Harrison and W. Leal Filho (eds) *Sustainable Tourism in Islands and Small States: Issues and Policies* (pp. 69–89). London: Pinter.

Harrison, D. (ed.) (2001) *Tourism and the Less Developed World: Issues and Case Studies.* Wallingford: CAB International.

Harrison, D. and Schipani, S. (forthcoming) Tourism in the Lao People's Democratic Republic. In M. Hitchcock, T. King and M. Parnwell (eds) *Tourism in South East Asia Revisited.* Copenhagen: NIAS.

Honey, M. (1999) *Ecotourism and Sustainable Development: Who Owns Paradise?* Washington: Island Press.

Jafari, J. (1989) Sociocultural dimensions of tourism: An English language literature review. In J.Bystrzanowski (ed.) *Tourism as a Factor in Social Change, Vol. I: A Sociocultural Study* (pp. 17–60). Vienna: International Social Science Council, European Coordination Centre for Research and Documentation in Social Sciences.

Jamieson, W. (2003) *Poverty Alleviation Through Sustainable Tourism Development*. Bankok: United Nations.

Johnston, A.M. (2006) *Is the Sacred for Sale?* London and Sterling, VA: Earthscan.

Kiss, A. (2004) Is community-based ecotourism a good use of biodiversity funds? *Trends in Ecology and Evolution* 19 (5), 232–237.

Lao National Tourism Administration (2006) *2005 Statistical Report on Tourism in Laos*. Vientiane: Planning and Cooperation Department Statistics Unit.

Lao People's Democratic Republic (Lao PDR) (1990) *National Plan for the Development of Tourism in the Lao People's Democratic Republic*. Vientiane: United Nations Development Programme.

Lao People's Democratic Republic (Lao PDR) (2004) *National Growth and Poverty Eradication Strategy*. Vientiane: Lao PDR.

Lao People's Democratic Republic (Lao PDR) (2006) Presentation on *Lao Investmnent Promotion at Tourism Round Table, Mekong Tourism Investment Summit, 'Expanding "Win-Win" Business Opportunities in the GMS'*, Luang Prabang, 28–30 March.

Lao People's Democratic Republic, United Nations Development Programme and the World Tourism Organisation (Lao PDR, UNDP and WTO) (1998) *National Tourism Development Plan for Lao PDR*. Vientiane: Lao PDR.

Lao People's Democratic Republic, United Nations Development Programme and the World Tourism Organisation (Lao PDR, UNDP and WTO) (1999) *National Tourism Marketing Plan for Lao PDR*. Vientiane: Lao PDR.

Lindberg, K., Enriquez, J. and Sproule, K. (1996) Ecotourism questioned: Case studies from Belize. *Annals of Tourism Research* 23 (3), 543–562.

Lyttleton, C. and Allcock, A. (2002) *Tourism as a Tool for Development: UNESCO-Lao National Tourism Authority Nam Ha Ecotourism Project–External Review July 6–18 2002*. Vientiane: NTAL and UNESCO.

Ministry of Foreign Affairs and Trade (1995) NZODA support for eco-tourism in Fiji: A report of a study. Wellington: Appraisal, Evaluation and Analytical Support Unit, Development Co-operation Division.

Momsen, J. (1972) *Report on Vegetable Production and the Tourist Industry in St. Lucia*. Canada: Dept. of Geography, University of Calgary.

Momsen, J.H. (1986) Linkages between tourism and agriculture: problems for smaller Caribbean economies. Seminar Paper 45, Dept. of Geography, University of Newcastle upon Tyne.

Mowforth, M. and Munt, I. (2003) *Tourism and Sustainability: Development and New Tourism in the Third World* (2nd edn). London: Routledge.

Nash, D. (1977) Tourism as a form of Imperialism. In V.L. Smith (ed) *Hosts and Guests: The Anthropology of Tourism* (pp. 33–47). Oxford: Blackwell.

Nash, D. (1996) *Anthropology of Tourism*. Oxford: Pergamon.

National Tourism Authority of Lao PDR (2004) *2003 Statistical Report on Tourism in Laos*. Vientiane: NTAL, Statistics, Planning and Co-operation Division.

National Tourism Authority of Lao PDR (2005) *National Ecotourism Strategy and Action Plan: 2004–2010*. Vientiane: NTAL.

Page, S. (1999) *Tourism and Development: The Evidence from Mauritius, South Africa, and Zimbabwe*. London: Overseas Development Institute.

Peters, M. (1969) *International Tourism: The Economics and Development of the International Tourism Trade*. London: Hutchinson.

Pro-Poor Tourism Partnership (2006) On WWW at http://www.propoortourism.org.uk/ppt_pubs_workingpapers.html. Accessed 18.4.06.

Rodenburg, E.E. (1980) The effects of scale in economic development: Tourism in Bali. *Annals of Tourism Research* 7 (2), 177–196.

Scheyvens, R. (2002) *Tourism for Development: Empowering Communities*. London: Longman.

Scheyvens, R. (2004) Tourism, globalisation and poverty-alleviation: Compatible goals? Paper presented at *DevNet Conference: 'Development on the Edge'*, Auckland University, 3–5 December.

Schipani, S. (2002) *Ecotourism Status Report: Lao PDR*. Vientiane: SNV Lao PDR.

Smith, V. (ed) (1978a) *Hosts and Guests: The Anthropology of Tourism*. Oxford: Blackwell.

Smith, V. (1978b) Introduction. In V.L. Smith (ed.) *Hosts and Guests: The Anthropology of Tourism* (pp. 1–14). Oxford: Basil Blackwell.

Smith, S. (1983) Class analysis versus world system: critique of Samir Amin's typology of development. In P. Limqueco and B. McFarlane (eds) *Neo-Marxist Theories of Development* (pp. 73–86). London: Croom Helm.

SNV (2006) SNV: Lao PDR. On WWW at http://www.snv.org.la. Accessed 2.1.06.

Telfer, D. (2002) Evolution of tourism and development theory. In. R. Sharpley and D.J. Telfer (eds) *Tourism and Development: Concepts and Issues* (pp. 35–79). Clevedon: Channel View Publications.

Timothy, D.J. and Wall, G. (1997) Selling to tourists: Indonesian street vendors. *Annals of Tourism Research* 24 (2), 322–340.

Torres, R. and Henshall Momsen, J. (2004) Challenges and potential for linking tourism and agriculture to achieve pro-poor tourism objectives. *Progress in Development Studies* 4 (4), 294–318.

United Nations Development Programme (UNDP) (2005) *Human Development Report 2005*. Oxford: UNDP/Oxford University Press.

UNESCO (2005) *Nam Ha Ecotourism Project Phase II, Project Document*. Bangkok: Office of the UNESCO Regional Advisor for Culture in Asia and the Pacific.

van den Berghe, P.L. (1994) *The Quest for the Other: Ethnic Tourism in San Cristobal, Mexico*. Seattle and London: University of Washington Press.

Walpole, M.J. and Goodwin, H.J. (2000) Local economic impacts of dragon tourism in Indonesia. *Annals of Tourism Research* 27 (3), 559–576.

Warner, R. (1997) *Shooting at the Moon: Story of America's Clandestine War in Laos*. Vermont: Steerforth Press.

Weaver, D.B. (1998) *Ecotourism in the Less Developed World*. Wallingford: CAB International.

Wheeller, B. (1993) Sustaining the ego. *Journal of Sustainable Tourism* 1 (2), 121–129.

Wilson, D. (1979) The early effects of tourism in the Seychelles. In E. de Kadt (ed.) *Tourism: Passport to Development?* (pp. 205–236). Oxford: Oxford University Press.

World Bank (2005) Country Assistance Strategy for the Lao People's Democratic Republic (PDR). Report No. 31758 LA, 10 March. East Asia and Pacific Region: Southeast Asia Country Unit.

World Tourism Organisation (WTO) (1996) *Compendium of Tourism Statistics: 1990–1994*. Madrid: WTO.

World Tourism Organisation (WTO) (1999) *Compendium of Tourism Statistics: 1993–1996*. Madrid: WTO.

World Tourism Organisation (WTO) (2001) *Compendium of Tourism Statistics: 2001 Edition*. Madrid: WTO.

World Tourism Organisation (WTO) (2002) *Tourism and Poverty Alleviation*. Madrid: WTO.

World Tourism Organisation (WTO) (2005) *Compendium of Tourism Statistics: Data 1999–2003. 2005 Edition*. Madrid: WTO.

Exploring the Tourism-Poverty Nexus

Regina Scheyvens
School of People, Environment and Planning, Massey University,
Palmerston North, New Zealand

Current discourse surrounding 'pro-poor tourism', a term emerging out of the writing of UK researchers in the late 1990s, suggests that tourism can effectively work as a tool to alleviate poverty. This proposition is alluring given that tourism is a significant or growing economic sector in most countries with high levels of poverty. Consequently the idea of utilising tourism to eliminate poverty has been embraced by donors, governments, non-governmental organisations, conservation organisations and tourism bodies, including the World Tourism Organisation. Academic views on the relationship between poverty and tourism have however varied widely over the past half century. While in the 1950s tourism was identified as a modernisation strategy that could help newly-independent Third World countries to earn foreign exchange, in the 1970s and 1980s many social scientists argued that poor people and non-Western countries are typically excluded from or disadvantaged by what tourism can offer. It is thus fascinating to see how there has been a concerted push towards a reversal of this thinking in the 1990s, coinciding with the development industry's global focus on poverty alleviation. This paper will detail this evolution of thinking and in doing so, explore theoretical debates on the tourism-poverty nexus.

doi: 10.2167/cit318.0

Keywords: poverty, development, pro-poor tourism

Introduction

Poverty is rife in our world. Despite decades of development planning, aid projects and programmes, grants, loans and structural adjustment, limited progress has been made in eliminating poverty. In fact, the number of countries with LDC (least developed country) status has grown from 25 in 1971 to 49 in 2002 (Saraogi, 2004). It is in this context that poverty-alleviation has become the leading development agenda in the past decade and 'pro-poor' discourse has come to the fore. However this 'poverty consensus' has been criticised because it tends to overlook important environmental, social and political issues: 'the pro-poor development paradigm ... is considerably circumscribed in its premise of economic growth as the foundation of development' (Mowforth & Munt, 2003: 34).

Nevertheless 'tourism' and 'poverty-alleviation' are being increasingly linked. The tourism industry, it is argued, offers an ideal avenue through which poorer countries can open up to the benefits of globalisation. There does seem to be significant potential to deliver more benefits from tourism to the poor, as tourism is a significant or growing economic sector in most countries with high levels of poverty. In over 50 of the world's poorest countries tourism is one of the top three contributors to economic development (World

Tourism Organisation, 2000, cited in Sofield, 2003: 350). The tourism industry already employs over 200 million people world wide, and there has been a 9.5% annual growth in arrivals to developing countries since 1990, compared to 4.6% worldwide (IIED, 2001). While tourism accounts for up to 10% of GDP in Western countries, in the developing world it contributes up to 40% of GDP (Sofield *et al.*, 2004: 2). Meanwhile, many countries are being forced to look beyond their traditional agricultural exports because of the declining value of these products have (e.g. bananas, cocoa, coffee and sugar). Comparing the value of such crops with tourism receipts for South Pacific countries over a 20-year period, it has been found that '*in every case* the value of these primary products in real terms has declined and the only sector to demonstrate a continuous upward trend has been tourism' (Sofield *et al.*, 2004: 25–26). Furthermore, the United Nations Conference on Trade and Development (UNCTAD, 1998) refers to tourism as the 'only major sector in international trade in services in which developing countries have consistently had surpluses'. It is argued that tourism as a sector 'fits' nicely with pro-poor growth because

> It can be labour-intensive, inclusive of women and the informal sector; based on natural and cultural assets of the poor; and suitable for poor rural areas with few other growth options. (Ashley & Roe, 2002: 61)

Thus support for tourism as a means of poverty alleviation has grown considerably since 1990. However, there is a need for caution as tourism statistics can be interpreted differently depending on what argument you wish to make. For example despite good growth in the tourism sector, Plüss and Backes (2002: 10) stress that in 10 of the 13 countries which are home to 80% of the world's people who live in extreme poverty, tourism has not been able to reduce poverty. Some advocates of tourism are also prone to exaggerate claims for what tourism can achieve. These claims extend well beyond rosy economic projections for tourism earnings, with some suggesting that tourism is a universal panacea for overcoming poverty, inequality, and even conflict (see IIPT, 2004).

It is thus apparent that there is a need for critical reflection on the origins and approaches associated with pro-poor tourism (PPT), which has in the new millennium captured the interest and imagination of a wide range of tourism and development organisations. Speaking of the most popular tourism term of the 1990s, 'ecotourism', Brennan and Allen (2001: 219) contend that it is 'essentially an ideal, promoted by well-fed whites'. Could the same be said of PPT, or is it likely to deliver genuine, wide-ranging benefits to the poor? This paper will explore the growth of interest in tourism as a means of poverty reduction, firstly, by reflecting on the poverty agenda that has come to absorb so much of the energy and resources of the development industry, and then considering how the evolution of PPT fits within this context. Secondly, the paper looks at different theoretical perspectives on the relationship between tourism and development, and then uses these theories to analyse the different approaches to PPT adopted by various agencies. The paper concludes with reflections on the poverty-tourism nexus, and highlights concerns that need to be addressed if tourism is to work effectively to reduce poverty.

The Poverty Agenda

'Pro-poor tourism' (PPT), which was coined to mean 'tourism that generates net benefits for the poor' (Ashley & Roe, 2002: 62) was first used in the development literature in 1999 (see Deloitte & Touche, 1999). It was inspired broadly by the development industry's move in the 1990s to establish poverty alleviation as the number one development agenda. Thus before explicitly discussing the evolution of PPT, it is important to gain an understanding of what has been driving the global development industry in recent times.

A pro-poor focus in the development industry arose in direct response to criticisms of the effects of structural adjustment programmes (SAPs) which had been imposed on many developing countries from the 1970s onwards. SAPs were driven by the logic that structural reforms could lead these countries out of indebtedness and put them on the road to economic recovery. In fact the impacts of SAPs on many societies were extremely harsh due to reductions in government support for various industries and the requirement of fiscal constraint (particularly, cuts in social spending), meaning poverty was in some cases entrenched (Dent & Peters, 1999). Widespread criticism of SAPs lead to reforms such as 'Adjustment with a Human Face', a softer approach to SAPs endorsed by UNICEF, being adopted in the late 1980s (Storey *et al.*, 2005).

It was however the decade of the 1990s that heralded a new approach to development, one which centred on poverty alleviation. This focus on poverty proved alluring: 'It has provided a powerful rallying cry – a new development mantra – for those in development practice and charged with garnering flagging political and financial support for aid programmes' (Storey *et al.*, 2005: 30). The World Bank and UNDP came out in favour of this approach in 1990, followed by the Development Assistance Committee of the OECD which established International Development Targets (the precursors of the Millennium Development Goals) in 1996. Concurrently a number of multilateral and bilateral donors also came on board to endorse the poverty agenda, e.g. DFID in 1991, and AusAID in 1997. By 1999 the IMF introduced Poverty Reduction Strategy Papers (PRSPs) as a more participatory, poverty-focused alternative to SAPs. Interestingly, in 80% of PRSPs tourism is identified as an important economic sector (Mann, 2005: iv), leading to the suggestion tourism can be effectively targeted towards benefiting the poor through PRSPs. However PRSPs are not dramatically different from SAPs: they still work on the principle of attaching conditionality to loans, and the main focus remains private sector development, macroeconomic growth, and liberalisation (Storey *et al.*, 2005).

This period was characterised by what many see as a consensus on poverty, including the belief that poverty results from poor governance and protected economies, and that globalisation offers a path out of poverty. Thus blame for economies that were failing was placed squarely with those countries themselves rather than recognising the roles that outside structures and institutions, historically and contemporarily, play in producing the conditions for poverty (Erbelei, 2000). In this way the poverty consensus does not reject the dominant neoliberal development path, rather, it compliments and builds upon this (Storey *et al.*, 2005). Policies which have been introduced under neoliberalism, including efforts to privatise basic services such as electricity and water, or to individualise ownership of communally held resources, can be seen as contrary to the interests of the poor in many circumstances.

Associated with the poverty consensus are the Millennium Development Goals, a set of eight goals that are almost universally supported, having been agreed upon by all 191 Member States of the United Nations:

(1)   eradicate extreme poverty and hunger;
(2)   achieve universal primary education;
(3)   promote gender equality;
(4)   reduce child mortality;
(5)   improve maternal health;
(6)   control HIV/AIDS, malaria and other diseases;
(7)   ensure environmental sustainability;
(8)   develop a global partnership for development.

The World Tourism Organisation has endorsed the MDGs and claims that increasing tourism will help countries to fight the 'war on poverty':

> For poor countries and small island states, tourism is the leading export – often the only sustainable growth sector of their economies and a catalyst for many related sectors. It can play a key role in the overall achievement of the Millennium Development Goals by 2015. (World Tourism Organisation, 2005)

However there are critics of the MDGs. Bond (2006) argues that the development of the MDGs has been led in a top-down fashion by countries and organisations whose policies directly undermine the well-being of the poor in much of the world, namely, the G8, World Bank, International Monetary Fund, World Trade Organisation, and third world elites. If we look closely at some of these organisations, it is clear that there is a significant mismatch between rhetoric and reality with relation to their commitment to poverty alleviation. The IMF, for example demands budget surpluses yet this undermines possibilities for social spending (Öniş & Şenses, 2005). We can also consider the World Trade Organisation's policies with respect to agriculture. As Torres and Momsen (2004) note, agriculture ideally should be able to compliment tourism. However the World Trade Organisation has effectively undermined the agricultural sector in many countries by allowing dumping of food surpluses from protected Western markets in developing country markets at prices lower than cost, supporting the removal of trade barriers and thus allowing large agribusiness companies to dominate agricultural production in some areas, and by preventing Third World governments from providing certain forms of support for local farmers (Bond, 2006).

Thus attention to poverty reduction from the organisations and individuals referred to above leads women's development advocate, Peggy Antrobus, to suggest that the MDGs are simply a 'Major Distraction Gimmick' (cited in Bond, 2006: 341). The implication here is that the emphasis on poverty reduction is a means of window dressing which may deflect criticism of earlier neoliberal policies, when the fundamental neoliberal orthodoxy on which the operations of many development-related organisations are based has barely changed: '... one gets the strong impression that the Bretton Woods institutions are using the poverty issue as a pretext for broadening and deepening the neoliberal agenda' (Öniş & Şenses, 2005: 280).

Other movements have been inspired by the MDGs including 'Make Poverty History', which at one high point in July 2005 saw 250,000 people march on the streets of Edinburgh to demand that leaders attending the G8 summit in Gleneagles made poverty history, and the Live8 rock concerts held at the same time. While these initiatives were a powerful expression of public concern over global poverty and garnered much popular support for the cause, they assume that powerful institutions can be reformed from within. This leads Bond to suggest that such initiatives 'all suffer from the direction of their gaze – to the powerful' (Bond, 2006: 342).

It is important now to consider how the evolution of pro-poor tourism is linked to this consensus on poverty.

The Evolution of Pro-Poor Tourism

The emergence of PPT is strongly associated with the development industry's 1990s-onwards global focus on poverty alleviation. Specifically, however, it evolved out of UK-sponsored research on sustainable livelihoods in southern Africa (see e.g. Ashley & Roe, 1998), and a comparative study of tourism, conservation and sustainability issues in protected areas of Indonesia, India and Zimbabwe (PPT Partnership, 2005a). Tourism began to emerge as an industry which had considerable potential to improve the well-being of rural communities in some parts of the work, thus the UK's Department for International Development (DFID) together with the Department for Environment, Transport and the Regions (DETR) commissioned a paper to be written on Sustainable Tourism and Poverty Elimination (Goodwin, 1998). The British delegation to the 1999 meeting of the UN Commission on Sustainable Development (CSD7), then used this information to get tourism as a means of poverty alleviation on the agenda in light of the framework of the Rio conference which had emphasised the need to consider both development and the environment when devising strategies for sustainable development. After CSD7, governments were urged to 'maximise the potential of tourism for eradicating poverty by developing appropriate strategies in cooperation with all major groups, indigenous and local communities' (IIED, 2001b: 41).

In 2000 the Overseas Development Institute (ODI) initiated a research project focused on analysing the theoretical basis of PPT and examining case studies of tourism in practice (Ashley *et al.*, 2001). This study was conducted by the Pro-Poor Tourism Partnership, a collaboration of Harold Goodwin (International Centre for Responsible Tourism), Dilys Roe (International Institute for Environemnt and Development), and Caroline Ashley (Overseas Development Institute). Since then the PPT Partnership has been responsible for a wide range of studies on PPT, often funded by DFID and the ODI (see e.g. Ashley & Roe, 2002; Roe *et al.*, 2002).[1] For example, it has been involved in a major 'PPT Pilots' programme in South Africa which works with a small number of private sector tourism enterprises to develop more pro-poor initiatives and linkages (e.g. procurement from small, locally based enterprises) (PPT Partnership, 2005a).

The next major player to take on board the idea of PPT was the World Tourism Organisation which, together with UNCTAD initiated its ST-EP programme ('Sustainable Tourism–Eliminating Poverty') in 2002. ST-EP was launched at the World Summit on Sustainable Development in Johannesburg with the aim of promoting sustainable tourism development as a means of poverty alleviation. It has since been developed in terms of a three part framework: a Foundation to generate funds for poverty-alleviation through tourism; a research network to link poverty alleviation and sustainable tourism; and a mechanism to provide seeding money for model projects (Sofield *et al.*, 2004: 17). A US$5 million donation from the government of the Republic of Korea in 2003 has led to the ST-EP Foundation being based in this country. The WTO has since established a Trust Fund for ST-EP which aims to attract funds from multiple donors and to use these funds for technical assistance towards tourism development that aims to reduce poverty. SNV, the Netherlands development organisation, was the initial founder contributing €2 million for 2005 and 2006, while the Italian government provided a smaller contribution for 2005 (PPT Partnership, 2005a).

A range of other agencies have also demonstrated commitment to PPT. They include development agencies and donors (e.g. German agency GTZ), tourism industry organisations (e.g. Pacific and Asia Travel Assocation – PATA), NGOs (e.g. IUCN – the World Conservation Union), research centres/universities (e.g. the Cooperative Research Centre for Sustainable Tourism in Australia, Asian Institute of Technology in Bangkok, George Washington University, and London Metropolitan University) and multilateral organisations (e.g. the Asian Development Bank). Other UN agencies supporting poverty alleviation through tourism include the United Nations Development Programme and United Nations Environment Programme.

Theoretical Perspectives on Tourism and Development

Clearly PPT has, in a relatively short period of time, attracted attention from a wide range of institutions. In this context it is wise to consider motivations behind the push for pro-poor tourism: for example is this coming from organisations that genuinely want a greater share of the multi-million dollar tourism industry to be directed towards the poor, or is it influenced more by neoliberal free trade and economic growth logic? In order to explore motivations behind the wave of interest in PPT, this next section will examine ways in which the relationship between tourism and development has been conceptualised over time. Figure 1 provides a summary of the ideas to be discussed, focusing on several theoretical approaches: liberal/neoliberal, critical, alternative development and post-structuralist. The arrows indicate that while all of these approaches have in some ways contributed to the growth of interest in PPT, it has been particularly influenced by neoliberal and alternative development thinking.

Liberal perspectives

The early liberal approach to tourism is epitomised by the logic of modernisation theory, which informed development practice particularly from the

Liberal/neo-liberal	Critical	Alternative Development	Post-structuralist
[1950s–1960s] Tourism can contribute to modernisation through economic growth, employment generation and the exchange of ideas; benefits will trickle down to the poor. [1980s onwards] Tourism offers a way out of indebtedness: 'trade your way out of poverty'. It encourages foreign investment and private sector development while providing employment and generating foreign exchange. [late 1990s onwards] Tourism is promoted hand-in-hand with free trade, democratisation and anti-poverty agendas. Investment in tourism in third world countries gives foreign companies a presence in major or growing markets. Poverty Reduction Strategy Papers identify tourism as an economic sector that can reduce poverty. Public-private partnerships encouraged. Tourism is seen as a means of helping to overcome the poverty and inequality which can breed terrorism.	[1970s – 1980s] Tourism is associated with enclave development, dependence on foreign capital and expertise, growing social and economic disparities, and repatriation of profits. It often undermines local cultures, social networks and traditional livelihoods e.g. when people are resettled so national parks can be created. [1990s onwards] Anti-globalisation lobby sees tourism as a means of advancing the forces of capitalism into more remote places and cultures. Postcolonial writers comment on the allure of the 'other' – poverty attracts tourists as poor places are associated with 'authentic' experiences of culture and nature. Strong class differences between 'hosts' and 'guests' are noted.	[late 1970s onwards] Alternative forms of tourism that are small-scale, involve education of tourists and more local control over tourism, are seen as worthy of promotion. e.g. justice tours, conservation tours. [1980s onwards] The 'green agenda' of the 1980s and the UN Summit in Rio in 1992 lead to renewed emphasis on the environment including ecological and social sustainability. Ecotourism comes to the fore. [1990s onwards] Tourism offers poor communities a means of diversifying their livelihood options. Communities can actively participate in tourism and be empowered through their experiences.	[1990s onwards] Rejects reductionist thinking: tourism is neither 'good' nor 'bad'. Stresses the need to take a holistic view which sees tourism as a complex system in which local people can exert power: they may be able to resist, subvert, manipulate, or transform tourism to their own benefit. Important to acknowledge dissenting viewpoints.

Tourism for Poverty Reduction Programmes

The work of the Pro-Poor Tourism Partnership, the World Tourism Organization's ST – EP (Sustainable Tourism – Eliminating Poverty) programme, SNV (Netherlands' development agency) and other proponents of tourism for poverty alleviation is influenced to varying degrees by these different theoretical frameworks.

Figure 1 Theoretical perspectives on the relationship between tourism and poverty[4]

1950s through to the 1970s. From this perspective tourism is regarded as 'a catalyst for modernisation, economic development and prosperity in emerging nations in the third world' (Williams, 1998: 1), an industry which generates jobs and foreign exchange, while also bringing beneficial sociocultural change in terms of demonstrating 'modern' ways of life to people living in traditional cultures. This approach thus endorses tourism as a means of bringing develop- ment to poorer countries and as such it accords with what Jafari (2001: 29–30), in his analysis of scholarly work on tourism, calls the 'advocacy platform'. It could also be described as a 'Tourism First' approach, which seeks expansion of the sector, sanctions globalisation and the needs of the tourism industry, as opposed to a 'Development First' approach which is more concerned with sustainable development of tourism and the needs of local people (Burns, 2004: 26).

Critical perspectives

When it became clear that economic growth often did not 'trickle-down' to benefit the poor, there was a backlash against liberal development thought from scholars inspired by dependency and political economy theory. Adopting explicitly critical perspectives, these scholars suggest that the prospects for international tourism to erode inequalities between people in different parts of the world are slim, and that in fact tourism in many cases exploits, highlights, and entrenches these differences (Britton, 1982; Brohman, 1996). Numerous studies have made this point, from work in the 1970s which signified a major shift in thinking away from the idea that tourism auto- matically led to poverty alleviation (see e.g. de Kadt, 1979; Nash, 1977; Smith, 1977), through to contemporary studies still drawing heavily on dependency theory (e.g. Mbaiwa, 2005).

Critics are concerned that the push for poor regions and countries to develop tourism is centred squarely on a combination of beautiful 'untouched' natural and cultural attractions: 'Tourism is promoted today as an industry that can turn poor countries' very poverty into a magnet for sorely needed foreign currency. For to be a poor society in the late twentieth century is to be "unspoilt"' (Enloe 1990:31). Combined with these unspoilt characteristics, poor countries also offer cheap labour: 'to some extent tourism always feeds off the poverty of host regions' (Plüss & Backes, 2002: 12). While governments will invest in infrastructure to meet the needs of tourists, local people often have to live without the basics. Thus there may be plenty of fresh water for the resort swimming pool or golf course, but insufficient water to irrigate nearby crops and no provision of piped drinking water to adjacent villages (Richter, 2001: 50). Postcolonial scholars note that tourism embodies power relations between 'the West' and 'the Rest', building on inequalities established through colonial relationships (Hall & Tucker, 2004). Thus tourists' travel fan- tasies may be fuelled by images of dark skinned porters, waiters, masseurs and other modern day service industry workers who will be at their beck and call.

The critical perspectives of tourism concur with what Jafari (2001: 29–30) refers to as the 'cautionary platform', a particular body of tourism scholarship which proclaims that tourism has a wide range of negative impacts, including cultural commodification, social disruption, and environmental degradation.

In addition, it is argued, the economic benefits of tourism are minimised because foreign companies, which dominate many developing countries, repatriate their profits. UNCTAD estimates that an average of 40–50% of foreign exchange earnings returns to the home countries of the tourists (Plüss & Backes, 2002: 11). There are further concerns that the expansion of capitalist relations can undermine sustainable livelihoods (Mowforth & Munt, 2003: 273). Governments cannot legislate to protect national interests by, e.g. providing subsidies to support domestic tourism businesses because under the General Agreement on Trade in Services, this is seen as 'trade-restrictive' (Mowforth & Munt, 2003: 266). Overseas companies and investors which come into a country under pro-globalisation policies (e.g. tax breaks and other investment incentives) can push out small, local investors or businesses who find they cannot compete. And when multinational companies and international agencies loan funds for infrastructure development for tourism, they gain increasing control over the industry in the destination area (Telfer, 2003: 100).

Neoliberal perspectives

The liberal approach discussed above was followed, in the 1970s and 1980s, by a surge of support for neoliberalism which stressed the importance of econ-omic rationalism and efficiency, market liberalisation, and a minimal role for the state, whose institutions were seen as interfering with free market processes (Öniş & Şenses, 2005). Such policies, packaged together and based on an 'unquestioning belief in the benefits of the free market', came to be known as the 'Washington Consensus' on poverty alleviation (Hart, 2001: 286). Key financial institutions such as the World Bank and IMF were quick to pick up on such neoliberal thinking, as it rose to the fore in the face of the indebtedness of many developing countries. In order to facilitate developing countries to pay off their debts, the World Bank and IMF introduced the structural adjustment programmes (SAPs) referred to earlier. International tourism was seen to fit nicely into a strategy of encouraging indebted countries to grow the economy and trade their way out of poverty (Brohman, 1996). However this outward-oriented approach whereby state action is heavily influenced by the neoliberal agendas of multilateral institutions to whom they are indebted, has meant government decisions do not always concur with the interests of local communities (Carbone, 2005). With regards to tourism planning, this can mean for example that tax breaks are given to foreign investors developing large resorts, while small-scale local entrepreneurs find it difficult to access credit or training needed to improve their enterprises.

The early 1990s heralded a period of serious challenges to the Washington Consensus, as it had become clear that inequalities between developed and developing world economies were growing. Liberalisation of economies did not automatically lead to enhanced economic growth, rather, it often left a vacuum in terms of the state's capacity to manage development and thus corruption increased (Öniş & Şenses, 2005). Meanwhile studies had revealed that the 'miracle' of growth in certain East Asian economies was spurred, in part, by interventionist state strategies and protection of infant industries. Thus there is now talk of a Post-Washington Consensus, or a New Poverty Agenda, supported to a certain extent by the major financial institutions (more so the

WB than the IMF) who have shown willingness to respond to some critiques of global neoliberalism (Hart, 2001; Öniş & Şenses, 2005; Storey *et al.*, 2005).

The emerging PWC is characterised by an emphasis on enhancing the role of the state, rather than letting markets rule unimpeded, an appreciation of the importance of strong institutions, support for democratic governance, and a move to more effectively target the poor and vulnerable (Öniş & Şenses, 2005: 273–275). Thus, for example there is renewed interest in the role of the state in regulating tourism development and facilitating linkages between the private sector and local communities (Sofield, 2003).

If neoliberal perspectives prioritise global, and sometimes national, interests, then the alternative perspectives to be discussed next prioritise local interests.

Alternative perspectives

While acknowledging the concerns of those coming from a critical perspective, some scholars suggest that tourism can contribute to development if it is approached in an alternative way to that proposed by liberal or neoliberal thinkers (Smith & Eadington, 1992). Potter (1993: 97) thus asserts that 'the needs of the poor should be met *in priority* to externally-oriented growth imperatives' (emphasis added).

Alternative approaches to tourism generally support small-scale or locally-based tourism initiatives which attempt to bring benefits to poorer communities, minimise harm to the environment, and aim to build good relationships between 'hosts' and 'guests' (Krippendorf, 1989). They also support the notion that local residents should play an active role in tourism planning and decision-making forums (Murphy, 1985), and support tourism that is fair, just and equitable (Scheyvens, 2002). This thinking accords with Jafari's (2001: 31) notion of the 'Adaptancy Platform', whereby community-focused forms of tourism are proposed as an alternative to the excesses of mainstream tourism. Some of the alternative forms of tourism proposed include 'soft tourism', 'green tourism' (Dann, 2002), 'altruistic tourism' (Singh, 2002), 'volunteer tourism' (Wearing, 2001) and 'justice tourism' (Scheyvens, 2002).

The alternative approaches to tourism as a means of development are informed by a number of bodies of thinking. A sustainable livelihoods perspective has influenced PPT in that tourism is seen as another means of diversifying the livelihood options of the poor. Similarly sustainable development thinking has also supported the growth of interest in PPT as people and poverty, not just the environment, have become central to sustainable development discourse (Neto, 2003), as evidenced by discussions at the 2002 World Summit on Sustainable Development in Johannesburg. Alternative development perspectives centred on grassroots development and embracing ideas on participation, equity, gender-sensitivity and empowerment (Telfer, 2002), have also been used to drive a number of initiatives to make tourism more focused on meeting the needs of the poor. Such initiatives include the 'Fair Trade in Tourism South Africa' campaign and 'Tourism for Rural Poverty Alleviation Programme' in Nepal (PPT Partnership, 2005a).

Jafari (2001) argues that while alternative forms of tourism such as ecotourism, responsible tourism and sustainable tourism, are well-intentioned, they account for only a small proportion of the total tourism product.

Alternative, community-based initiatives are often not successful because of factors ranging from the lack of business skills of community members to the lack of connections to mainstream tourism enterprises. Even when they are successful, they may be limited in reach and they are unlikely to replace other forms of tourism (Harrison, 2003). Endorsement of community tourism is coupled with an assumption that communities will not want to pursue mass tourism (de Kadt, 1992; Jafari, 2001), when in practice this can be seen as more manageable, profitable, and less invasive than alternative forms of tourism (Butler, 1990; Thomlinson & Getz, 1996). Thus, argues Burns,

> Exhortations to 'leave only footprints' … carry an ironic and unintentional truth because footprints with no dollars attached do little to develop the industry to a level of critical mass that can supply large-scale employment and a reliable stream of tax revenues to be used to implement beneficial government policies including health, education, and welfare. (Burns, 2004: 25)

The very focus of alternative development approaches on 'communities' has also been criticised because too often it is assumed that communities are homogeneous entities with shared interests, when in reality most communities are made up of distinct interest groups. Often communities are split into various factions based on a complex interplay of class, gender and ethnic factors, and certain families or individuals are likely to lay claim to privileges because of their apparent status. Elites often co-opt and come to dominate community-based development efforts and monopolise the benefits of tourism (Mowforth & Munt, 2003). Indeed, the poorest of the poor may be excluded from community structures, thus making them very difficult to target if adopting a community-based approach.

In addition, local empowerment alone is not sufficient to corner the benefits of tourism (Sofield, 2003: 346). Rather, it is often necessary for states to intervene to provide appropriate legislation (e.g. to protect local rights to land and to encourage joint venture arrangements, as well as ensuring adequate environmental standards are adhered to) and support in the way of information and training. Hampton's (2005) research in Indonesia thus suggests that tourism departments and local authorities should provide more support for communities living in the vicinity of tourist attraction through providing business training, ensuring local people have access to capital, and rewriting their tourism plans to incorporate priorities of local residents.

Overall, and despite various limitations, alternative development perspectives have provided a strong critique of forms of tourism dominated by outside interests and offered some viable alternative ideas on tourism development which is more in line with local interests. They have been less effective, however, in tackling the need for change in the most important market, mass tourism.

Post-structuralist perspectives

Post-structuralists are interested in how people and places are socially constructed for tourism (Pritchard & Morgan, 2000), and in issues of representation, identity-formation, and ideology (see e.g. Hutnyk, 1996). They reject reductionist views of the world which see tourism as either a force of good or evil. Many tourism researchers still essentialise identity categories and use power binaries to frame their analysis, suggesting for example that foreign investors are 'exploitative' while local communities supposedly work together for the good of all. Thus neoliberal, critical and alternative development theorists could all be judged as making too many generalisations about the relationship between tourism and development: '... while there are a great number of reports rendering prominent the linkages between tourism and poor people ... few indepth studies have been carried out to understand the complexity of these interrelationships' (Gössling *et al.*, 2004: 132). Post-structuralist views thus appear to accord with Jafari's (2001: 31–32) fourth and final platform of scholarly knowledge on tourism, the knowledge-based platform. Based on this platform researchers are interested in a holistic view of the structures and functions of the tourism industry, rather than focusing on impacts (like the advocacy and cautionary platforms) or on alternative forms of tourism, as occurs under the adaptancy platform.

It is thus suggested that rather than focusing too much on tourism's 'impacts', we need detailed studies of systems, processes, places, and interactions between people, in order to understand how culture and power influence the actions of tourism stakeholders (Cheong & Miller, 2000; Davis, 2001). Teo (2003: 460), commenting on the global system as a whole, argues that it should be conceived as a 'multi-layered and intricate web of structures, agents and interactions that interweaves external conditions with local ones in both cooperative as well as competitive ways'. In this way we can consider how communities engage in tourism in complex ways that reflect their interests as well as those of other tourism stakeholders. They are not simply victims of a destructive global industry rather, they have power to respond to tourism, adapt it, embrace it, or reject it. Malam (2005) demonstrates this clearly in her research on the microgeographies of power and identity in Koh Phangan, Thailand, as played out in relationships between young Thai male workers and young Western female backpackers. Rather than positing the young men as less powerful actors in their romantic/sexual relationships with the backpacker women, Malam clearly articulates how the power balance varies over time and space, and that it is predicated by axes of education, gender, culture and economics. Thai male bar and bungalow workers have used the space of the beach bar to exert their masculinity even though they are effectively a poorly paid group of migrant workers.

Furthermore, we are urged to work with 'an active civil society' to identify appropriate paths for tourism development (Burns, 2004: 25). This means recognising dissenting voices regarding tourism development, just as Bond (2006) suggests that supporters of poverty alleviation world wide should have greater recognition of and support for 'organic' social struggles such as resistance of communities to certain developments (e.g. golf courses, tourist resorts), anti-debt movements, and labour strikes.

Different Approaches to Pro-Poor Tourism

PPT has in a very short period of time enjoyed increasing popularity, being embraced by some rather powerful organisations, although sometimes using different banners (e.g. ST-EP). While there has been a small amount of scholarly interest in PPT to date (see e.g. Binns & Nel, 2002; Mowforth & Munt, 2003; Neto, 2003; Torres & Momsen, 2004), PPT has not been subject to rigorous scrutiny. This article does take a critical perspective on PPT however, particularly in reflecting on the various approaches to PPT that have been adopted by a range of agencies who do not share the same vision of poverty reduction through tourism.[2] An understanding of various theorisations of the relationship between tourism and development such as that provided above is useful in allowing us to unpack the strategies adopted by different stakeholder groups over time. Below, the approaches of the PPT Partnership, the World Tourism Organization, and the World Bank, are discussed.

The PPT partnership

The PPT Partnership stresses that PPT is not a product, it is an *approach* to tourism which seeks to bring a wide range of benefits to the poor, including social, environmental and cultural benefits in addition to economic benefits. PPT does *not* aim to expand the size of the sector, but to 'unlock opportunities for the poor within tourism, at all levels and scales of operation' (PPT Partnership, 2005b: 1). This is interesting, as it does not focus on growth of tourism, and rather than just focusing at the community level where, for example villagers might be encouraged to establish a cultural tourism homestay or craft ventures, the PPT approach asserts that a wide range of stakeholders, from local entrepreneurs to government officials and international tour companies, will need to make concerted efforts if poverty reduction is to occur:

> Pro-Poor Tourism is about changing the distribution of benefits from tourism in favour of poor people. It is not a specific product. It is not the same as ecotourism or community-based tourism, nor is it limited to these niches. Any kind of tourism can be made pro-poor. PPT can be applied at different levels, at the enterprise, destination or country level. (Pro-Poor Tourism Partnership 2005a: 1)

Thus rather than focusing on alternative 'types' of tourism, the members of the PPT Partnership encourage mainstream tourism providers to change their practices. In a briefing paper, for example, they clearly explain why poverty should be of concern to tourism companies, and provide a detailed 'to do' list of action points (Roe *et al.*, 2002). The 'core activities' of PPT according to the PPT Partnership are then:

- to increase access of the poor to economic benefits (e.g. training, employment, supply linkages, information to tourists on community tourism ventures and the importance of buying local);
- to address the negative environmental and social impacts of tourism (e.g. loss of access to natural resources associated with creation of protected areas, social disruption);
- to reform policies and processes (e.g. to encourage partnerships with the private sector and to promote active participation of the poor in decision-making) (IIED, 2001).

The PPT Partnership seem to have a broad, holistic notion of poverty-alleviation which is inspired at least in part by alternative development theory. For example, they draw attention to the value of a number of non-economic benefits of PPT such as the development of new skills, better access to education and health care, and infrastructural improvements in terms of access to potable water and improved roads or transport. They also explain how intangible benefits of tourism can make a significance difference to the lives of the poor, including greater opportunities for communication with the outside world and improved access to information, better knowledge of market opportunities, strengthening of community institutions, and enhanced pride in one's culture and the skills and knowledge which exist within the community (Ashley & Roe, 2002). While this approach does accord somewhat with alternative development thinking, the PPT Partnership clearly aims well beyond the local level (often the focus of alternative development perspectives) in practice. For example the people behind the PPT Partnership firmly believe that it is important to bring about changes in mainstream tourism, including challenging corporates to change the way they operate, rather than to establish numerous community-run bungalow-style ventures with dubious business prospects.

World Tourism Organisation and ST-EP (sustainable tourism – eliminating poverty)

World Tourism Organisation has a mandate from the United Nations to promote and develop tourism on behalf of its 138 government tourist board members and 350 affiliate members (tourism associations, airlines, and hotel groups): it has no explicit interest in reflecting critically on tourism. As noted by Gössling *et al.* (2004: 145), 'The WTO currently seeks to establish a positive image of tourism by promoting the industry's vast job and income generating potential, and by emphasising its pro-environmental and pro poor effects'. Thus the green agenda and the pro-poor agenda have led to new initiatives within the World Tourism Organisation in recent years, such as ST-EP, but their main motivation is still to promote economic growth through tourism. This is not surprising given the origins of an initiative like ST-EP. The ST-EP programme emerged out of an earlier World Tourism Organisation programme entitled 'Liberalisation with a Human Face', and its partner in ST-EP is UNCTAD, an organisation focused on promotion of international trade. Thus, it can be argued, 'Anything the World Tourism Organisation does outside tourism promotion is just window dressing' (Anonymous informant, personal communication, 1/9/05).

The World Tourism Organisation has identified seven different ways of addressing poverty through tourism which it suggests can be applied in almost every country:

(1) Employment of the poor in tourism enterprises.
(2) Supply of goods and services to tourism enterprises by the poor or by enterprises employing the poor.
(3) Direct sales of goods and services to visitors by the poor (informal economy).

(4) Establishment and running of tourism enterprises by the poor – for example micro, small and medium sized enterprises (MSMEs), or community based enterprises (formal economy).
(5) Tax or levy on tourism income or profits with proceeds benefiting the poor.
(6) Voluntary giving/support by tourism enterprises and tourists.
(7) Investment in infrastructure stimulated by tourism also benefiting the poor in the locality, directly or through support to other sectors.

(Yunis, 2005: 3)

While a wide range of strategies appear to be presented here, they focus mainly on the local level, without addressing changes at national and global levels which could be of far greater significance. For example, it is relatively straightforward (and good for public relations) to pump money into community tourism initiatives, but it is far more difficult and controversial to endorse labour rights for all tourism sector workers worldwide, or to challenge the control that foreign companies and local elites often have over the tourism sector.

The World Tourism Organisation also refers to how tourism can be used in the 'war on poverty' (WTO, 2005). This is interesting language which obviously reflects the 'war on terror' waged by the United States' government on certain Middle Eastern countries. The two 'wars' are not unrelated. Democratic governance and security are seen as key components of a neoliberal poverty agenda. Thus in part the interest of organisations like the World Tourism Organisation in using tourism for poverty alleviation is motivated by the 11 September 2001 terrorist attacks in the United States, which some analysts interpreted as evidence that 'endemic poverty underlies instability in many parts of the world' (Sofield, 2003: 350). Specifically, pro-poor initiatives are attempt to overcome some of the inequalities which are seen since 9/11 as contributing to global insecurity.

World Bank

While the World Bank does not have a specific 'tourism for poverty alleviation' programme, it is currently providing significant funding for tourism projects and programmes around the globe with the intention that this will lead to development and reduce poverty over time. In Mann's (2005) account of the World Bank's approach to tourism over the past 40 years, it is fascinating to detect several phases which reflect different theoretical understandings of the relationship between tourism and development. In the first phase, the World Bank began funding tourism projects as a means of generating economic development in 1966, soon after commercial air travel started to generate large numbers of tourists to long haul destinations. This could be interpreted as a liberal perspective prioritising modernisation and economic growth. In the second phase starting in 1979, however, the World Bank closed its tourism department and pulled most of its funding from the tourism sector due to: (1) the neoliberal emphasis on allowing markets to drive growth, and (2) criticisms of the social and economic impacts of tourism which then required agencies like the World Bank to spend more money when preparing their projects. Thus during this second phase it was a combination of neo-liberal logic and critical perspectives on tourism which encouraged the World Bank to withdraw from

Table 1 Funding for tourism at the World Bank, 1970–2004

	Funding for tourism (in constant prices)
1970s	$1115 million
1980s	$180 million
1990s	$600 million
2000s	$2926 million

Source: Mann (2005: 2).

tourism projects. The World Bank was prompted to invest considerable sums of money in tourism once again in the third phase, however, in the 1990s, due to widespread calls to support environmental projects and sustainable development following publication of the Brundtland Report in 1987 and the Rio Earth Summit in 1992. To some extent, therefore, the World Bank was in this third phase responding to concerns raised under an alternative development approach. It was however the endorsement of tourism as a means of alleviating poverty at the UN General Assembly in 1999, a stance which accorded with the World Bank's new emphasis on poverty reduction, which led to larger sums of money than ever before being directed to the tourism sector (Mann, 2005) (Table 1).

In its renewed focus on tourism the World Bank endorses preservation of important natural and cultural resources and encourages participation of local communities in tourism, however it stresses that this needs to be backed up by a commitment from governments to 'make markets work for tourism' (Christie, 2002: 36). Neoliberal logic is clearly being applied here. For example, it is suggested that any 'enlightened' government will recognise that in order to achieve development through tourism it is vital to adopt certain reforms, such as guaranteeing investors clear title to land (Christie, 2002: 36). Yet to do this may mean undermining customary land ownership and traditional decision-making structures, something which those adopting a critical or alternative development perspective would see as contrary to attempts to make development 'pro-poor'.

Reflections on Different Approaches to Pro-Poor Tourism

The discussion above reveals that neoliberal orthodoxy is a key driver behind both World Bank and World Tourism Organisation initiatives launched in the name of poverty alleviation, even though these organisations also draw quite heavily on alternative development rhetoric (e.g. 'participation', 'empowerment', 'capacity building') in their written documents. As Storey *et al.* (2005: 35) note, however, such '. . . alternative development concepts and terminology . . . have been selectively incorporated into the mainstream'. There is more evidence of an alternative development approach being applied in practice, however, in the work of the PPT Partnership, although they clearly do not want to focus their work at the local level as they argue that changes at national and global levels, for example working with governments and corporates, are vital to securing more benefits of tourism for the poor. Overall, therefore, as suggested in Figure 1, a somewhat awkward combination of alternative and neoliberal development thought has had the greatest influence on the rationale and practice of PPT to date, although critical and post-structuralist perspectives have also had a role to play.

When recognising the extent to which neo-liberal logic pervades PPT discourse, it is clear that more critical reflection on this concept, rather than unadulterated support, is needed. Thus for example

> it is not unreasonable to consider the degree to which pro-poor tourism analysis and promotion is a repackaging of existing initiatives so that they fit within the prevailing development paradigm with an emphasis on poverty reduction, sustainable livelihoods and a focus on the poor and pro-poor growth. (Mowforth & Munt, 2003: 273)

That focus on pro-poor growth is based squarely within a neoliberal agenda. It is likely then that some organisations are adopting PPT rhetoric primarily as a means of promoting trade liberalisation, market-led growth and private sector development, while calling for minimum government 'interference' in market mechanisms. Rather, the role of governments may be seen as to smooth the way for outside investors, assisting them with gaining access to prime tourism sites.

Concerns about the enthusiastic push for PPT echo broader concerns about the poverty consensus, which, despite the reforms outlined earlier, is still essentially top-down in fashion and does not significantly challenge the limitations of neoliberal policy: 'the New Poverty Agenda ... fails to contain a self-critique of the very global agendas (such as globalisation, structural adjustment, debt repayments and the like) that remain intact despite this shift to a concern for poverty' (Storey *et al.*, 2005: 31). Referring to the related Post Washington Consensus, Öniş and Şenses (2005: 285) argue that its fundamental problem is 'the inability or unwillingness to address major issues pertaining to power and its distribution both at the domestic and international levels'. Thus the actions of local elites, company directors, and government leaders are not questioned. Also domestic policy reforms are adopted, rather than more broad-ranging global reforms such as regulation of the activities of transnational corporations and the continued protectionism of western markets. The pro-poor policies put forward are then to take place in the context of existing structures of power hierarchies, which leads Öniş and Şenses (2005: 281) to conclude that it unlikely that widespread poverty reduction will occur.

While much of the push for PPT is based on the logic that tourism is a growth industry in the world and one which has not been fully tapped by developing countries, it does not follow that a country must adopt neoliberal policies in order to take advantage of this expanding market (Desforges, 2000: 188). There are for example countries which have chosen to adopt tourism policies which clearly prioritise the interests of local people and seek to ensure that tourism development does not impinge on local well-being (Milne, 1997). Thus in Samoa, effective, budget-style tourism enterprises have been established on communal lands, allowing communities to retain control over tourism and ensuring a wide range of multiplier effects (Scheyvens, 2005). The tourism industry is largely made up of small to medium sized enterprises that are locally owned and operated. Thus neoliberal imperatives have not guided the development of tourism in Samoa yet tourism still earns more foreign exchange than any other sector, it provides numerous formal and informal sector jobs, and it has effectively rejuvenated a number of rural villages (Scheyvens, 2005). The Himalayan kingdom of Bhutan has also thwarted the neoliberal model of growth. It takes a 'middle path' approach to economic development whereby there are strict controls over the type and amount of tourism, in order to maximise revenue while minimising negative effects on religion, culture and the environment. This approach accords with the King's aim: to preserve GNH (Gross National Happiness). 'Happiness' is defined in both a material and spiritual sense, thus the focus is not a move towards a more individualistic, consumer-oriented, commodity-focused world, rather, there is strong recognition of the value of Bhutanese culture (Brunet *et al.*, 2001: 257).

Meanwhile in some countries which have clearly taken a neoliberal path, the poor have seen few benefits from the growth of tourism. For example in Peru, neo-liberal policies adopted under Fujimori from 1990 onwards, contributed to a three-fold increase in tourist arrivals between 1992 and 1996. While this did result in some macroeconomic benefits, poverty has been entrenched and the agricultural sector has decreased in size (Desforges, 2000). Similarly in Ghana, which has been hailed as a structural adjustment success story for Africa, tourist arrivals increased from around 85,000 in 1985 to over 286,000 in 1995, and tourist receipts increased from US$20 m to US$233 over the same period. However spatial disparities have become entrenched, the quality of life of many Ghanaians has declined and increasing rates of foreign ownership of tourism infrastructure are leading to higher leakages. Devaluation of the cedi enabled travellers to see Ghana as a 'cheap destination', while making it difficult for locals to afford imported products such as medicine (Konadu-Agyemang, 2001: 194).

These examples provide evidence that an alternative path to PPT – which does not mean an approach limited to alternative *forms* of tourism – can reap substantial rewards, including greater control and self-determination, not just revenue-generation. However, they also indicate that there is a need for effective governance structures if tourism is to maximise benefits for the poor. It is relatively easy for donors or governments to embrace PPT rhetoric while failing to ensure this occurs in the context of an appropriate policy and regulatory framework. This strategy could entrench existing economic and social inequalities while threatening the environment in many countries. Early case studies of PPT show 'trickle down' does not work, and that 'a proactive interventionist approach is needed' whereby governments target the poor and establish legislation to back up affirmative action strategies (Briedenhann & Wickens, 2004; Sofield, 2003: 351). Governments need to ensure that local people are empowered with appropriate knowledge and skills and access to networks, so they are not sidelined from active involvement in tourism. In many cases for example, economic opportunities for small farmers are being lost because of inadequate linkages between them, agricultural extension officers and hoteliers (Momsen, 1998; Torres & Momsen, 2004). Governments also need to find ways of supporting local industry through training and information, and through provision of a supportive policy environment. Appropriate policies and legislation could for example support the establishment of local tourism businesses on communal land, as in Samoa, without transferring rights of use or ownership to outsiders.

While the role of governments is thus vital to implementing effective PPT policies and strategies, we must recognise that past policies have in many cases undermined the capacity and perceived legitimacy of government institutions, making it difficult for them to implement pro-poor policies in practice: 'The neoliberal practices of the past two decades may also have had a lasting impact on state agents and officials alike, impairing their ability to readjust to a new agenda involving fresh thinking in spheres such as poverty alleviation' (Öniş & Şenses, 2005: 279). It is very difficult for proposed partnerships between the market and state to work in such circumstances rather, the market continues to dominate, and this can certainly inhibit pro-poor initiatives.

Critical perspectives have not played a very strong role in the development of PPT initiatives, perhaps because as Oppermann (1993) noted, they focus on critique and stop short of considering effective strategies whereby developing countries could work to secure greater benefits of tourism development. The critical views of an author like Britton (1982), for example, writing about tourism and underdevelopment in small island states, largely failed to acknowledge the fact where there are high levels of local ownership and strong economic linkages between tourism and other local industries, the benefits can be great (Milne, 1997). Britton also did not consider the significant role that local governments and people can play in managing the development of their tourism industries (ibid). However critical perspectives should not be unduly dismissed by proponents of PPT as they still have value in identifying power relations at national and international levels which can provide constraints to the implementation of effective PPT strategies.

Post-structuralist perspectives too deserve more consideration for two major reasons. Firstly, poststructuralism encourages us to develop a nuanced understand of the links between tourism and poverty reduction: tourism is neither panacea nor the root of all problems for developing countries. Thus, urges, Gössling *et al.* (2004: 132) '... there is a need to understand better the complexity of tourism-related development processes in the context of marginalized population groups living in absolute poverty'. As noted by both Jafari (2001) and Sofield (2003), tourism is a system involving multiple levels and dimensions, and a wide range of actors, from the private and public sectors and civil society. This then provides the opportunity for tourism to be directed by social and environmental motives, rather than just neoliberal economic motives (Wearing *et al.*, 2005), and to be more centred on the needs of the poor. This viewpoint appears to be supported by Burns (2004) who urges us to move beyond the polarizing 'development first' and 'tourism first' conceptions of tourism development – it is not necessary to choose *either* to work for enhancing community well-being, *or* for improving national economic prospects. In reality, however, there may be a need for trade-offs (Kontogeorgopoulos, 2004).

A second important contribution of poststructuralism is it recognition of the value of social movements and alternative voices. As Storey *et al.* (2005), who object to the notion of a poverty *consensus* argue, there should be vigorous debate among both scholars and practitioners of concerning questions of poverty. It is thus imperative that we hear the debates about tourism develop-ment, the critical voices, especially from local residents, environmental groups and people's organisations in areas most affected by tourism development, but also by international labour organisations, NGOs, or lobby groups. This is in line with Bond's (2006) argument that advocates of poverty reduction should pay attention to the pleas of a wide range of justice and anti-poverty move-ments around the globe. PPT proponents could learn much, for example, from listening to the views of those handing out leaflets protesting at charter flights at Goan airports (Lea, 1993: 709), those protesting at development of another foreign-owned resort (d'Hauteserre, 2003), or those campaigning about the rights of porters in mountain areas or the rights of tourism sector workers globally (see www.tourismconcern.org.uk).

Conclusion

There is certainly potential for tourism to contribute to poverty-alleviation, however in analysing this potential we need to carefully scrutinise the approaches of the agencies concerned to see whose interests are central to their agenda. While a number of agencies have been keen to adopt PPT rhetoric, it is likely that for some the interests of the poor are peripheral to their main operations. Thus the views of different stakeholder groups on the notion of poverty alleviation through tourism vary widely, even when most speak out in favour of the concept. In practice, some prioritise the interests of the tourism industry as a whole, that is, in growing the sector, expanding markets and enhancing profits, while others focus more directly on utilising this large, global industry to improve the well-being of impoverished peoples.

While there are positive examples of PPT initiatives around the globe (see PPT Partnership, 2005a), influencing a wide range of mainstream tourism sta-keholders to make their practices more pro-poor will be a major challenge. It will be difficult for well-intentioned governments to move beyond the rhetoric and into the practice of prioritising the interests of the poor if powerful elites and private sector lobby groups (such as hotel associations) with strong politi-cal connections resent PPT initiatives, such as positive discrimination towards poorer tourism providers. Thus a supportive policy environment is important, but not sufficient, to promote PPT. Even though the government and NGOs in South Africa have a strong commitment to promoting fair trade in tourism and using tourism as a means of regenerating local economies (Binns & Nel, 2002), the government is struggling to get the industry to commit to and make changes (Briedenham, 2004). Most mainstream tourism industry ventures carry on as usual.

It is at the level of large, private sector stakeholders that perhaps the greatest changes in support of PPT still need to occur. Hoteliers and resort owners may willingly use grey water on their gardens and provide donations to societies that protect turtle nesting sites, but they may be less keen to develop partner-ships with the poor[3] or to support implementation of effective labour rights legislation. Instead, in order to remain competitive, pay rates and labour con-ditions of tourism workers may be compromised (James, 2004). They may support token community tourism projects that assist a small number of people, rather than making long term changes so that their practices, including employment, training and procurement, are more pro-poor. If the World Tourism Organisation wants to demonstrate a strong commitment to reducing poverty, rather than making platitudes about the need to build capacity among communities and to find ways in which they can gain more of the benefits of tourism, it should be pressurising its members to consider joint venture arrangements with local communities, to ensure corporates abide with acceptable labour standards, and to minimise leakages from conventional forms of mass tourism.

Overall there needs to be more debate about the value of PPT as an approach to poverty reduction. To date, few critical views on PPT have been aired. This belies the reality, that is, while there are certainly circumstances in which tourism has helped to alleviate poverty, there are also situations in which it has deepened the fissures separating rich and poor, and where it has impoverished people culturally, socially, or environmentally, even when the economic benefits have been real. There should not be a consensus that tourism reduces poverty, akin to the poverty consensus, as debate is critical if we are to gain a full understanding of both tourism's potential and its limitations.

Correspondence

Any correspondence should be directed be to Dr Regina Scheyvens, School of People, Environment and Planning, Massey University, PB 11222 Palmarston North, New Zealand (r.a.scheyvens@massey.ac.nz).

Notes

1. NB the PPT Parternship website, www.propoortourism.org.uk, lists a wide range of publications which are mostly accessible on line.
2. In a recent document the Pro-Poor Tourism Partnership (2005a: 6) themselves noted that their vision of PPT may be different from that being put forward by the WTO through ST-EP.
3. When researching the poor linkages between hotel chefs and farmers in Quintana Roo, Mexico, Torres and Momsen found that 'This is mainly due to a lack of communication and the deep mistrust that exists between farmers, who are generally Maya, and the local non-Maya entrepreneurial elites and tourism industry suppliers and hotel buyers' (2004: 301).
4. Thanks to John Overton and Donovan Storey for sharing their thoughts on the constitution of this diagram.

References

Ashley, C. and Roe, D. (1998) *Enhancing Community Involvement in Wildlife Tourism: Issues and Challenges.* IIED Wildlife and Development Series No. 11, London, UK.

Ashley, C. and Roe, D. (2002) Making tourism work for the poor: Strategies and challenges in southern Africa. *Development Southern Africa* 19 (1), 61–82.

Ashley, C., Roe, D. and Goodwin, H. (2001) *Pro-Poor Tourism: Putting Poverty at the Heart of the Tourism Agenda.* Natural Resource Perspectives, Number 51, Overseas Development Institute, London.

Binns, T. and Nel, E. (2002) Tourism as a local development strategy in South Africa. *Geographical Journal* 168, 235–247.

Bond, P. (2006) Global governance campaigning and MDGs: From top-down to bottom-up anti-poverty work. *Third World Quarterly* 27 (2), 339–354.

Brennan, F. and Allen, G. (2001) Community-based ecotourism, social exclusion and the changing political economy of KwaZulu-Natal, South Africa. In D. Harrison (ed.) *Tourism and the Less Developed World: Issues and Case Studies* (pp. 203–221). New York: CABI Publishing.

Briedenham, J. (2004) Corporate social responsibility in tourism: A tokenistic agenda? *In Focus* 52, 11.

Briedenham, J. and Wickens, E. (2004) Tourism routes as a tool for the economic development of rural areas – vibrant hope or impossible dream? *Tourism Management* 25 (1), 71–79.

Britton, S. (1982) The political economy of tourism in the third world. *Annals of Tourism Research* 9 (3), 331–358.

Brohman, J. (1996) New directions in tourism for the Third World. *Annals of Tourism Research* 23 (1), 48–70.

Brunet, S., Bauer, J., De Lacy, T. and Tshering, K. (2001) Tourism development in Bhutan: Tensions between tradition and modernity. *Journal of Sustainable Tourism* 9 (3), 243–263.

Burns, P.M. (2004) Tourism planning: A third way? *Annals of Tourism Research* 31 (1), 24–43.

Butler, R. (1990) Alternative tourism: Pious hope or trojan horse? *Journal of Travel Research* 28 (3), 40–45.

Carbone, M. (2005) Sustainable tourism in developing countries: Poverty alleviation, participatory planning, and ethical issues. *The European Journal of Development Research* 17 (3), 559–565.

Cheong, S. and Miller, M. (2000) Power and tourism: A Foucauldian observation. *Annals of Tourism Research* 27 (2), 371–390.

Christie, I. (2002) Tourism, growth and poverty: Framework conditions for tourism in developing countries. *Tourism Review* 57 (1&2), 35–41.

Dann, G. (2002) Tourism and development. In V. Desai and R. Potter (eds) *The Companion to Development Studies*. (pp. 236–239). London: Arnold.

Davis, J.B. (2001) Commentary: Tourism research and social theory – Expanding the focus. *Tourism Geographies* 3 (2), 125–34.

de Kadt, E. (ed.) (1979) *Tourism: Passport to Development?* New York: Oxford University Press.

de Kadt, E. (1992) Making the alternative sustainable: Lessons from development for tourism. In V. Smith and W. Easington (eds) *Tourism Alternatives: Potential and Problems in the Development of Tourism* (pp. 47–75). Philadelphia: University of Pennsylvania Press.

Deloitte and Touche (1999) *Sustainable Tourism and Poverty Elimination: A Report for the Department of International Development*. London: IIED and ODI.

Dent, M. and Peters, B. (1999) *The Crisis of Poverty and Debt in the Third World*. Aldershot: Ashgate.

Desforges, L. (2000) State tourism institutions and neo-liberal development: A case study of Peru. *Tourism Geographies* 2 (2), 177–192.

d'Hauteserre, A. (2003) A response to 'Misguided policy initiatives in small-island desintations: Why do up-market tourism policies fail?' by D. Ioannides and B. Holcomb. *Tourism Geographies* 5 (1), 49–53.

Enloe, C. (1990) *Bananas, Beaches and Bases: Making Feminist Sense of International Politics*. Berkeley: University of California Press.

Erbelei, W. (2000) Taking the lead in the fight against poverty: World Bank and IMF speed implementation of their new strategy. *Development and Cooperation* 3, 23–24.

Goodwin, H. (1998) *Sustainable Tourism and Poverty Elimination*. DFID/DETR Workshop on Sustainable Tourism and Poverty, 13 October 1998.

Gössling, S., Schumacher, K., Morelle, M., Berger, R. and Heck, N. (2004) Tourism and street children in Antananarivo, Madagascar. *Tourism and Hospitality Research* 5 (2), 131–149.

Hall, C.M. and Tucker, H. (2004) *Tourism and Postcolonialism: Contested Discourses, Identities, and Representations* London: Routledge.

Hampton, M. (2005) Heritage, local communities, and economic development. *Annals of Tourism Research* 32 (3), 735–759.

Harrison, D. (2003) Themes in Pacific Island tourism. In D. Harrison (ed.) *Pacific Island Tourism* (pp. 1–23). New York: Cognizant Communication Corporation.

Hart, G. (2001) Development critiques in the 1990s: *Cul de sacs* and promising paths. *Progress in Human Geography* 25 (4), 649–658.

Hutnyk, J. (1996) *The Rumour of Calcutta: Tourism, Charity and the Poverty of Representation.* London: Zed.

International Institute for Environment and Development (IIED) (2001) Pro-poor tourism: Harnessing the world's largest industry for the world's poor. On WWW at http://www.iied.org/docs/wssd/bp_tourism_eng.pdf. Accessed May 2001.

International Institute for Peace Through Tourism (IIPT) (2004) *January Newsletter.* On WWW at http://www.iipt.org/newsletter/January2004.html. Accessed 1.12.04.

Jafari, J. (2001) The scientification of tourism. In V.L. Smith and M. Brent (eds) *Hosts and Guests Revisited: Tourism Issues of the 21st Century* (pp. 28–41). New York: Cognizant Communication.

James, G. (2004) Riding the wave: Working within a globalised tourism economy. *In Focus* 52, 12–13.

Konadu-Agyemang, K. (2001) Structural adjustment programmes and the international tourism trade in Ghana, 1983–99: Some socio-spatial implications. *Tourism Geographies* 3 (2), 187–206.

Kontogeorgopoulos, N. (2004) Conventional tourism and ecotourism in Phuket, Thailand: Conflicting paradigms or symbiotic partners? *Journal of Ecotonmism* 3 (2), 87–108.

Krippendorf, J. (1989) *The Holidaymakers.* Oxford: Butterworth-Heinemann.

Lea, J. (1993) Tourism development ethics in the Third World. *Annals of Tourism Research* 20, 701–715.

Malam, L. (2005) Encounters across difference on the Thai beach scene. PhD thesis, Australian National University, Canberra.

Mann, S. (2005) Tourism and the World Bank. Paper presented at the *Development Studies Association Conference*, Milton Keynes, 7–9 September 2005.

Mbaiwa, J.E. (2005) Enclave tourism and its socio-economic impacts in the Okavango Delta, Botswana. *Tourism Management* 26 (2), 157–172.

Milne, S. (1997) Tourism, dependency and South Pacific microstates: Beyond the vicious cycle? In D.G. Lockhart and D. Drakakis-Smith (eds) *Island Tourism: Trends and Prospects* (pp. 281–301). London: Pinter.

Momsen, J.H. (1998) Caribbean tourism and agriculture: new linkages in the global era? In T. Klak (ed.) *Globalization and Neoliberalism: The Caribbean Context* (pp. 115–134). Lanham: Rowman and Littlefield.

Mowforth, M. and Munt, I. (2003) *Tourism and Sustainability: Development and New Tourism in the Third World* London: Routledge.

Murphy, P. (1985) *Tourism: A Community Approach.* New York: Methuen.

Nash, D. (1977) Tourism as a form of imperialism. In V.L. Smith (ed.) *Hosts and Guests: The Anthropology of Tourism* (pp. 33–47). Philadelphia: University of Pennsylvania Press.

Neto, F. (2003) A new approach to sustainable tourism development: Moving beyond environmental protection. *Natural Resources Forum* 27 (3), 212–222.

Öniş, Z. and Şenses, F. (2005) Rethinking the emerging post-Washington consensus. *Development and Change* 36 (2), 263–290.

Opperman, M. (1993) Tourism space in developing countries. *Annals of Tourism Research* 20 (3), 535–556.

Plüss, C. and Backes, M. (2002) *Red Card for Tourism? 10 Principles and Challenges for a Sustainable Tourism Development in the 21st Century.* Freiburg: DANTE (NGO Network for Sustainable Tourism Development).

Potter, R. (1993) Basic needs and development in the small island states of the Eastern Caribbean. In D.G. Lockhart, D. Drakakis-Smith and J. Schembri (eds) *The Development Process in Small Island States* (pp. 92–116). London: Routledge.

Pritchard, A. and Morgan, N. (2000) Constructing tourism landscapes: Gender, sexuality and space. *Tourism Geographies* 2 (2), 115–139.

Pro-Poor Tourism Partnership (PPT Partnership) (2005a) *Pro-Poor Tourism: Annual Register 2005*. London: Pro-Poor Tourism Partnership.

Pro-Poor Tourism Partnership (PPT Partnership) (2005b) *Key Principles and Strategies of Pro-Poor Tourism*. London: Pro-Poor Tourism Partnership.

Richter, L.K. (2001) Tourism challenges in developing nations: Continuity and change at the millennium. In D. Harison (ed.) *Tourism and the Less Developed World: Issues and Case Studies* (pp. 47–59). New York: CABI Publishing.

Roe, D., Goodwin, H. and Ashley, C. (2002) *The Tourism Industry and Poverty Reduction: A Business Primer*. London: Pro-Poor Tourism Briefing No. 2/2002.

Saraogi, B. (2004) A ray of hope? *Travel Wire News*. On WWW at http://www.travelwire news.com/cgi-script/csArticles/articles/000020/002001-p.htm. Accessed 11.10.04.

Scheyvens, R. (2002) *Tourism for Development: Empowering Communities*. Harlow: Prentice Hall.

Scheyvens, R. (2005) Growth of beach *fale* tourism in Samoa: The high value of low-cost tourism. In C.M. Hall, and S. Boyd (eds) *Nature-Based Tourism in Peripheral Areas: Development or Disaster?* (pp. 188–202). Clevedon: Channelview Publications.

Singh, T.V. (2002) Altruistic tourism: Another shade of sustainable tourism – the case of Kanda Community. *Tourism* 50 (4), 361–370.

Smith, V.L. (1977) *Hosts and Guests: The Anthropology of Tourism*. Philadelphia: University of Pennsylvania Press.

Smith, V.L. and Eadington, W.R. (1992) *Tourism Alternatives: Potentials and Problems in the Development of Tourism*. Philadelphia: University of Pennsylvania Press.

Sofield, T. (2003) *Empowerment for Sustainable Tourism Development*. Oxford: Pergamon.

Sofield, T., Bauer, J., De Lacy, T., Lipman, G. and Daugherty, S. (2004) *Sustainable Tourism – Eliminating Poverty: An Overview*. Australia: Cooperative Research Centre for Sustainable Tourism.

Storey, D., Bulloch, H. and Overton, J. (2005) The poverty consensus: Some limitations of the 'popular agenda'. *Progress in Development Studies* 5 (1), 30–44.

Telfer, D.J. (2002) The evolution of tourism and development theory. In R. Sharpley and D.J. Telfer (eds) *Tourism and Development: Concepts and Issues* (pp. 35–78). Clevedon: Channel View Publications.

Telfer, D.J. (2003) Development issues in destination communities. In S. Singh, D.J. Timothy and R.K. Dowling (eds) *Tourism in Destination Communities* (pp. 155–180). New York: CABI Publishing.

Teo, P. (2003) Striking a balance for sustainable tourism: Implications of the discourse on globalization. *Journal of Sustainable Tourism* 10 (6), 459–474.

Thomlinson, E. and Getz, D. (1996) The question of scale in ecotourism: Case study of two small ecotour operators in the Mundo Maya region of Central America. *Journal of Sustainable Tourism* 4 (4), 183–200.

Torres, R. and Momsen, J.H. (2004) Challenges and potential for linking tourism and agriculture to achieve pro-poor tourism objectives. *Progress in Development Studies* 4 (4), 294–319.

United Nations Conference on Trade and Development (UNCTAD) (1998) Developing countries could target tourism to boost economic growth. On WWW at http://www.unctad.org/Templates/Webflyer.asp?docID=3243&intItemID=2068&lang=1. Accessed 9.6.98.

Wearing, S. (2001) *Volunteer Tourism: Experiences that Make a Difference*. Wallingford: CABI.

Wearing, S., McDonald, M. and Ponting, J. (2005) Building a decommodified research paradigm in tourism: The contribution of NGOs. *Journal of Sustainable Tourism* 13 (5), 424–439.

Williams, S. (1998) *Tourism Geography*. London: Routledge.

World Tourism Organization (WTO) (2005) 'Use tourism on war on poverty' world leaders urged. 15 September 2005. On WWW at http://www.asiatraveltips.com/news05/159-Tourism.shtml. Accessed 7.3.06.

Yunis, E. (2005) Tourism enriches? Poverty reduction, tourism and social corporate responsibility. Presentation on 16 June 2005, Wageningen University, Netherlands. On WWW at http://www.idut.nl/Yunis.doc. Accessed 7.3.06.

Nature-Based Tourism and Poverty Alleviation: Impacts of Private Sector and Parastatal Enterprises In and Around Kruger National Park, South Africa

Anna Spenceley
International Centre for Responsible Tourism, South Africa

Harold Goodwin
International Centre for Responsible Tourism, University of Greenwich, UK

International programmes and national policies around the world have identified tourism as an appropriate mechanism for sustainable development, poverty alleviation and biodiversity conservation. To evaluate the impact of nature-based tourism on the poor, socio-economic assessments were undertaken at enterprises based within South African protected areas. Comparisons were made between local economic interventions reported by enterprises and neighbouring community member's perceptions of their initiatives. Socioeconomic impacts evaluated included employment, gender equality, procurement, corporate social responsibility, dependency on tourism and access to markets. The studies demonstrate that isolated efforts from individual tourism companies have little tangible impact on the majority of people living in highly populated rural communities but impacts are substantial for the few people who directly benefit. Implications of these findings for future socio-economic initiatives through tourism, and options to increase net benefits to the poor are explored.

doi: 10.2167/cit305.0

Keywords: South Africa, socioeconomic, SUNTAT, poverty, protected area, Kruger National Park, private nature reserve

Introduction

The purpose of this paper is to present information on socioeconomic interventions by tourism enterprises and their impacts on poverty and the rural livelihoods of people living in neighbouring communities. The employment, purchasing practices, and corporate social responsibility (CSR) initiatives of four nature-based tourism enterprises in South African protected areas are described. Tangible impacts and perceptions of local people among local community members reveal the extent to which these activities have affected their quality of life. The work highlights the need for well-intentioned responsible tourism enterprises to consider local engagements carefully, particularly in relation to local needs and constraints. Researchers and tourism managers interested in measuring socioeconomic impacts of tourism will find the studies and their results useful in directing future work. This study supports the argument that poverty is a multi-faceted problem, and that the expectations of both individual tourism enterprises and local people should not be unrealistically raised regarding their potential to transform local economic situations.

South African context

The social and political environment of the South African tourism industry has been influenced by apartheid and subsequent actions taken to rectify historical inequalities. The decade following South Africa's 1994 democratic elections saw the development of various policies and programmes designed to bring about a more equitable and non-discriminatory society. The *Constitution of the Republic of South Africa* formed the basis for this transform-ation, by prohibiting discrimination based on any grounds while promoting affirmative action for previously disadvantaged individuals (PDIs). PDIs were people discriminated against during the apartheid period, namely black people (i.e. African, Indian and coloured), women and the disabled (Government of South Africa, 1996a).

An extensive national consultation process led to the *White Paper on the Development and Promotion of Tourism*, which outlines the objective for sustain-able tourism development in South Africa, (Government of South Africa, 1996b). The White Paper identified factors that had previously constrained the industry's potential to create jobs, empower PDIs, uplift communities and develop small, medium and micro-enterprises (SMMEs). Factors con-straining communities included limited integration of local communities and PDIs into tourism; lack of market access and knowledge; lack of interest among enterprises to build partnerships with local communities; lack of infor-mation and awareness; and a lack of appropriate institutional structures (Government of South Africa, 1996b). The tourism White Paper promoted 'responsible tourism', meaning:

> Tourism that promotes responsibility to the environment through its sustainable use; responsibility to involve local communities in the tourism industry; responsibility for the safety and security of visitors and responsible government, employees, employers, unions and local communities. (Government of South Africa, 1996b: vi)

The White Paper was subsequently supported by *Tourism in GEAR*; a policy that promoted entrepreneurship, community shareholding in tourism and the sustainable use of both cultural and natural resources (DEAT, 1997). From this basis the Department of Environmental Affairs and Tourism (DEAT) embarked on a consultative process to develop national responsible tourism guidelines to enable industry stakeholders to measure and monitor performance across the 'triple bottom line' of sustainability (Spenceley *et al.*, 2004). The guidelines were released in 2002 prior to the World Summit on Sustainable Development (DEAT, 2002).

Tourism is the fastest growing sector of the South African economy, contri-buting 7.4% of total economic activity in 2004 (WTTC, 2004). Although globally tourism shrank from 714 million international tourist arrivals in 2002 to 694 million in 2003 (down 2.8%), South Africa's foreign arrivals grew by 1.2% in 2003 and foreign direct spend grew 10.5% from R48.8 billion in 2002

(~US$7.0 billion, assuming R7 to $1) to R53.9 billion in 2003 (~$7.7 billion) (South African Tourism, 2004).

The World Travel and Tourism Council's satellite accounts estimate that $4562 million was generated in personal travel and tourism, generating 491,700 jobs from the industry in 2003 (WTTC, 2003). Scenery and wildlife in South Africa are primary factors attracting foreign tourists to South Africa. Market research indicates that at least 45% of South Africa's foreign air arrival market visits at least one nature or wildlife reserve during their visit. In addition to these 900,000 tourists, an estimated 5 million South Africans fall within the Game or Bush Lover segment of South African domestic market (Seymour, 2003). In the province of KwaZulu-Natal the nature-based tourism industry accounts for 21% (~$59 million) of the gross geographical product and 30% of total employment in the north east of the province (Aylward, 2003). Cassim *et al.* (2004) suggest that nature-based tourism is a fast-growing sector of tourism in South Africa.

Poverty and tourism

Poverty can be defined both using 'economic' and 'non-economic' approaches (Sultana, 2002). The 'economic' approach typically defines poverty in terms of income and consumption. The 'non-economic' approach incorporates concepts such as living standards, basic needs, inequality, subsistence, and the human development index. In recent years poverty analyses have also included issues such as vulnerability, isolation, social exclusion, powerlessness, personal dignity, security, self-respect and ownership of assets (Sultana, 2002). The range of characteristics integrated within the notion of poverty means that definitions of the term may differ both within and between societies, institutions, communities and households. For simplicity, this research adopted the definition of poverty used within this goal, as individuals living on less than US$1 per day (DFID, 2000).

Globally, 1.2 billion people are living in extreme poverty, of which about a quarter live in sub-Saharan Africa and three quarters work and live in rural areas. Poverty is characterised by hunger, malnutrition, poor health, lack of access to water and sanitation, lack of participation in education, lack of marketable skills, insecurity and vulnerability. More than 800 million people (15% of the world's population) suffer from malnutrition while the life expectancy at birth in the least developed countries is under 50 years: 27 years less than in developed countries (UNDP, 2003). The United Nations classifies 49 nations as least developed countries (LDCs), due to their low GDP per capita, weak human assets and high economic vulnerability: 34 of these are in Africa. The United Nations Development Programme (UNDP) argues in their Human Development Report that development is ultimately a process of enlarging people's choices not just raising national incomes (UNDP, 2003).

There is a growing perception that tourism can be used as a tool in the fight against poverty. This has been reflected in international initiatives, such as the World Tourism Organization's (WTO) *Global Code of Ethics for Tourism* (WTO, 1997). The code argues that local populations should share equitably in the economic, social and cultural benefits generated from tourism, and in particular from employment opportunities (WTO, 1997). The seventh session of the United

Nation's Commission on Sustainable Development urged governments to maximise the potential of tourism to eradicate poverty by developing appropriate cooperative strategies with major groups, indigenous and local communities (CSD, 1999). This agenda was further promoted when *Principles for the Implementation of Sustainable Tourism* were released by the United Nations Environment Programme (UNEP, 2001), and a year later at the World Summit on Sustainable Development (WSSD) the WTO released a paper specifically on poverty alleviation and tourism (WTO, 2002). During WSSD the WTO in collaboration with UNCTAD (the United Nations Commission on Trade and Development) launched the 'Sustainable Tourism – Eliminating Poverty' (ST-EP) programme. The programme aims to alleviate poverty through sustainable tourism by financing research and development, and also providing incentives for good practice (WTO, undated). A broader key outcome of the WSSD in 2002 was a reaffirmation of the Millennium Development Goal to halve the number of people living in poverty by 2015 (UN/DESA, 2002).

Clearly tourism can make a substantial contribution to economic development on a national scale. For example, the tourism performance of Botswana was a major factor in its graduation from the list of LDCs in 1994 (WTO, 2004). In 2000, tourism was a principal export for 83% of developing countries, and the principal export for one third of these. Between 1990 and 2000 the export value of tourism grew by 154% in developing countries, and by 47% in the LDCs. Some LDCs are particularly dependent on tourism, with a high proportion of their GDP generated by international tourism receipts (e.g. 57.7% of the Maldives' GDP) (WTO, 2002). However, Sharpley (2002) asks whether tourism can realistically form a development panacea, since it is associated with social and environmental costs. The impacts of tourism should therefore be regarded critically to evaluate whether it is an empowering sustainable development strategy for host communities (Mitchella & Reidb, 2001).

It is for this reason that the work of the Pro-Poor Tourism Partnership has emphasised the importance of looking at tourism and poverty from a livelihoods perspective, tourism and can have both positive and negative social, economic and environmental impacts on local communities, it is essential that a broad view is taken when assessing likely impacts and determining whether or not to proceed with particular initiatives. At a local level, tourism's potential to generate net benefits for the poor, or to be 'pro-poor', lies in four main areas (Ashley *et al.*, 2001; DFID, 1999): First, tourism is a diverse industry, which increases the scope for wide participation of different stakeholders and businesses, including the involvement of the informal sector; second, the customer comes to the product, which provides considerable opportunities for linkages to emerging entrepreneurs and small, medium and micro-enterprises (SMMEs); third, tourism is highly dependent upon natural capital (e.g. wildlife and culture), which are assets that the poor may have access to – even in the absence of financial resources; and fourth, tourism can be more labour intensive than other industries such as manufacturing. In comparison to other modern sectors a higher proportion of tourism benefits (e.g. jobs and informal trade opportunities) go to women.

Tourism has been promoted as an economic option for community development and poverty alleviation in South Africa: through employment (Binns &

Nel, 2002; Mahony & van Zyl, 2002; Poultney & Spenceley, 2001); small enterprise development (Kirsten & Rogerson, 2002); and enterprise ownership (Mahony & van Zyl, 2002; Ntshona & Lahiff, 2003). Tangible socioeconomic benefits have been documented in South Africa in relation to community based tourism enterprises (e.g. Amadiba Adventures: Ntshona & Lahiff, 2003), joint ventures with the private sector (e.g. Wilderness Safaris: Poultney & Spenceley, 2001), and where tourism enterprises have channelled donations into community initiatives (e.g. Conservation Corporation Africa: Spenceley, 2001). In addition, planning gain has been used by protected area managers across South Africa to commercialise parks and lever quantifiable local economic benefits through concession contracts (Fearnhead, 2004; Relly, 2004; Spenceley, 2004). This paper considers three private sector and one parastatal-owned nature-based tourism enterprises, and their impacts on local communities from business and corporate social responsibility perspectives.

Private sector tourism associations have become increasingly involved in the promotion of responsible tourism. Associations including the Federated Hospitality Association of South Africa (FEDHASA) and the Bed and Breakfast Society of South Africa have developed their own responsible tourism guidelines (DEAT, 2002). FEDHASA actually repackaged its environmental award as the Imvelo responsible tourism award in 2002, promoting the quantitative reporting of responsible economic, social and environmental actions (Spenceley *et al.*, 2004). The initiative has provided good publicity for the winners and theoretically acts to ratchet up standards across the industry (Spenceley, 2003b). A survey by the Tourism Business Council of South Africa in 2003 of 30 tourism enterprises, bodies and groups indicated that while 53% of companies had affirmative procurement policies, and 75% had at least one black director, only a fifth reported above 25% black ownership (Sykes, 2003).

A southern African pro-poor tourism pilot project was established in May 2002 to promote strategies that could be used by tourism companies to create and enhance linkages with local people or enterprises that make business sense to the company. The project worked closely with five 'pilot' tourism enterprises in southern Africa to promote and facilitate local linkages (Ashley *et al.*, 2005). Over the course of three years, the project facilitated a range of initiatives with the pilot enterprises to strengthen local linkages and enhance local economic development. Their efforts have led to increased local employment (e.g. at Spier), increased use of local contractors and suppliers (e.g. a new laundry and purchases of food and craft at Spier), upgrading existing product development facilities (e.g. glass making enterprise near Sun City) and stronger local relationships (e.g. Wilderness Safaris and the Mqobela community) (PPT, 2005). The results of the programme and lessons learned are now in the process of being compiled for stakeholders.

There has been limited uptake of international environmental management systems such as ISO 14001 or Green Globe21 within the South Africa tourism industry to date. Other locally developed systems tend not to contain measurable, performance-based criteria for certification (Koch *et al.*, 2002). In addition, efforts have been made by individual tourism companies to audit environmental and social responsibility using independently developed internal appraisal systems (e.g. Conservation Corporation Africa) or to enact the Global Reporting Initiative (e.g. Spier).

Non-governmental organisations have also played a role in the development of responsible tourism in South Africa. Fair Trade in Tourism South Africa (FTTSA) is a non-profit initiative that has developed a set of predominantly socioeconomic standards against which tourism products can be assessed and certified for Fair Trade practices. Gender equality, employee benefit, the protection of vulnerable groups and community support and empowerment are priority areas (Seif & Spenceley, in press). By March 2007 21 enterprises had obtained the FTTSA trademark (www.fairtourism.org.za).

Despite the presence of strong supportive policies and attempts by various stakeholders to generate socioeconomic benefits for local people through tourism, there are still questions regarding the extent to which tourism growth and investment actually benefits South Africa's poor. The capacity of PDIs and community-based enterprises to find and exploit entry points in a highly competitive industry is questionable. Appreciating that growth does not automatically equate to poverty reduction is critical to the long-term sustainability of the tourism industry, in addition to the realisation of meaningful socioeconomic growth and development in a democratic South Africa (Seif & Spenceley, in press).

Despite increasing numbers of publications regarding tourism and poverty alleviation in South Africa, there is little quantitative research that provides comparable data. Case studies tend to be written up in general terms with little standardisation or comparative analysis of economic data. This makes the evaluation of best practice strategies very difficult, even in cases where researchers have been requested to apply identical assessment methodologies (e.g. Ashley *et al.*, 2001: Tables 4 and 5). Few studies tangibly indicate how tourism activities have impacts on poverty, but instead tend to quantify financial and qualitative livelihood changes. However some researchers have begun to develop comparative quantitative analysis of socioeconomic impacts of tourism within local economies (e.g. Spenceley & Seif, 2003).

The purpose of this paper is to move the debate further by indicating how simple comparative analyses can be used to highlight the impacts of economic interventions on local communities. These assessments can be used to identify effective strategies that utilise the realistic capacity of enterprises to generate local benefits in relation to the needs and constraints of local people.

Assessment of Tourism Interventions

Study methods

The methodological tool used to evaluate the socioeconomic impacts of tourism in this study was Sustainable Nature-Based Tourism Assessment Toolkit (SUNTAT) (Spenceley, 2003a). The tool was developed during doctoral research through a process that included: a literature review to identify sustainability factors and assessment methodologies; a Delphi consultation to prioritise factors relevant to stakeholder experts in southern Africa; and four case studies to field test its practicality in application. The aim of developing the SUNTAT was to address the need for a holistic evaluation tool for rapid and reliable assessment of sustainable tourism in developing countries. The early stages of the SUNTAT's evolution are described elsewhere (Spenceley, 2003a, 2005a, in press) while this paper describes the socioeconomic aspects of the case studies.

Case studies entail empirical investigations of contemporary phenomenon in their real life context using multiple sources of evidence (Robson, 1993). Ngala Private Game Reserve, Pretoriuskop Camp, Jackalberry Lodge and Sabi Sabi were selected as the four case study sites to exhibit differences on a range of independent variables (see Table 1). Ngala and Jackalberry are located within the province of Limpopo, while Sabi Sabi and Pretoriuskop are in

Table 1 Variation of independent variables between enterprises

Ngala	*Pretoriuskop*	*Jackalberry*	*Sabi Sabi*
Conservation status			
National Park	National Park	Private Nature Reserve	Private Nature Reserve
Area land			
~147 km² within ~789 km² PNR	~620 km² for region within ~20,000 km² park	~ 43 km² within ~124 km² PNR	~ 32 km² within ~750 km² PNR
Land ownership			
Privately owned land	Government owned land	Privately owned land	Privately owned land
Number other operations managed by same organisation			
22 lodges in six African countries	18 national parks in South Africa. In KNP: 13 rest camps (plus six bushveld & five private camps)	None	None
Capacity			
One camp with 21 rooms (42 beds)	One camp with 136 units (352 beds) & 40 camp sites	One camp with 5 rooms (10 beds)	Three camps with 46 rooms (92 beds)
Price range (approximate figures given where converted from Rands)			
US$340 to $475 p/p per night Price includes meals, game drives, game walks	~$7 to ~$245 per site/room/guest house Accommodation only	~$170 to ~$205 p/p sharing Price includes meals, game drives, game walks	~$410 to ~$1050 p/p sharing Price includes meals, game drives, game walks
Closest rural community			
Welverdiend (3 km)	Numbi (1 km)	Timbavati (2 km)	Huntingdon (5 km)

Source: Spenceley (2003a).

Mpumalanga. The four enterprises operate photographic safari tourism as their core business, working within lowveld savannah habitats that wildlife such as elephant, rhino, buffalo, lion and leopard inhabit. Each enterprise is located within a protected area either in or near to Kruger National Park (KNP) and is neighbored by a different rural community. A brief description of each enterprise is provided below.

Ngala Private Game Reserve (PGR) is privately owned by the South Africa National Parks Trust (SANPT) on land within the Timbavati Associated Private Nature Reserve. The land is managed by South African National Parks (SANParks) as part of KNP, as the reserve is adjacent to the national park and unfenced from it. The SANPT has leased the lodge and exclusive traversing rights on the reserve to Conservation Corporation Africa since 1992. Ngala PGR operates luxury, high-cost and low-density tourism, and foreign tourists form the majority of their clientele, paying US$450 per person per night. The Welverdiend community lies within the Mnisi Tribal Authority, to the south of Ngala PGR. In 1996 the community was populated by around 7000 people (Spenceley, 2000).

Pretoriuskop Rest Camp lies within the Pretoriuskop section of the KNP, located in the south-east of the park. The camp has been owned and operated by SANParks since its initial development in 1931. Although it began with just four chalets, the camp now has 352 beds available within 136 accommodation units, which constitutes 10% of the accommodation available in the park. The quality includes basic campsites and chalets with communal ablutions and cooking facilities; cottages with fitted kitchens and bathrooms; and luxury guest house. The prices range between R65 and R2200 per unit per night (~US$8 and $253), and can therefore accommodate most visitor budgets. The majority of tourists are self-drive, and some travel organised tour groups, but the camp also offers official game drives and bush barbeques (Spenceley, 2002a). Pretoriuskop neighbours the Numbi Community, which lies either side of a tarred road to the Numbi Gate of KNP in the Mdluli Tribal Authority. The Numbi Community included 4720 people the year 2000, and of these only 24% men and 15% of women had an income. Of those earning an income, 73% men and 88% women were earning less than R1000 per month (Urban Dynamics Middleburg Inc., 1999).

Jackalberry Lodge is a privately owned safari lodge within the Thornybush Game Reserve. The reserve consists of aggregated and contiguous privately owned game farms that are operated under a common constitution. Although reserve is divided into northern and southern management areas, it is managed as a whole to promote wildlife, biodiversity conservation and tourism. Jackalberry lodge offers 10 beds at nightly rates of between R1650 and R1950 (~US$189 and $223), and operates photographic safari tours mainly for foreign tourists (Relly & Koch, 2002). The managers of the lodge diversify their sources of income by occasionally offering hunting packages, and by breeding tuberculosis-free buffalo for live sales (Spenceley, 2002b). To the south of the Thornybush reserve lies the Timbavati Community of around 11,200 people, located within the Mnisi Tribal Authority. There is a very low estimated employment rate of 3% in women and 15% in men (Spenceley, 2002c).

The Sabi Sabi Private Game Reserve lies within the Sabi Sand Wildtuin (SSW) – a reserve that covers approximately 57,000 hectares (750 km^2), and lies adjacent to the KNP. The SSW is comprised of about 48 unfenced farms with different landowners. Similarly to the Timbavati, the SSW is unfenced from KNP, and so wildlife can move freely between the national park and the private reserve. The SSW is overseen by a consortium of local landowners, which is governed by a constitution whose objectives include the promotion, conservation and protection of wildlife, fauna and flora within the reserve (Spenceley, 2002d). Sabi Sabi has three lodges on its property – Bush, Earth and Selati lodges – each of which provides a different experience for guests through different styles of architecture and facilities. In all, the lodge offers 92 beds at nightly rates between R3700 to R9500 (~US$424 to $1088) for different types of room. Guests are taken on photographic safari tours in open-top land rovers, and have the option of bush walks and visits to hides on the property. The majority of guests are from Europe (~40%) but there is are also substantial African visitors (~25%) (Spenceley, 2002d). The Huntingdon community lies to the west of the Sabi Sand Wildtuin, inhabited by approximately 6500 people within the Khosa Tribal Authority. There was a low level of employment (35% in women and 40% in men: Mhlongo, 2001), the main source of employment being the lodges within the SSW (Spenceley, 2002d).

A variety of simple tools from the SUNTAT were used to assess the local socioeconomic impacts of the enterprises. These included literature review, observation and stakeholder interviews. Documentation reviewed included internal policies, financial reports, human resources information, staff training materials, codes of practice/conduct and social development reports. Direct observation was used to confirm the physical presence of infrastructure that enterprises had developed or facilitated in neighbouring rural communities. Semi-structured interviews were undertaken with managers and heads of departments within the enterprises regarding social and economic issues. This type of interview lies between a fully structured, quantitative approach and an unstructured qualitative approach (May, 1993). The evolving SUNTAT provided the guide to this process (Spenceley, 2003a).

Local field assistants undertook structured interviews with members of local communities. The field assistant candidates were recruited from the specific communities assessed with the assistance of local Tribal Authorities, a university research field station, and SANParks staff. The field assistants were fluent in English and their respective local language (either Shangaan or Swazi) and had a high standard of written English. Their educational level ranged from matric (the South African equivalent of GCSEs) to masters, and the majority had teaching diplomas (Spenceley, 2003a). They were trained and then paid to carry out structured interviews with members of their village regarding socioeconomic issues in order to: ensure that interviews were carried out in local languages with culturally specific phrases; avoid problems with low literacy levels; maximise the number of community interviews that could be undertaken during the study period; and avoid culturally specific investigator bias (Myrdal, 1973). The training process addressed interview techniques that promoted the collection of standardised and unbiased data, valid sampling techniques and confidentiality. Role-plays and question-answer sessions during the training allowed the researcher to assess the confidence and linguistic skills of the field assistants prior to employing them (Spenceley, 2003a).

A Local Community Questionnaire (LCQ) was developed for the local field assistants to use during the surveys within the communities. This was designed to solicit information regarding specific toolkit factors from respondents based in rural neighbouring communities, and also sought baseline demographic and socioeconomic information (Spenceley, 2003a). The structured questionnaires were written in English; with simple and carefully phrased questions; used uniformly accepted meanings; that were not ambiguous; were not leading (Hay, 2000) and avoided dual-meaning statements (Wilkinson, 2000). Questionnaire techniques have been criticised for assuming that collective responses from individuals reflect an underlying social norm (May, 1993), but they may be used to highlight variations within a population (Walpole, 1997). Alternative investigation techniques such as rapid rural appraisal, focus groups and community meetings were discarded as options for this research. It was considered that intimate and anonymous face-to-face interviews would solicit a better representation of individual's views, by avoiding subjecting them to peer pressure from other community members (Spenceley, 2003a).

The way in which the field assistants were deployed to implement the surveys evolved over the course of the four case studies, but some factors remained consistent. In all cases, a base map of the village was created and was used by the field assistants to record where in the village they had conducted each interview. They were requested to stratify their sampling by systematically requesting interviews from people at every third house they came to. If there was not someone to interview at that house they were requested to move on to the next house. This method of sampling was engaged to systematically obtain a relatively even distribution of people across different geographical areas of the community. The gender and age of participants were recorded so that equivalent numbers of men and women and a relatively even distribution of ages would be represented within the sample (Spenceley, 2003a). Overlap was avoided by comparing the maps annotated by each field assistant. Therefore a hybrid of purposive and stratified sampling was effectively employed.

Regular meetings were held with the field assistants during each case study. These meetings improved the reliability of the surveys by ensuring that the field assistants understood the type of information to be collected, had sufficient materials, and allowed timely resolution of any logistical problems (Spenceley, 2003a).

Table 2 describes sample sizes from the communities in each case study, in addition to basic demographic and socioeconomic information. Between 2.4% and 5.5% of the local community populations participated in the surveys, with roughly equal numbers of men and women represented. All interviewees participated anonymously (Spenceley, 2003a).

The four case studies took place between 23 July 2000 and 4 May 2001.

Table 2 : Community samples (Spenceley, 2003a)

Welverdiend	*Numbi*	*Timbavati*	*Huntingdon*
Population			
7,000 (1996 census)	4,130 (1996 census)	11,240 (1999 census)	6,507 (1999 census)
No. interviewees (and proportion of the community surveyed)			
168 (2.4%)	226 (5.5%)	314 (2.8%)	350 (5.4%)
Numbers of men and women interviewed			
78 men, 90 women	119 men, 147 women	158 men, 156 women	164 men, 186 women
Ages			
19–90 years	18–90 years	18–85 years	18–80 years
Average 44 years	Average 40 years	Average 44 years	Average 40 years
Levels of employment			
18% sample employed.	23% sample employed.	36% sample employed.	12% sample employed.
63% of employees earned <R1000 p/m	78% of employees earned <R1000 p/m	77% of employees earned <R1000 p/m	35% of employees earned <R1000 p/m

Socioeconomic Impacts

The socioeconomic impacts of Ngala Private Game Reserve, Pretoriuskop Camp, Jackalberry Lodge and Sabi Sabi are presented below in relation to issues of employment and gender equality, procurement, corporate social responsibility, dependency on tourism and access to markets. The implications of the interventions for poverty alleviation in rural areas are inferred.

Local employment

The majority of employees at Ngala and Jackalberry lived within 25 km of the enterprise, while at Pretoriuskop the opposite was true (see Table 3).

During the last case study, at Sabi Sabi, the extent to which tourism employment affected levels of poverty in the local area was evaluated. The level of local earnings from the tourism enterprise was estimated, and then related to the proportion of local people living above the international poverty line ($1 per day: DFID, 2000) that was determined during surveys within local communities. This evaluation at Sabi Sabi subsequently indicated that approximately 70% of the monthly wage bill was paid to 140 people living within 20 km of the enterprise, and that the average monthly wage was R2500 (~$357). Local employees effectively earned $12 per day and therefore had the capacity to support their estimated seven to eight dependents to a level just above the poverty line, on $1.5 per person, per day (Spenceley & Seif, 2002). The survey within the rural community adjacent to Sabi Sabi, Huntingdon, had revealed that only 12% of the sample was employed, and 40% of these people received wages that would be sufficient to support seven to eight dependents above the international absolute poverty line of $1 per day (DFID, 2000). Cumulatively,

Table 3 Proximity of employees homes

Distance from protected area border	Proportion of total staff			
	*Ngala**	*Pretoriuskop*	*Jackalberry*	*Sabi Sabi*
≤25 km	58%	27%	69%	59%
≥26 and ≤50 km	36%	37%	11%	12%
≥51 and ≤100 km	4%	8%	–	4%
Total ≥101 km	2%	28%	20%	25%
Average distance	52 km	199 km	166 km	127 km
% staff in the sample	57%	56%	97%	94%

*Note that data was only collected for employees in non-management positions, who tended to live in closer proximity to the lodge than management.

Table 4 Local perceptions of work in tourism

	Ngala: Welverdiend (n = 168)	*Pretoriuskop: Numbi* (n = 226)	*Jackalberry: Timbavati* (n = 314)	*Sabi Sabi: Huntingdon* (n = 350)
Proportion of community members interviewed wishing to				
Work locally	85%	66%	82%	91%
Work in tourism	68%	81%	66%	89%
How do people find jobs with tourism companies?				
Friends or relatives	63%	47%	18%	22%
Applications	20%	30%	23%	67%
Education/ skill	1%	–	1%	33%
Luck	1%	1%	1%	–
Do not know	13%	20%	51%	7%

therefore, local employment from Sabi Sabi was estimated to have lifted between 980 and 1120 dependents in the local area above the poverty line: approximately 4.1% of the local population (Spenceley & Seif, 2002). By comparison, the contribution of revenue from other employment options reported during the community survey inferred additional capacity to lift another 4.3% of the population above the poverty line. Critically, this form of comparative analysis revealed the economic significance of local employment from just one tourism enterprise was almost a doubling of the proportion of local people living above the poverty line. Put simply, increasing the proportion of local people lifted out of poverty due to employment through tourism improves its economic sustainability (Spenceley, 2003a).

The context of the employment data from the enterprises was local perceptions of opportunities for employment in tourism. Table 4 indicates the proportion of people who wanted to work in the tourism industry and also local perceptions of recruitment mechanisms.

Local interviewees predominantly wished to remain working in the area and with between 66% and 89% of interviewees wishing to work in the tourism industry. In addition, the majority of respondents from Welverdiend and Numbi stating that they needed family members to tell them about jobs in companies they were working for (32% and 47% respectively), while the overwhelming perception in Huntingdon was that people applied for jobs (67%). The local perceptions of enterprise recruitment strategies were relatively accurate. New employees at Ngala and Jackalberry tended to be sought by management through asking existing staff if they knew of people who needed work. Family and friends would be informed of the vacancies and would visit for an interview. By contrast, neither Sabi Sabi nor Pretoriuskop operated such systems and had formal human resources policies that described their recruitment processes (Spenceley, 2003a).

Procurement

The operational goods and services procured locally at the enterprises were assessed. Table 5 indicates that although Jackalberry purchased nearly 60% of its products locally only 0.2% of expenditure was on locally made products. Sabi Sabi had made more significant efforts to obtain high value laundry and gardening services locally than it had on products purchased. Comparable data was only available for both of these enterprises.

Assessments of expenditure during the case studies highlighted the need to discriminate between relative expenditure on services and products sold by local companies, and also relative expenditure on products manufactured by local companies. Although procurement from both manufacturers and retailers of products would benefit the local economy and provide employment, in the latter less tourism expenditure would be leaked out of the local area.

Surveys in the neighbouring rural communities supported this data from the enterprises, indicating little procurement of products or services by tourism enterprises or tourists within the Timbavati and Huntingdon communities (see Table 6). The data also indicates a similar situation in Welverdiend, but a

Table 5 Expenditure at Jackalberry and Sabi Sabi

Position	*% of expenditure*	
	Jackalberry	*Sabi Sabi*
Local products made within 50 km	0.2%	0%
Local products purchased within 50 km	59.6%	5.3%
Local services within 50 km	38.3%	65.0%
Local Products made/purchased from historically disadvantaged individuals (HDIs), or black economic empowerment (BEE) companies	0.2%	33.0%

Table 6 Local perceptions of tourism procurement

	Ngala: *Welverdiend* *(n = 168)*	*Pretoriuskop:* *Numbi* *(n = 226)*	*Jackalberry:* *Timbavati* *(n = 314)*	*Sabi Sabi:* *Huntingdon* *(n = 350)*
Tourism companies purchase				
Nothing	80%	9%	44%	65%
Arts and crafts	3%	5%	31%	12%
Food and drink	6%	–	6%	4%
Tourists purchase				
Nothing	75%	–	82%	69%
Arts and crafts	6%	72%	12%	19%
Food and drink	15%	21%	7%	3%

Note: Proportions do not add up to 100% as there were some blank answers while others answered more than one type of response.

high proportion of people in the Numbi survey reported tourists purchasing arts and crafts in the community. Numbi was the only one of the four communities that had a craft market where local artisans made and sold artwork.

Corporate social responsibility initiatives

The level of investment in community development initiatives by Ngala, Jackalberry and Sabi Sabi are indicated in Table 7. Note that comparable data is not available from Pretoriuskop, as KNP's Social Ecology Unit (rather than the camp itself) funds initiatives centrally.

Discriminating between different financial mechanisms used to generate funds for local community benefits was addressed during the case studies.

Table 7 Investment on local community development

	Ngala	*Jackalberry*	*Sabi Sabi*
Year	*1999/2000*	*2000/2001*	*2000/2001*
Enterprise investment			
Proportion of enterprise turnover spent annually (%)	0%	1%	1%
In-kind support	–	Accommodation for community members	Accommodation for visiting teachers and children
Donations channelled from third parties			
Education/training	~$11,900	–	–
Infrastructure	~$30,100	–	~$50,000
In-kind donations	Computers	Computers	–

Table 8 Financial contributions to community education initiatives

Ngala: Welverdiend		Jackalberry: Timbavati		Sabi Sabi: Huntingdon	
Funded by donations		Funded by tourism		Funded by tourism	
3 day Bush schools	~$12,860	Environmental education at local school	~$1360	Ecotourism units in 'reach and teach'	~$5140
Conservation lessons	~$730				
Wildlife competitions	~$1430	Wildlife show	~$290		

Ngala's CSR initiatives were financed through donations, while Jackalberry and Sabi Sabi allocated revenue from both turnover and donations for CSR activities. The use of donations, turnover, or staff time for CSR has different implications both for, and due to, the commercial viability of a tourism enterprise: CSR financed by turnover is dependent upon the commercial profitability of the enterprise, while CSR financed through donations is dependent upon the willingness of tourists and philanthropic institutions to support it.

With specific regard to local education, the case studies found that all of the private sector enterprises provided environmental education opportunities to local community members. Ngala channeled donations into academic bursaries, conservation lessons, environmental debates and educational weekend trips for local community members. In collaboration with the other landowners in the Thornybush Game Reserve, Jackalberry Lodge funded conservation education for local children at a nearby environmental centre. Sabi Sabi supported the rehabilitation of a community-owned building to create a community environmental education centre and library – using both donations and its own funds. The extent of enterprise assistance observed appeared to depend upon the extent of enterprises' financial and human resource capacities, and also their access to donations and support from other organisations and individuals. A breakdown of the type of environmental education benefits is provided in Table 8, which could be used to monitor contributions over time.

Local economic dependency and access

Local perceptions of dependency on tourism reported during the community surveys are illustrated in Table 9, which also outlines the perceptions of difficulties preventing them from engaging within the industry.

This data indicates that only the majority of the Numbi community sample perceived that they were dependent upon tourism. This may have been related to the fact that Numbi was the only village among the four that was bisected by the main access road to the enterprise; the others lay adjacent to the main roads and therefore tourists did not need to travel through the communities to reach the enterprise. This community was the only one to suggest that they would actively promote the return of tourists and tourism, should it fail (Spenceley, 2003a).

Table 9 Dependency and access

	Ngala: Welverdiend (n = 168)	Pretoriuskop: Numbi (n = 226)	Jackalberry: Timbavati (n = 314)	Sabi Sabi: Huntingdon (n = 350)
Do you think that your community depends upon tourism?				
% 'No'	81%	36%	69%	69%
% 'Yes'	13%	58%	29%	26%
What would you do differently if tourism and the protected area were not here?				
Farming	81%	8%	63%	28%
Sell something	10%	–	–	1%
Alternative work	3%	3%	8%	8%
Work to bring back the tourists	–	22%	–	–
Nothing	3%	52%	27%	50%
What are the main difficulties preventing you from becoming involved in tourism?				
Lack of education/ skills	32%	36%	8%	23%
Lack of money	5%	14%	–	12%
Lack of information about jobs	–	4%	24%	1%
No friends or relatives working in tourism	–	–	4%	11%
No difficulties	–	8%	28%	38%

Note: Proportions do not add up to 100% as there were some blank answers while others answered more than one type of response.

Conclusions

The aim of this paper was to describe activities conducted by nature-based tourism enterprises that had socioeconomic impacts on neighbouring communities. Quantification of the impacts and reporting local perceptions of the interventions was undertaken through use of the Sustainable Nature-Based Tourism Assessment Toolkit (SUNTAT). The toolkit provided simple mechanism quantifying the local impacts on poverty and rural livelihoods, and to compare different enterprises.

SUNTAT assessments undertaken at Ngala, Pretoriuskop, Jackalberry and Sabi Sabi in South Africa elicited tangible information regarding their levels of local employment, procurement and philanthropy. Interviews with members of neighbouring communities revealed the level of dependency on tourism, access to the industry, and the impacts of the enterprises on poverty.

The majority of employees at the three private nature-based tourism enterprises (Ngala, Jackalberry and Sabi Sabi) lived locally, and on average 62% of staff resided within 25 km of the establishment. Only 27% of Pretoriuskop's staff lived locally. Local employment by Sabi Sabi effectively ensured that 4.1% of the Huntingdon population was lifted above the absolute poverty line of $1 per day (Spenceley, 2003a). Although only a relatively small proportion of the community benefited from direct employment at this 92-bed lodge, the impacts on those individuals were tangible and significant. To increase the net benefits of employment to poor people, enterprises could improve the level of access to vacancies information locally (e.g. not only advertising through existing staff). Rocktail Bay lodge in KwaZulu-Natal has an innovative mechanism of selecting local people for interview, whereby the manager approaches the Community Trust and Induna, who place the names of all prospective candidates in a hat. The names drawn are selected for interview by the lodge (Poultney & Spenceley, 2001). Such an approach may not be practical at all enterprise, but the mechanism for advertising jobs equitably, such as the formal systems in place at Pretoriuskop and Sabi Sabi, should be carefully considered. The majority of local people interviewed in communities neighboring the enterprises were interested both working locally and in working in the tourism industry, but the availability of information regarding recruitment processes was a barrier to access.

Little or no purchasing of locally produced goods (within 50 km) was practiced by the enterprises, although Sabi Sabi outsourced its laundry and gardening services to local businesses. Only within the Numbi community, close to Pretoriuskop camp, did a substantial proportion of people indicate that tourists purchased goods directly from them – and these were mainly arts and crafts sold to people who drove through the village on the way to Kruger National Park. Enterprise purchasing of operational products and services in the local economy can provide a reliable opportunity for the poor to supplement their livelihood activities. Where appropriate capacity to provide suitable goods or services does not exist, a nature-based tourism enterprise located in remote areas may find it cost-effective to build that capacity. For example, Ngala needed to transport employees from their homes in local villages to the lodge. They provided around $150 in micro credit to a local entrepreneur for the purchase of a vehicle. Through the payments made by Ngala for his taxi services, he was able to generate a reliable income and pay off the loan (Spenceley, 2000). Eventually he sought additional credit from the lodge to purchase two other vehicles and employed three drivers to operate them (Spenceley, 2005b). This initiative provided a win-win situation: the enterprise solved its transportation problem and a local entrepreneur established a business that had employment opportunities for other members of the community. Facilitating the development of small enterprises in the local economy can provide alternative livelihood options for the poor, especially when they need little financial input and require resources that are readily available. Tourism enterprises may also be able to support local SMMEs with base materials for products. In the North West province, Sun City provided seed funding of around US$20,000 to a local craft project – Craft Planet – where 12 women transform discarded linen from Sun City into attractive soft furnishings.

The cushions and throws are not only sold to Sun City, but also to other customers (Spenceley & Seif, 2003). Regular support of local agricultural activities by purchasing fruit, vegetables and meat grown close to the enterprise can also provide people in rural areas with an important source of income. Interviews with enterprise managers indicated that considerable time and effort is required to build local business capacity, and small tourism enterprises on tight budgets have difficulty in allocating time and resources to local business development. By using the SUNTAT to evaluate barriers that people in rural areas face in becoming involved in tourism, enterprises can develop more tightly focused initiatives with a greater likelihood of success in alleviating poverty. In impoverished rural areas with high levels of unemployment and marginal opportunities for agriculture, nature-based tourism enterprises can be one of the few businesses to generate substantial income, and therefore they have the potential to alleviate poverty in localised areas.

Philanthropic activities provide a valuable source of capital investment social utilities and services, such as schools and clinics. Although government should arguably be responsible for funding these facilities, rural areas in South Africa are impoverished and the lack of social infrastructure as a legacy of the apartheid period yet to be rectified. Among the private sector enterprises assessed two strategies for investment were observed: financing from donations or from tourism turnover. The former of these provided the majority of monies pushed into local initiatives, but enterprises also made in-kind donations of staff time and equipment. Donations are inherently less sustainable than dividends from company equity or revenue from employment or goods and services procured, as they rely on the ability of an enterprise to solicit monies from tourists and other donors. However, Ngala has a formal and institutionalised basis for donations, through the use of the Africa Foundation. This foundation has been operating since 1992, and sources donations from guests and philanthropic agencies to support development in communities around all of Conservation Corporation Africa's lodges: including Ngala. Brochures are provided in guest rooms to promote the Africa Foundation's activities, and encourage people to provide support. With the majority of interviewees living near Ngala, Jackalberry and Pretoriuskop indicating that a major barrier to their involvement in tourism was education and skills, capacity building activities facilitated by tourism enterprises could address this need by focusing on literacy, business skills and continuing their support of environmental education.

The lack of dependency on tourism and protected areas that people from neighbouring communities reported is in part a reflection of the lack of local ownership of tourism and the low level of local procurement by the enterprises. Levels of unemployment in these areas were far higher than the 1997 national average of 37% (DEAT, 1999) in all of the communities, ranging from 60% of men and 65% women in Huntingdon to 85% of men and 97% of women in the Timbavati community (interview with P. Mhlongo, Bushbuckridge Municipality, Easter D.C., 2001). This indicates that their lack of dependence was not a result of alternative employment in other industries.

The scale of the poverty in rural areas bordering protected areas highlights the need for both tourism enterprises and local people to proactively seek mutually beneficial business linkages. Although the expectations of the enterprises and local people should not be unrealistic regarding the opportunities for tourism to transform local economic situations, focused interventions can make major differences to the livelihoods of individuals and their families.

This study demonstrates that poverty is major problem in for the people living in rural areas around protected areas. Implementation of equitable local employment practices has made a tangible impact on the livelihoods of small numbers of people and their dependents. However, a low level of operational purchasing in local communities has largely been a missed opportunity, both for local people and the tourism enterprises. Some efforts have been made to stimulate the development of community-based businesses that can supply the tourism sector, but reports indicate that the level of procurement has not yet reached a state where local people in general perceive tangible benefits. Local reports revealed that positive interventions would include improving access to education and training, and information about employment, product and service provision opportunities in the industry.

Although it is clear that the selection of these four particular nature-based tourism enterprises for assessment was not random, they are establishments that are highly regarded in terms of responsible tourism in the region. For example, since the SUNTAT assessments took place Sabi Sabi has been awarded the Fair Trade in Tourism South Africa trademark, which is an independent certification award indicating (among other factors) beneficial socioeconomic impacts on local people. However, it is clear that none of the enterprises had local shareholdings, and therefore lessons from joint venture operations, such as Wilderness Safaris operations in Namibia and South Africa (Ashley & Jones, 2001; Poultney & Spenceley, 2001) should also be considered regarding the impact of nature-based tourism on poverty.

By providing a reliable mechanism for comparing the economic impacts of different nature-based tourism enterprises in local communities, application of the SUNTAT has generated comparable qualitative and quantitative data from four enterprises. The importance of triangulation, and evaluating activities from the perspective of both enterprise staff and members of local communities is vital. Although the local employment and donations by enterprises initially appeared to be proactive and generous, the majority local people reported little knowledge or appreciation of those benefits. Quantifying interventions with the SUNTAT provides a framework to systematically assess local economic interventions in a comparable way and a mechanism for enterprises to determine whether their activities are generating tangible benefits. By objectively ascertaining their local economic impacts at a particular point in time, enterprises can have baseline information from which they can set targets to improve their impacts on local levels of poverty. Quantifying the level of financial input and the local benefit perceived also provides enterprises and researchers with a realistic understanding of local needs and constraints, allows them to identify gaps and alternative interventions, and also allows them to highlight activities are most effective. Not only could the tool be used by enterprises to improve their own performance, but also by reporting the impacts of their activities they could motivate tourists to visit. Market research is increasingly indicating a growth in the number of holidaymakers who desire a socially responsible holiday (Goodwin & Francis, 2003;

Tearfund, 2001, 2002), and use of the SUNTAT could facilitate enterprise efforts to capitalise on this market niche.

Further application of the SUNTAT will allow researchers to quantify and compare the interventions of nature-based tourism enterprises on local levels of poverty. The SUNTAT allows information to be gathered locally that can be used to identify appropriate interventions to reduce barriers the poor face when engaging with the tourism sector. Factors that can contribute towards implementation of pro-poor initiatives by tourism enterprises include the presence of a 'champion' who can invest time and energy; top management support with staff incentives; managed expectations; the ability to form new partnerships and a willingness to turn first failures into improvements (McNab, 2005). Over time, repeated use of the toolkit will allow researchers and enterprises to monitor their performance and quantify reductions in poverty and improvements in local economic activities over time. By evaluating reports from individual enterprises, private sector associations and government will be able to generate a database of information regarding tangible impacts that tourism has on poverty, and to compare its impacts with other industries and livelihood options. Using the nature-based tourism industry as a tool for poverty alleviation in rural areas will become a more realistic objective when the processes of generating mutual benefits are better understood.

Correspondence

Any correspondence should be directed to Anna Spenceley, Transboundary Protected Areas Research Initiative, University of the Witwatersrand, Private Bag X3, 2050, Wits, South Africa (annaspencley@hotmail.com).

Acknowledgements

Many thanks to the managers and staff of Ngala, Pretoriuskop, Jackalberry Lodge and Sabi Sabi, members of the communities of Welverdiend, Numbi, Timbavati and Huntingdon who agreed to participate, and especially Louis Hlabane and Johannes Moreko. The Leverhulme Trust generously funded this research, which was in part used to towards a doctorate from the International Centre for Responsible Tourism at the University of Greenwich.

References

Ashley, A., Haysom, G. and Poultney, C. (2005) *Pro-Poor Tourism Pilots in Southern Africa. Practical Implementation of Pro-Poor Linkages by Tourism Companies.* South Africa: Mboza Tourism and London: Overseas Development Institute.

Ashley, C. and Jones, B. (2001) Joint ventures between communities and tourism investors: Experience in Southern Africa. *International Journal of Tourism Research* 3, 407–423.

Ashley, C., Roe, D. and Goodwin, H. (2001) *Pro-Poor Tourism Strategies: Making Tourism Work for the Poor: A Review of Experience.* Pro-poor tourism report No. 1. April 2001. ODI/IIED/CRT. Nottingham: The Russell Press.

Aylward, B. (2003) The actual and potential contribution of nature tourism in Zululand. In B. Aylward and E. Lutz (eds) *Nature Tourism Conservation and Development in KwaZulu-Natal, South Africa* (pp. 1–40). Washington, DC: The World Bank.

Binns, T. and Nel, E. (2002) Tourism as a local development strategy in South Africa. *The Geographical Journal* 168 (3), 235–247.

Cassim, R., Jackson, W. and Gavera, L. (eds) (2004) *International Trade in Services and Sustainable Development: The Case of Tourism in South Africa.* Trade Knowledge Network, April 2004. Geneva: International Institute for Sustainable Development.

Commission on Sustainable Development (CSD) (1999) Report on the seventh session. 1 May and 27 July 1998, and 19–30 April 1999, Economic and Social Council Official Records, 199, Supplement No. 9. New York: United Nations.

Department for International Development (DFID) (1999) *Tourism and Poverty Elimination: Untapped Potential.* London: DFID.

Department for International Development (DFID) (2000) *Halving World Poverty by 2015: Economic Growth, Equity And Security.* London: DFID.

Department of Environmental Affairs and Tourism (DEAT) (1997) *Tourism in GEAR.* Pretoria: Department of Environmental Affairs and Tourism.

Department of Environmental Affairs and Tourism (DEAT) (1999) *The National State of the Environment Report.* Pretoria: Department of Environmental Affairs and Tourism.

Department of Environmental Affairs and Tourism (DEAT) (2002) *Guidelines for Responsible Tourism Development.* Pretoria: Department of Environmental Affairs and Tourism.

Fearnhead, P. (2004) Commercialisation in national parks. In A. Spenceley (ed.) *Proceedings of the SASUSG Annual Members Meeting,* Addo Elephant National Park, 5–7 May 2004 (pp. 54–61). IUCN Southern African Sustainable Use Specialist Group.

Goodwin, H. and Francis, J. (2003) Ethical and responsible tourism: Consumer trends in the UK. *Journal of Vacation Marketing* 9 (3), 271–284.

Government of South Africa (1996a) Constitution of the Republic of South Africa Act 108 of 1996.

Government of South Africa (1996b) *White Paper on the Development and Promotion of Tourism in South Africa.* Pretoria: Department of Environmental Affairs and Tourism.

Hay, I. (ed.) (2000) *Qualitative Research Methods in Human Geography.* Oxford: Oxford University Press.

Koch, E., Massyn, P.J. and Spenceley, A. (2002) Getting started: The experiences of South Africa and Kenya. In M. Haney (ed.) *Ecotourism and Certification: Setting Standard in Practice* (pp. 237–264). Washington: Island Press.

Kirsten, M. and Rogerson, C.M. (2002) Tourism, business linkages and small enterprise development in South Africa. *Development Southern Africa* 19 (1), 29–59.

Mahony, K. and van Zyl, J. (2002) The impacts of tourism investment on rural communities: Three case studies in South Africa. *Development Southern Africa* 19 (1), 83–103.

May, T. (1993) *Sharing the Land: Wildlife, People and Development in Africa.* Harare: IUCN Regional Office for Southern Africa.

McNab, D. (2005) South African corporates piloting pro poor linkages: Procurement, partnerships, and products. In A. Spenceley (ed.) *Tourism in the Great Limpopo Transfrontier Conservation Area: Relating Strategic Visions to Local Activities that Promote Sustainable Tourism Development.* Workshop Proceedings, 14–16 April 2005, Wits Rural Facility, Nr. Kruger National Park, South Africa, (pp. 53–55). Johannesberg: Transboundary Protected Areas Research Initiative.

Mhlongo, P.P. (2001) 'Information Huntington Village and Timbavati Village: Bushbuckridge municipality'. Letter to Anna Spenceley, 28 May 2001.

Mitchella, R.E. and Reidb, D.G. (2001) Community integration: Island tourism in Peru. *Annals of Tourism Research* 28, 112–139.

Myrdal, G. (1973) The beam in our eyes. In D. Warwick and S. Osherson (eds) *Comparative Research Methods* (pp. 89–99). Englewood Cliff, NJ: Prentice Hall.

Ntshona, Z. and Lahiff, E. (2003) *Community-Based Eco-Tourism on The Wild Coast, South Africa: The Case of the Amadiba Trail.* Sustainable Livelihoods in South Africa Research Paper 7. Brighton: Institute of Development Studies.

Poultney, C. and Spenceley, A. (2001) Practical strategies for pro-poor tourism. Wilderness Safaris South Africa: Rocktail Bay and Ndumu Lodge. Pro-poor tourism working paper No. 1. ODI/CRT/IIED.

Pro-Poor Tourism (PPT) (2005) Update on pro poor tourism pilots, April 2005. Pro-poor tourism pilots: Southern Africa. PPT in Practice.

Relly, P. (2004) Employment and investment in Madikwe Game Reserve, South Africa. MA dissertation in Tourism Studies, University of Witswatersrand.

Relly, P. and Koch, E. (2002) Case study assessment Jackalberry Lodge – Thornybush Game Reserve, National Responsible Tourism Guidelines for the South African Tourism Sector, Application of the Guidelines to the Nature-based tourism sector, March 2002.

Robson, C. (1993) *Real World Research*. Oxford: Blackwells.

Seymour, J. (2003) KwaZulu-Natal's Nature-Based Tourism Market. Tourism KwaZulu-Natal Occasional Paper No. 12.

Sharpley, R. (2002) Tourism management: Rural tourism and the challenge of tourism diversification: The case of Cyprus. *Tourism Management* 23, 233–244.

Seif, J. and Spenceley, A. (in press) Assuring community benefit in South Africa through 'Fair Trade in Tourism' Certification. In R. Black and A. Crabtree (eds) *Quality in Ecotourism*. Oxon: CABI.

South African Tourism. (2004) *2003 Tourism Annual Report*. Pretoria: South Africa Tourism Strategic Research Unit.

Spenceley, A. (2000) Sustainable nature-based tourism assessment: Ngala Private Game Reserve. Unpublished report to Ngala Private Game Reserve.

Spenceley, A. (2001) A comparison of local community benefit systems from two nature-based tourism operations in South Africa. Industry and Environment: Ecotourism and sustainability. *United Nations Environment Programme* 24 (3–4), 50–53.

Spenceley, A. (2002a) Sustainable nature-based tourism assessment: Pretoriuskop Camp, Kruger National Park, Unpublished report to South African National Parks, December.

Spenceley, A. (2002b) Overview report of three case studies: Pretoriuskop Camp, Jackalberry Lodge, and Coral Divers. National Responsible Tourism Guidelines for the South African Tourism Sector, Application of the Guidelines to the Nature-based tourism sector. Report to DFID/DEAT, March 2002.

Spenceley, A. (2002c) Sustainable nature-based tourism assessment: Jackalberry Lodge. Confidential report to Jackalberry Lodge.

Spenceley, A. (2002d) Sustainable nature-based tourism assessment: Sabi Sabi Game Reserve. Confidential report to Sabi Sabi.

Spenceley, A. (2003a) Managing sustainable nature-based tourism in Southern Africa: A practical assessment tool. PhD dissertation in earth and environmental sciences, University of Greenwich.

Spenceley, A. (2003b) *Tourism, Local Livelihoods and the Private Sector in South Africa: Case Studies on the Growing Role of the Private Sector in Natural Resources Management*. Sustainable Livelihoods in South Africa Research Paper 8. Brighton: Institute of Development Studies.

Spenceley, A. (2004) Responsible nature-based tourism planning in South Africa and the commercialisation of Kruger National park. In D. Diamantis (ed.) *Ecotourism: Management and Assessment* (pp. 267–280). London: Thomson Learning.

Spenceley, A. (2005a) Environmental sustainability of nature-based tourism enterprises in protected areas: Four case studies from South Africa. *International Journal of Sustainable Tourism* 13 (2), 136–170.

Spenceley, A. (2005b) *CCAfrica: Tourism for Tomorrow 'Investors in People Award'*. Unpublished report to the World Travel and Tourism Council, March 2005.

Spenceley, A. (in press) Sustainable nature-based tourism: An African Delphi Consultation. *Tourism Geographies*.

Spenceley, A. and Seif, J. (2003) Strategies, Impacts and Costs of Pro-poor Tourism Approaches in South Africa. Pro-Poor Tourism working paper No. 11. January 2003.

Spenceley, A. and Seif, J. (2002) Sabi Sabi Imvelo Responsible Tourism Assessment, Confidential report to the Federated Hospitality Association of South Africa. Cited in A. Spenceley and J. Seif (2003) Strategies, Impacts and Costs of Pro-poor Tourism Approaches in South Africa. Pro-Poor Tourism working paper No. 11. January 2003.

Spenceley, A., Goodwin, H. and Maynard, W. (2004) Development of responsible tourism guidelines for South Africa. In D. Diamantis (ed.) *Ecotourism: Management and Assessment* (pp. 281–297). London: Thomson Learning.

Sultana, N. (2002) *Conceptualising Livelihoods of the Extreme Poor.* Working paper 1, January 2002 Department for International Development, UK, 12 December 2002.

Sykes, P. (2003) *South African Tourism Industry Empowerment and Transformation Annual Review 2003.* Pretoria: Tourism Business Council of South Africa and W.K. Kellog Foundation.

Tearfund (2001) *Guide to Tourism: Don't Forget Your Ethics!* 6 August 2001.

Tearfund (2002) *Worlds Apart: A Call to Responsible Global Tourism.* January 2002.

United Nations/DESA (UN/DESA) (2002) Key outcomes of the summit, Johannesburg Summit 2002. World Summit on Sustainable Development, Johannesburg South Africa, 26 August–4 September. United Nations.

United Nations Environment Programme (UNEP) (2001) *Principles for the Implementation of Sustainable Tourism.* UNEP.

United Nations Development Programme (UNDP) (2003) *Human Development Report 2003.* UNDP.

Urban Dynamics Middleburg Inc. (1999) Land Development Objectives – Hazyview Local Council, HAZ 103. Cited in Spenceley, A. (2002a) op. cit.

Walpole, M. (1997) Dragon Tourism in Komodo National Park, Indonesia: Its contribution to conservation and local development. PhD dissertation in conservation and ecology. University of Kent.

Wilkinson, D. (2000) *The Researcher's Toolkit: The Complete Guide to Practitioner Research.* Falmer: Routledge.

World Tourism Organization (WTO) (1997) *Global Code of Ethics for Tourism.* Madrid: World Tourism Organization.

World Tourism Organization (WTO) (2002) *Tourism and Poverty Alleviation.* Madrid: World Tourism Organization.

World Tourism Organization (WTO) (2004) *Tourism and Poverty Alleviation Recommendations for Action.* Madrid: World Tourism Organization.

World Tourism Organization (WTO) (undated) *(ST-EP) Sustainable Tourism–Eliminating Poverty.* Madrid: World Tourism Organization.

World Travel and Tourism Council (WTTC) (2003) *Country League Tables Travel and Tourism: A World of Opportunity.* The 2003 Tourism & Travel Economic Research. London: WTTC.

World Travel and Tourism Council (WTTC) (2004) *South Africa: Travel and Tourism Forging Ahead.* The 2004 Travel and Tourism Economic Research. London: WTTC.